Cost Engineering Health Check

High quality cost estimating gives a business leader confidence to make rational financial decisions. Whether you are a business leader or a cost estimating manager, you have a vested interest in understanding whether you can depend on your organisation's ability to generate accurate cost forecasts and estimates. But how can business leaders have confidence that the cost information that they are being provided with is of high quality? How can a cost estimating manager be sure that their team is providing high quality cost information?

QinetiQ's Cost Engineering Health Check is used as a capability benchmarking tool to identify improvement opportunities within their clients' cost estimating capability, enabling them to focus on areas that have the potential to increase their competitiveness. High quality estimating leads to accurate budgets, a reduced potential for cost growth, accurate evaluation of risk exposure, and the opportunity to implement effective earned value management (EVM).

The Cost Engineering Health Check employs a standardised competency framework that considers all aspects of cost estimating capability, and provides an objective assessment against both best practice and the industry standard. This framework is based on QinetiQ's long established, tried and tested, Knowledge Based Estimating (KBE) philosophy comprising Data, Tools, People and Process, with additional consideration given to cultural and stakeholder assessments.

Dale Shermon has been estimating since 1984 and parametric cost estimating since 1987. He has presented courses in hardware estimating, software estimating, life cycle cost, cost estimating relationships, information technology, risk analysis and supplier assessment in the UK, Italy, USA, Sweden, Australia, Taiwan and Germany. He has also conducted consulting assignments in cost estimating in UK, Italy, France, Australia, Switzerland, Canada and the Netherlands. Dale was the first European to become an International Society of Parametric Analysts (ISPA) Certified Parametric Practitioner (CPP) in 2003 and be awarded the Frank Freiman award in 2009. He has presented and published widely on cost engineering and parametrics and is a QinetiQ Fellow. Dale is also author of *Systems Cost Engineering*, Gower Publishing 2009.

Mark Gilmour has a PhD in Cost Engineering from Queens University, Belfast and is a Certified Cost Estimator and Analyst with Parametric specialism (CCEA/P) from the International Cost Estimating and Analysis Association (ICEAA). In 2013 Mark was awarded a QinetiQ Engineering, Scientific and Technical Recognition Award for the development of the Cost Engineering Health Check. During his time at QinetiQ Mark managed the Cost Estimating and Analysis Team and he continues to lead through life cost and risk management and analysis activities in support of UK aerospace and defence programmes. Mark is an active member of the Society for Cost Analysis and Forecasting (SCAF) and ICEAA, and is a regular contributor to professional cost analysis journals and conferences.

Cost Engineering Health Check

How Good are Those Numbers?

Dale Shermon and Mark Gilmour

LONDON AND NEW YORK

First published 2017
by Routledge
2 Park Square, Milton Park, Abingdon, Oxon OX14 4RN

and by Routledge
711 Third Avenue, New York, NY 10017

Routledge is an imprint of the Taylor & Francis Group, an informa business

British Library Cataloguing in Publication Data
A catalogue record for this book is available from the British Library

Library of Congress Cataloging-in-Publication Data
A catalog record for this book has been requested

ISBN: 978-1-4724-8407-9 (hbk)
ISBN: 978-1-315-57443-1 (ebk)

Typeset in Times New Roman
by Apex CoVantage, LLC

Contents

List of figures   vi
List of tables   x
Glossary   xi
Acknowledgements   xii

1   Foreword   1

2   Introduction   3

3   Knowledge Based Estimating (KBE)   5

4   What is the Cost Engineering Health Check (CEHC)?   10

5   The CEHC methodology   15

6   Data gathering, normalisation and application   25

7   Tool development and usage   50

8   People's skills, professionalism and knowledge   81

9   Process existence and utilisation   122

10   Culture, leadership and management   151

11   Stakeholders' engagement and acknowledgement   157

12   Conducting assessments   165

13   Summary   175

References   178
Index   181

Figures

3.1 The four foundational building blocks of a credible and justified cost estimate   6

4.1 Results from the QinetiQ Risk Maturity Model (QRMM) applied to cost deviation identified in the NAO major projects report   11

4.2 Results from the QinetiQ Risk Maturity Model (QRMM) applied to schedule deviation identified in the NAO major projects report   12

4.3 The motivation for conducting the Cost Engineering Health Check   13

4.4 The levels of maturity in a Cost Engineering Health Check   14

5.1 The application of the Cost Engineering Health Check   16

5.2 An e-voting handset can record the input from each individual to the maturity assessment   16

5.3 The current and potential maturity assessment of an organisation   18

5.4 A simple Cost Engineering Health Check dashboard   19

5.5 An example of maturity assessments for detailed areas showing the range of outcomes   20

5.6 An example of potential migration of capability with the implementation of recommendations   22

5.7 An example of the timeline for potential improvements   22

5.8 The Cost Engineering Health Check implemented in AWARD®   23

6.1 Example of an operating and support data collection database   26

6.2 Two-phase approach to generating a cost model   27

6.3 The relationship between cost influenced by overhead related activities and those which are task related   30

6.4 The migration of a project from the dependency on assumptions to the mature data   32

6.5 The productivity metric for different suppliers   35

6.6 The correct approach to process historical cost data   36

6.7 The effects of cost improvement or learning curves   37

6.8 Relationship between the PBS, WBS and CBS with example products, work packages and functions   40

6.9 The importance of the inflation rates applied to constant prices to establish outturn prices   45

6.10 As the number of nations increases, the development costs grow. Individual nations benefit if they share equally the non-recurring costs.   48

6.11 FOREX prediction is necessary in a mature cost estimating environment   48

7.1 Understanding the organisation's productivity is essential in a mature cost engineering environment   52

7.2	The relationship between risk and uncertainty	56
7.3	Varying degrees of complexity in risk analysis	56
7.4	Relative outcomes of the Monte Carlo analysis	59
7.5	Traditional V diagram of systems engineering leading to waterfall software development	62
7.6	Alternative software development methods	63
7.7	The flow of data through the tools at the hands of a mature project control function	65
7.8	Price build-up of the cost and non-cost	66
7.9	The flow process necessary for the development of a cost model on a mature organisation	68
7.10	An example of a simple cost model requirements database in a mature cost engineering function	69
7.11	The relationship between cost model calibration and verification and validation	71
7.12	Regression analysis of data	74
7.13	The non-linear relationships and the mathematical transformations to create a straight line	76
7.14	Cost estimating methods are applicable at different times in a project life cycle	78
8.1	Challenges faced by cost engineers	82
8.2	The need for cost engineering	82
8.3	The experience of a cost engineer	83
8.4	The data sources of a cost engineer; meeting the needs	85
8.5	Modelling capability	85
8.6	Cost engineering capability improvement model	87
8.7	Life cycle of a car	92
8.8	Statistically superior	93
8.9	Superior CER	94
8.10	Considering the population and outliers through standard deviation	96
8.11	Example of an 80/20 share ratio for an incentive contract	100
8.12	Life cycle development of costing	102
8.13	Establishing recurring and non-recurring costs	102
8.14	Indirect and direct allocation of costs	104
8.15	How the addition or removal of an operational unit affects the overheads	105
8.16	From assumption to data over a project life cycle	105
8.17	Spreading constant cost with the same base year	108
8.18	Understanding of base year and constant costs	109
8.19	Explanation of base year and outturn costs	109
8.20	The cash flow of example options 1 and 2	110
8.21	Work breakdown structure (WBS)	113
8.22	Sample network	114
8.23	Point cost estimate	114
8.24	Uncertainty quantified as minimum, most likely and maximum	115
8.25	Analysis of the uncertainty using Monte Carlo	116
8.26	Risks or potential deviations for the baseline plan	116
8.27	Pre-mitigation risks quantified as probability and impact	117
8.28	Uncertainty and pre-mitigated risk analysis	117

8.29	Mitigation actions identified to avoid the risks	118
8.30	Mitigation actions added to the baseline uncertainty	118
8.31	Post-mitigation risk analysis	119
8.32	Monte Carlo analysis	120
9.1	A defence budget is too large to handle in one part and hence it is broken down	123
9.2	Different analysis techniques are used at different levels of the budget	124
9.3	The decision making process	125
9.4	The costs need to include all costs necessary to deliver a capability, not just the equipment costs	126
9.5	The COEIA will replace MOE with benefits when appropriate	127
9.6	Major elements of a cost engineering process	128
9.7	Example cost estimating schedule	132
9.8	Integration of costing with other project analysis processes on a typical defence project	133
9.9	Interlinking of project processes to generate a combined operational effectiveness and investment appraisal	134
9.10	Example of a task calculator for cost engineers	135
9.11	A risk management process with governance	137
9.12	Sensitivity analysis tornado chart	139
9.13	The risk management of two work packages	140
9.14	Two work packages split into four work packages	141
9.15	Correlation added to four-work package	142
9.16	Austerity Handbook: "Hints and tips on how to make a project affordable"	143
9.17	Price to win	144
9.18	Estimating uncertainty funnel	146
9.19	A typical EVM chart of a plan, actual and progress	146
9.20	The use of multiple estimating methods provides confidence to the decision maker	147
9.21	Multiple estimating methodology approach	148
9.22	The verification and validation process	149
10.1	The storage of data in an accessible format is an indication of maturity	153
11.1	The perfect cost engineer experiences considerable stakeholder pressure	158
11.2	The dimensions of the cost engineering stakeholder community and knowledge	159
11.3	The reassuring presence of data gives stakeholders a warm feeling	160
11.4	An example output from the FACET cost model	161
11.5	Cost engineering process with stakeholder reviews clearly identified	163
12.1	CEHC database – indicator A1 – senior management involvement – all individuals' perspectives	166
12.2	CEHC database – indicator A5 – estimators' understanding of project – all individuals' perspectives	167
12.3	CEHC database – indicator B1 – historical financial data – all individuals' perspectives	168
12.4	CEHC database – indicator B3 – historical technical data – all individuals' perspectives	169
12.5	CEHC database – indicator C4 – risk analysis tools – all individuals' perspectives	170

12.6 CEHC database – indicator C5 – software estimating tools – all
      individuals' perspectives   171
12.7 CEHC database – indicator D3 – planning and communication – all
      individuals' perspectives   172
12.8 CEHC database – indicator D13 – use of multiple estimating processes –
      all individuals' perspectives   173
12.9 CEHC database – multiple indicators – range of average
      organisational scores   174
13.1 A dashboard showing the organisation relative to the quartile ranges
      of the competition   176

Tables

5.1	An example of Category 1 recommendations – designed to improve the organisation's ability to generate credible estimates	21
5.2	An example of Category 2 recommendations – designed to further mature the confidence in the cost engineering capability	21
6.1	Types of schedules related to cost	30
6.2	Possible learner rates	38
6.3	The definitions of the ADORE analysis	39
6.4	Cost data maturity assessment matrix	44
6.5	Inflation rates applied individually and composite inflation rate calculation	46
6.6	Time phasing of costs	47
7.1	Advantages and disadvantages of adding a percentage	57
7.2	Treatment of risks as a certainty	57
7.3	Advantages and disadvantages of treating risk as a certainty	57
7.4	Weighted sum calculation	58
7.5	Advantages and disadvantages of the weighted sum approach	58
7.6	Advantages and disadvantages of the probabilistic modelling approach	59
7.7	The ESLOC calculations for four computer software configuration items	61
7.8	The terms used in earned value management (EVM)	67
7.9	RACI matrix	72
7.10	Risk and uncertainty terms	79
8.1	Advantages and disadvantages of the funding of a cost engineering function	88
8.2	Common types of distributions and their usage	97
8.3	The risk spectrum for contract types	99
8.4	Detailed and composite labour rates	103
8.5	A discounted cash flow example	110
8.6	Definitions of cost elements, uncertainty and risk	112

Glossary

CADMID / T	An abbreviation of the project life cycle including Concept, Assessment, Demonstration, Manufacture, In-service and Disposal / Termination
Cost Engineer	Terms used for individuals employed in the cost engineering function can include: Cost Engineer, Cost Analyst, Parametrician, Cost Forecaster and others, which are used interchangeably.
Organisational breakdown structure (OBS)	This is a formal arrangement of resources (labour and non-labour) which will need to be consumed or used to ensure successful completion of the project
Product breakdown structure (PBS)	This is a formal arrangement of technologies or software which will need to be acquired or built to ensure successful completion of the project
Programme	The term given to a collection of projects which belong to a portfolio, for example, project, programme and portfolio management (P3M)
Program	A software code used to make computers perform a useful function
Whole life cost (WLC)	For simplicity in this book we have used the term whole life cost as a reference to the financial measure of resources consumed throughout a project's life, also recognised as through life cost (TLC), life cycle cost (LCC), total ownership cost (TOC), cost of ownership (COO) and others.
Work breakdown structure (WBS)	This is a formal arrangement of activities or tasks which will need to be conducted to ensure successful completion of the project

Acknowledgements

We would like to acknowledge Steve Moreton and Chad Chandramohan at QinetiQ Commerce Decisions for their contributions regarding the AWARD® software.

1 Foreword

Public government perspective

By Dr Tim Sheldon, Head of Cost Assurance & Analysis Service (CAAS), MOD

The Ministry of Defence is charged with delivering a key component of the UK's National Security Strategy, as recently updated through the publication of the UK Strategic Defence and Security Review 2015. A key aspect of the MOD's role is the delivery of the UK Equipment Programme, valued at over £170Bn over the next decade, to provide effective military equipment and support to our Armed Forces. The Equipment Programme includes a range of challenging projects from new Armoured Fighting Vehicles through cutting edge fighter aircraft to new warships and nuclear submarines – a very diverse portfolio.

Understanding and effectively managing the costs of the MOD Equipment Programme remains absolutely critical, especially when one considers the macro financial challenge across the UK public sector. Set against this context, the MOD has made a significant investment over the past 5 years to modernise and strengthen its in-house cost management capability including cost forecasting, cost engineering, cost accounting and portfolio analytics. This book highlights the fundamental facets to achieve an effective cost management organisation, and as such I commend the approach, both in terms of 'what good looks like' and how that can be assessed to understand opportunities for improvement. I have learnt that this is a continuous process and one that requires constant focus to maximise the benefits to our customers, the UK's Armed Forces.

Private industry perspective

By Steve Elwell, Managing Director, Advisory Services, QinetiQ

As a senior manager in QinetiQ I am personally responsible for making multiple financial decisions each week. These range from private venture investment opportunities to the price to be included in a bid and proposal. The decisions I make can have a direct influence on the business as a whole and the share price of the company; they are strategically important and the decision lies with me.

For the technical element I have advisors such as technical directors and subject matter experts who can advise me on the viability of the solution, concept or proposal technical volume. On the financial side I can reach out to the finance and accounting director to ensure the correctness of the figures. However, this does not represent an opinion on the quality of the estimate. Finance will confirm whether the correct labour rates have been applied, the right exchange rate used and a realistic cash flow, but they don't know if the number of hours is justified. For this I use a cost engineering function, but how good are these guys?

The Cost Engineering Health Check (CEHC) gave me an independent analysis of the cost engineers in my organisation. It provided a benchmark against other organisations which work in our environment and identified areas for improvement and investment. I was able to see the return on this investment and the effect it will have on the decisions I will make.

The outcome? Well my cost engineers didn't score 100%, but they are in the upper quartile when compared to similar organisations in our domain. We have identified a number of investment areas for improvement which they were able to justify and although they are not perfect, they are better than our competitors, which means I have the ability to make decisions of higher quality than my competitors, which as a decision maker is the best outcome I can have! [37]

2 Introduction

2.1 Background

High quality cost estimating gives a business leader confidence to make rational financial decisions. Whether you are a business leader or a cost estimating manager, you have a vested interest in understanding if you can depend on your organisation's ability to generate accurate cost forecasts and estimates. But how can business leaders have confidence in the quality of the cost information that they are being provided? How can a cost estimating manager be sure that his or her team is providing high quality cost information? [25]

The Cost Engineering Health Check is used as a capability benchmarking tool to identify improvement opportunities within a cost estimating capability, enabling it to focus on areas that have the potential to increase the competitiveness. High quality estimating leads to accurate budgets being set, a reduced potential for cost growth, accurate evaluation of risk exposure and the opportunity to implement effective earned value management (EVM).

The Cost Engineering Health Check employs a standardised competency framework that considers all aspects of cost estimating capability, and provides an objective assessment against both best practice and the industry standard. This framework is based on QinetiQ's long established, tried and tested, Knowledge Based Estimating (KBE) philosophy comprising Data, Tools, People and Process, with additional consideration given to cultural and stakeholder assessments.

2.2 Purpose of this book

In these austere times decision makers are finding the financial impacts of their decisions coming under increasing levels of scrutiny by shareholders, chairmen, public accounts committees and other august bodies. But as decision makers typically do not generate the cost information on which they base their decisions, how can they be confident of the quality of the cost information that they are being provided to inform their decisions? Within the public sector there are a number of notable high profile events where the cost estimates being used to make decisions have been found to be significantly lacking in quality – for example in awarding the franchise for train operations on the UK's West Coast Main Line [1]. How can such situations be avoided in the future and how can decision makers act to protect themselves and their organisations from cost estimates of questionable maturity?

In response to this situation, QinetiQ has developed the Cost Engineering Health Check (CEHC). The Cost Engineering Health Check has the express aim to aid decision makers such as project and programme managers, Managing Directors, Chief Executive Officers and so forth, to evaluate their organisation's cost estimating capability. By evaluating their organisation's cost estimating capability relative to both best practice and their industry peers, these individuals can gain confidence in the information that they are being asked to base their decisions upon, or, where their organisation's capability is found to be deficient, to put measures in place to improve it.

2.3 Definition

There are a lot of flavours of cost engineering depending upon the industry and the environment in which you work. Terms used for individuals employed in the cost engineering function can include: Cost Engineer, Cost Analyst, Parametrician, Cost Forecaster and others, which are used interchangeably. In some organisations these terms have very specific and defined meanings. In this book the term Cost Engineer will be consistently used to describe a suitably qualified and experience person (SQEP) able to gather data, analyse it and generate a cost estimate. This is not intended to exclude staff who do not have the title Cost Engineer but is simply designed to make the writing of the book more consistent.

In a similar way there are both private industry and public bodies that deploy and depend upon cost engineering functions. For this reason this book will simply refer to the wider body as the organisation, as this Cost Engineering Health Check can equally apply to both the public and private domains.

Finally, there have been many initiatives to ensure that all costs associated with a project are considered. These have produced numerous terms including whole life cost (WLC), through life cost (TLC), life cycle cost (LCC), total ownership cost (TOC), cost of ownership (COO) and others. For simplicity in this book we have used the term whole life cost as a reference to the financial measure of resources consumed throughout a project's life.

3 Knowledge Based Estimating (KBE)

3.1 Introduction

QinetiQ cost forecasts and estimates are underpinned by its philosophy of Knowledge Based Estimating (KBE). This promotes the application of knowledge, skills and understanding as the basis of all credible and justifiable costs (see Figure 3.1). The building blocks that form the foundation of this philosophy are Data, Tools, People and Process.

Within the context of the KBE philosophy, data is defined as any information, both cost and technical, concerning historical projects and services that will be used as the basis for future estimates, whilst also extending out to information in relation to the technical or schedule characteristics of future projects or services. Tools are defined as the software systems that help cost engineers to interpret historical data, such as statistical tools that can be used to create cost estimating relationships (CER), historical trend analysis (HTA) [28] or other tools that allow the application of such relationships to generate estimates. Parametric cost models could fall into that category.

People within KBE are required to interpret historical data and predict the concepts for the new projects and services that will satisfy the perceived capability or requirements. Cost engineers need the qualifications to justify their professionalism and the skills to elicit the data from finance, project and technical staff as well as the customer. Finally, processes are necessary so that the people conduct an estimate in a rational, repeatable way, ensuring that the outputs are traceable to source data and assumptions.

The Cost Engineering Health Check has two additional outputs for the full assessment: Culture and Stakeholders. Information concerning both is inferred from the questions sets for Data, Tools, People and Process as opposed to being asked directly. Culture refers to the environment in which cost engineering is taking place. Stakeholders refer to anyone who has a vested interest in the cost inputs or outputs.

When considering the development of a benchmarking capability the KBE philosophy was an ideal structure to draw from. If the maturity of an organisation can be measured against the KBE framework, then this will be a sound measure for comparison with other organisations.

3.2 Why cost engineering?

Cost engineering has recently had an increased visibility in the minds of a lot of engineers. With the age of austerity, the costs of projects, systems and services have come more into focus [35]. Cost engineers have technical backgrounds; they are not accountants. For cost engineers, their focus is not watts, newtons, volts, amps or kilograms, but dollars, euros and pounds.

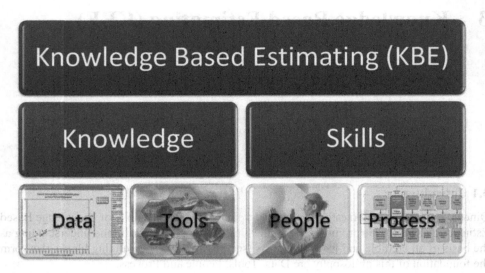

Figure 3.1 The four foundational building blocks of a credible and justified cost estimate

There is frequently a grey and hazy distinction between the terms cost estimator and cost forecasters; they both require technical understanding to appreciate the magnitude and complexity of the hardware, software or service that they are considering. For the purposes of this book we will define them as a category of cost engineer:

- Cost estimators consider the costs associated with current immediate projects, systems and services; while
- Cost forecasters tend to consider the next generation of projects, systems and services, perhaps one or two decades into the future.

They have a number of purposes to their work; cost predictions are not the end in itself. It is always necessary to consider the answer to the question, "What is the requirement?" Potential applications of cost engineering [56] include:

- Financial analysis, budgeting, investment and planning
- Analysis of alternatives (AoA)
- Economic analysis (EA)
- Cost benefit analysis (CBA)
- Business case analysis
- Contracting and project management
- Design and trade-off decisions
- Acquisition analysis, for example technology insertion [58]

In the generation of costs to satisfy these potential cost applications, it is necessary to consider the limitations of the cost estimate being produced. There have been some occasions when costs have been used out of context or inappropriately. You cannot use an economic analysis with cost calculated in net present value (NPV) to set the budget for a project, system or service.

It is not commonly appreciated that there are a number of different types of cost prediction which can be deployed suitably to different applications:

- Rough order of magnitude (ROM)
- Independent cost estimate (ICE)
- Whole life cost (WLC) or life cycle cost estimate (LCCE)
- Budget estimate
- Commercially committing proposal estimate
- Discounted cash flow and net present value (NPV)
- Parametric top-down forecast
- Should cost / would cost / could cost
- Operating and support cost or through life cost (TLC)
- Activity-cased costing (ABC)
- Price-to-win acquisition estimates

Common to all these types of estimate is the need for cost estimating data. This data and information needs to be documented to provide a legacy and corporate memory of the cost estimate. When completed a robust cost engineering output has a number of benefits.

3.3 Benefits of cost engineering

When an organisation with a mature costing function produces a cost estimate, there are a number of benefits which occur as a consequence. Such a function is likely to support the bidding or budgeting process by accurately linking the requirements to cost through the utilisation of cost drivers. If the magnitude of the cost drivers changes, then this linkage will directly influence the cost estimate either upwards or downwards depending upon the cost estimating relationships. With a robust cost estimate you will be able to assess the reasonableness of a bid/budget and effectively defend the value that you have generated. In a governance and scrutinised environment you will be able to justify the estimated cost. In an organisation with a mature cost engineering function you will be able to quickly and precisely determine the impact of costs to the predicted budget due to the direct relationship to the cost drivers.

The mature cost organisation will enhance the profits of the business in the private domain or enable more projects for the same funding in the public sector. This will be achieved through the comprehensive understanding of the cost estimate and the reduced management contingency required for cost growth attributable to inaccurate estimation [2]. A mature cost engineering organisation will work to identify all the cost, schedule and performance risks in the project and conduct a transparent analysis of these risks to form an objective quantification of their impact on the project, system or service.

There will be a financial basis for the evaluation of competing systems and initiatives within the project under consideration. When the options are purchased or commercial off the shelf (COTS), rather than developed and researched within the organisation, then the mature cost engineering organisation will have the luxury of financial evaluation of the options supporting the proposal pricing and evaluation of the proposals for reasonableness. When the COTS items need to be changed, any design decisions are supported by a design trade-off including a financial consideration. Design to cost, target costing and Cost as an Independent Variable or CAIV are all techniques which a mature cost engineering organisation will utilise.

When you work with a mature cost engineering function it is important that the cost estimates are characterised as:

- Accurate
- Comprehensive
- Replicable and auditable
- Traceable
- Credible
- Timely

There is a limitation to the use of cost engineering outputs, whether they are mature or not. There needs to be a recognition by decision makers that the output from a cost engineering process cannot be better than the data fed into the process. No amount of analysis will make poor information any better; garbage in, garbage out!

Cost engineering cannot be delivered just by following a process; the cost engineer needs to consider the context and deliver the output appropriate to the 'exam question' being asked. It is certainly true that when it comes to politics, if a certain outcome is desirable, no amount of sophisticated cost analysis will be able to influence the necessary outcome and decision. In conclusion, a cost engineering organisation, however mature, only makes a recommendation and the final decision is usually someone else's. Cost engineering cannot substitute for sound judgement, good management and reasonable control mechanisms.

3.4 The challenges to mature cost engineering

There are many difficulties, or challenges, that a mature cost engineering organisation must overcome to become effective. These are not placed in front of the cost engineering organisation to trip them up, but exist in the day-to-day working of the organisation for them to manoeuvre around or navigate through.

- Quality challenge – there is a need to answer the question, "What does good data look like?" Before it can be sourced there is a need to determine what it might look like when it's found. Primary data is desirable as secondary data might have been adjusted several times for different reasons before we receive it. Good quality data needs to be documented to ensure that we fully appreciate where it has originated, who owns the source, its content or definition, when it was last refreshed, and so forth.
- Coordination challenge – an estimate is not completed in a vacuum, even an independent cost forecast needs to engage with stakeholders. The challenge with stakeholders is being able to coordinate their inputs; for some reason they don't always see the cost forecasting as important, and don't give it the priority in their diary that it should naturally demand.
- Consistency challenge – the words a cost engineer dreads hearing are, "Can you explain the difference?" Producing a reconciliation between two cost forecasts is always tricky, even when they have been produced by the same organisation. Estimates generally migrate from one estimating methodology to another over a project life cycle, which means that the granularity of cost forecasts change over time. Comparing a top-down parametric estimate to a bottom-up analytical forecast is not simple, but occasionally necessary. The challenge is further problematic when the cost estimate needs to be compared to actuals or historical data of unknown or dubious origin.

- Security/access challenge – in engineering we are very cautious with information and data; knowledge is power. In the commercial world this is even more acute. Companies will seek to keep their costs classified or confidential to prevent other competitors gaining an understanding and a competitive advantage. This does, however, cause a challenge for a cost engineer when trying to develop a cost database. Companies will keep their numbers to themselves, denying a source of information to cost engineers. Finally, there is the possibility of data misuse: when data is made accessible, it can be misused out of context if it is not fully defined.

- Resource and schedule constraints challenge – "There is never enough time to do it properly, but always enough time to do it twice." Decision makers need to appreciate that for an estimating task the time given to the cost forecast is proportional to the quality of the resulting cost forecast. If you want an answer by 17:00, I will provide you with an estimate with appropriately large tolerances of accuracy. Between zero and 10 billion – now what did you want me to estimate? If you give me a month you will have more certainty and confidence in the output. Three to six months and I will be able to provide a solid, mature cost forecast that has had appropriate stakeholder review and endorsement.

4   What is the Cost Engineering Health Check (CEHC)?

4.1 Introduction

QinetiQ have been conducting maturity assessments on the risk management capabilities [4] of organisations for many years using the QinetiQ Risk Maturity Model (QRMM). It has been demonstrated through use of the RMM that projects that benchmark their capabilities to understand their areas of weaknesses, and then take action to improve upon these weaknesses, perform significantly better than projects that do not. An analysis of the National Audit Office (NAO) report on MOD's major equipment projects [3] identified overspending as a percentage of original estimate for a selection of projects, as shown in Figure 4.1.

This clearly showed that projects with a higher level of maturity in the area of risk management were less likely to deviate from their original cost forecast than projects with lower levels of maturity. But this result is not limited to the cost forecast; as you can see in Figure 4.2, it is possible to make the same observation of the schedule slippage; those projects which are more mature in their approach to risk appear to have experienced fewer problems.

4.2 Cost maturity and benchmarking

The authors of this book realised that there was a need for a similar assessment technique in the cost estimating, forecasting and analysis community. As a result, the authors invested their time and applied their experience to establishing a comparable maturity assessment framework for cost engineering.

Consider the growth in projects since approval [5], as shown in Figure 4.3, when combined with comments from Bernard Grey, UK Chief of Defence Materiel [6], who said "Another problem is the significant capability deficiencies in the [integrated project team] IPT. . . . In particular we found insufficient financial skills. The costing and estimating groups had been cut down in order to save money." He went on to say "I would have liked to have the time and resources to do more international benchmarking on a quantitative basis. . . . Some quantitative measurement may well have flushed out some further efficiencies."

Finally, in a National Audit Office report [7] on forecasting in government to achieve value for money, the key finding included: "Poor forecasting is an entrenched problem, leading to poor value for money and taxpayers bearing the costs. Since 2010, over 70 of our reports have identified forecasting weaknesses" and "there is insufficient information to assess the quality of departments' forecasting. Spending teams lack a consistent approach to assess and compare the quality of programme forecasting" (p. 6).

When considering the elements of maturity to be examined, and taking experience from the QRMM, the Cost Engineering Health Check has two more areas identified in addition

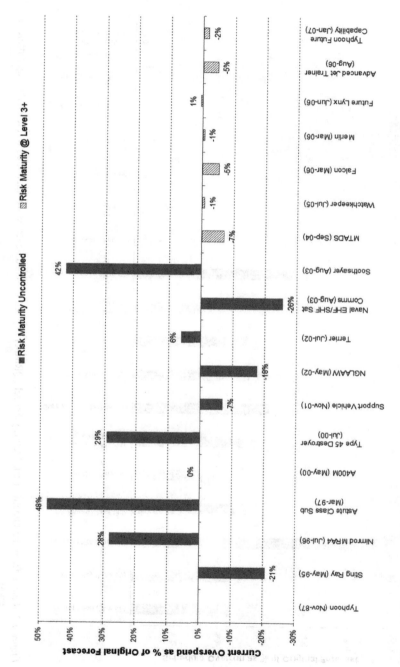

Figure 4.1 Results from the QinetiQ Risk Maturity Model (QRMM) applied to cost deviation identified in the NAO major projects report

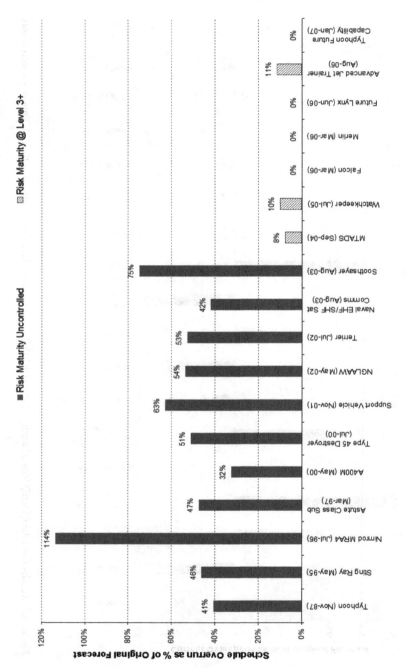

Figure 4.2 Results from the QinetiQ Risk Maturity Model (QRMM) applied to schedule deviation identified in the NAO major projects report

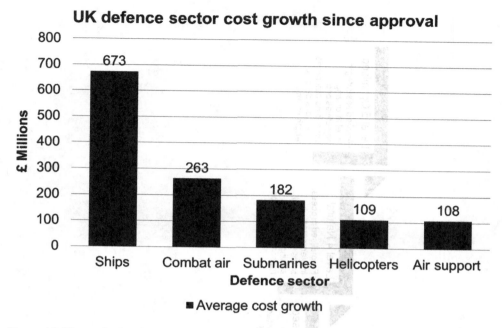

Figure 4.3 The motivation for conducting the Cost Engineering Health Check

to the four recognised in the KBE: Culture and Stakeholders. Culture refers to the level to which the cost engineers are integrated into the wider project environment and organisation policies. Stakeholders refer to anyone who has a vested interest in the cost inputs or outputs associated with the cost engineering function.

So why conduct a maturity assessment? The objective is not to determine the accuracy of the cost estimate; this can be determined through uncertainty analysis and Monte Carlo techniques that enable you to state the estimate is X with an accuracy of +/- Y%. The objective here is to examine the work that underpins the estimate. The Cost Engineering Health Check will assess the quality and consistency of the cost engineering consistently using five levels of maturity from Naive to Optimised as shown in Figure 4.4. It will support an understanding of the costs and their impacts across the enterprise and the interaction between the customer and supplier of the estimate. Cost Engineering Health Check can support the improvement of cost estimating and forecasting to inform better decision making across the organisation. This can be achieved through improved communications, where common issues are identified, and reduced duplication of effort, across the organisation. Finally, by taking this initiative the assessment can improve coherency and alignment, and share good practice throughout the organisation.

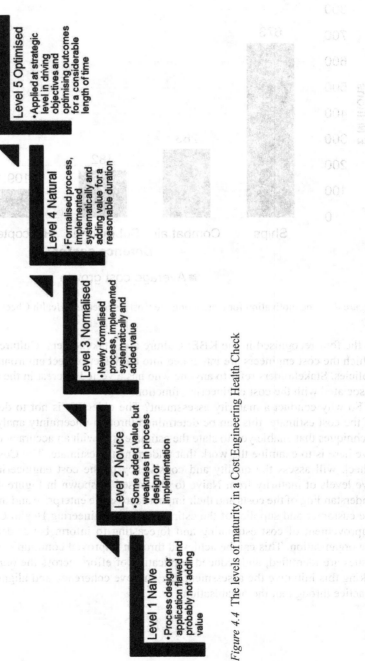

Figure 4.4 The levels of maturity in a Cost Engineering Health Check

5 The CEHC methodology

5.1 Introduction

Having a benchmarking capability is useful but to apply it consistently this needs to be conducted by trained consultants. Through experience and practice it is recognised that a four-stage model is best applied to the benchmarking of cost engineering as shown in Figure 5.1.

5.2 Pre-workshop

At the start of this process there needs to be a business case which identifies the benefits, both tangible and intangible, that will be realised through this process. This can be difficult if there is no perception of the value the cost engineering offers today, and can be a leap of faith on behalf of a senior manager to fund a benchmarking review prior to understanding the true benefit that will be achieved.

Having engaged in the benchmarking of a cost engineering function, there is a significant amount of work that can be conducted prior to any workshop. Conducting a pre-workshop analysis of the organisation's cost estimating process and documentation will save time in the workshop and familiarise the assessors with the organisation's capability, terminology and acronyms.

5.3 E-voting workshop assessment

In order to make an accurate assessment of the maturity of an organisation's capabilities you need to engage with the cost engineering managers and professional staff within that organisation. An effective way of undertaking this engagement is through electronic voting in a professionally facilitated workshop. E-voting is a well-established method of Group Decision Support. The technique is used in the operational analysis (OA) domain for the elicitation of opinion and can be adapted for use in CEHC. Participants use a small handset (Figure 5.2), similar in size to a mobile phone or television remote control, to register their votes in response to questions posed by the facilitator. The votes are anonymous, or participants can register their handset if they wish to have a record of their personal voting. The primary interest is the reason for the vote, not the vote itself. The electronic voting session needs to be conducted by an experienced facilitator to control the pace and stimulate discussion through the workshop. The e-voting provides a framework to consider arguments before expressing an opinion.

It is important to limit discussion to points of clarification before voting. The facilitator should ensure that participants fully understand the questions and supporting narrative, in

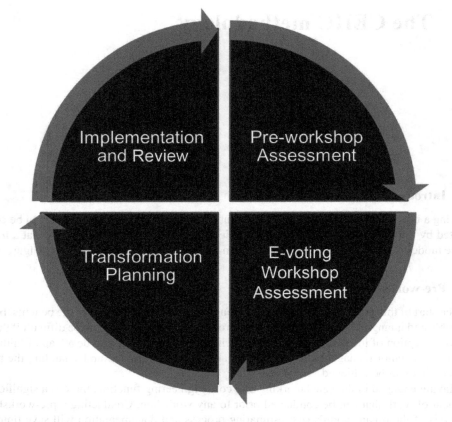

Figure 5.1 The application of the Cost Engineering Health Check

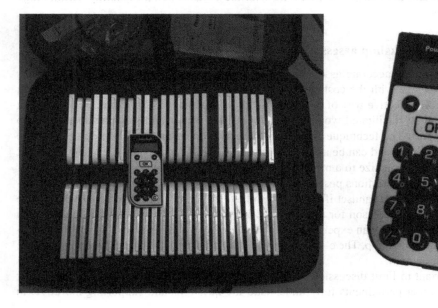

Figure 5.2 An e-voting handset can record the input from each individual to the maturity assessment

relation to cost engineering, prior to voting. The facilitator should also support an understanding of how the question and context relate to the organisation. Divergence in votes will thus provide additional insights into the issue under discussion, rather than resulting from uncertainty regarding the process.

These workshops should cover all disciplines involved in cost engineering delivery, including project management; complex project management [9]; and commercial, financial, technical and senior management. This ensures that the Cost Engineering Health Check assessment is objective and that the questions take account of the way in which all business functions affect the quality of cost engineering. The workshops proceed using a Delphi technique:

1   A question is posed.
2   The participants are given an opportunity to think! They consider the question and context. They are encouraged to put the questions in context of their organisation or experience.
3   Participants vote.
4   The workshop leader facilitates a discussion based upon the live voting results that are presented. Salient points are recorded for analysis and reporting. There is a record of the consensus view.
5   If necessary, there is a re-vote and a record of the subsequent consensus view.

The Cost Engineering Health Check tool is implemented in QinetiQ's AWARD® environment (see section 5.8) to provide traceability and a web-based user interface. AWARD® enables the tracking of the evidence required for the analysis, both pre-workshop evidence (such as copies of procedures, reports and guidelines) and evidence gathered during the workshop (such as voting scores and discussion points).

5.4 Definitions

Our experience has shown that providing adequate definitions and scope at the beginning of the workshop, and throughout it, is essential to ensure the success of a workshop. The participants need to have the workshop placed in context for them. You need to ask yourself prior to the workshop:

- Owning organisation – Who are you conducting the Cost Engineering Health Check for?
- The project – Is there a project or programme focus?
- End users, external customers or lead customer – Is there an ultimate customer organisation for this project or programme?
- Main estimators, cost analysts or cost forecasters – Who are the providers of these cost forecasts or estimates?
- Stakeholders – Which are the public and private organisations involved?
- Senior management – Who is the named internal customer receiving this financial information?

By analysing the data gathered during the workshop, you can identify weaknesses in an organisation's team and offer suggestions to enable a more reliable and accurate cost estimating ability. You can thus provide an organisation with the confidence to improve its cost estimates, and can identify development opportunities within the cost estimating capability to enable the organisation to focus on areas that have the potential to increase competitiveness and money saving efficiencies.

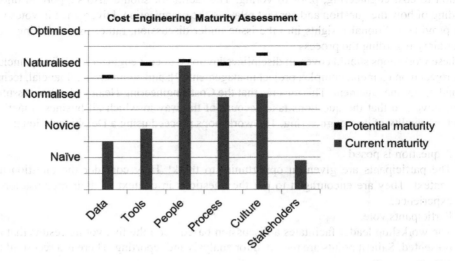

Figure 5.3 The current and potential maturity assessment of an organisation

5.5 Transformation planning

The output from the workshop will be a comprehensive report and analysis of the weak areas for improvement; however, this is likely to become 'shelf-ware' unless there are plans to implement its recommendations. You need to start with a prioritisation of the recommendations. Don't imagine that there will be a change just as a result of wishful thinking. This change process needs to be planned just like any other project, with objectives, a schedule and appropriate resources. Figure 5.3 is a great visualisation of the CEHC assessment that provides an indication of the current assessment and a vision of the future maturity state if the transformation planning is successful.

The two difficult areas to influence are the cultural environment and the stakeholder community. These will be given greater consideration in chapters 10 and 11 respectively.

5.6 Implementation and review

Finally, the plan needs to be put into practice. The organisation is endeavouring to transform the cost engineering function and all concerned need to understand the significance of the transformation.

In many transformation tasks, knowledge transfer is implicit in the requirements, as the team is expected to impart expertise during the course of a transformation project. In any change process there are distinct occasions where the transfer of knowledge must take place.

In situations where there are multiple candidates working on a task, concurrently and/or consecutively, the transformation team should ensure the successful transfer of knowledge from one person to another via briefing notes or meetings, as appropriate, thus ensuring that any inexperienced or less mature staff within the cost organisation are included in the knowledge transfer at all times.

Knowledge transfer between the inexperienced cost staff may occur in a variety of ways depending on the exact situation [43]. Appropriate methods for transferring knowledge and understanding of the outputs of the work include:

- Workshops – stakeholder meetings, facilitated by another part of the organisation or external facilitators, will seek to resolve areas of weakness in the team. It may be appropriate to form special interest groups (SIGs) to work upon particular niche areas for improvement and help the organisation maximise its potential.
- Formal training – a course may be provided to inexperienced cost staff to introduce new concepts, processes and methods for cost engineering. Tools may require specialist training to enhance their application and maximise the return on their investment, for example parametric models and statistic tools.
- Briefings and presentations – one-to-one meetings or mentoring can ensure that the inexperienced cost staff understand the methodology behind the work that has been done and the meaning of the outcome from this work. Learning from experience (LFE) briefings can focus on recent bids or projects – what went well or was problematic? – to provide useful insight for future cost work.

Formal handover activities, including lessons learnt, should occur as part of the project close down. These activities will include the transfer of project notebooks, files, copies of communication – both written and electronic – and other project records as appropriate to the task and as specified by the Transformation Team Leader. This will help ensure the maintenance of knowledge relating to the cost task(s) performed. In some cases there might also be scope for dissemination of research findings through papers and/or conference presentations, where the tasks allow information to be released into the public domain.

Reviewing progress is critical. It is necessary for all involved to see progress being made and that the organisation is benefitting from the changes and transformation. One of the easiest ways to achieve this is through a dashboard which you can maintain or update periodically and which shows the progress of the organisation during its 'get well' programme. A simple dashboard such as that in Figure 5.4 provides an indication of the organisation's movement towards an improving level of maturity.

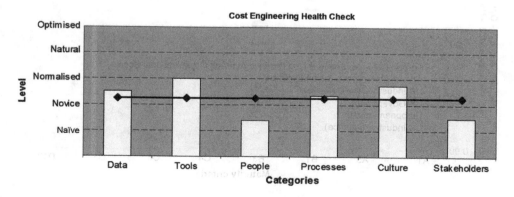

Figure 5.4 A simple Cost Engineering Health Check dashboard

As it is possible to see in Figure 5.4, the people and stakeholder maturity assessments are not progressing as rapidly are the other categories; you will need to focus more effort in these areas to enable the overall assessment of maturity to progress beyond the 'naïve' assessment that is currently registered.

Ideally, the organisation would wish to monitor itself against other peer organisations to provide context. It is not always necessary to strive to be classed as 'optimised' in your maturity; it is only necessary to be more mature than your peers. It is possible to see from the graph in Figure 5.5 the average maturity scores calculated from the e-voting for a number of assessments. Focusing on maturity criteria A5, regarding how well the cost engineering organisation understands its projects and the way that they function, there have only been average scores in the range 3.18 to 3.89 – nobody has scored an average of 5.0! The aim of any organisation should be to lie in the upper quartile or top 75% of this range; in this context an average score of 3.85 or above would be an excellent outcome.

Typically you will need to make recommendations as to the means of making improvements to areas of weakness. In the next example the recommendations have been split into two categories to make the transformation process seem less daunting and more achievable. The first set of recommendations should act to support a cost engineering capability that enables the development and generation of credible estimates, as shown in the example in Table 5.1.

These can be followed by Category 2 recommendations designed to enhance the capability further by providing confidence to management and wider stakeholders. These second category recommendations are focused on achieving best in class engineering approaches and new evolving principles (see Table 5.2).

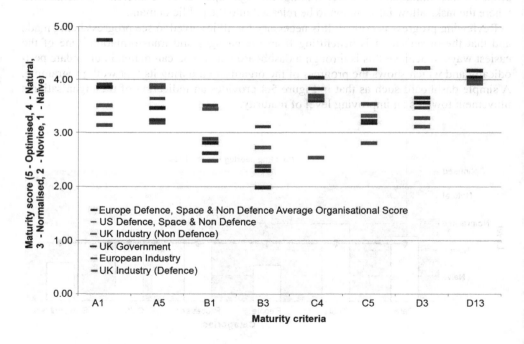

Figure 5.5 An example of maturity assessments for detailed areas showing the range of outcomes

Table 5.1 An example of Category 1 recommendations – designed to improve the organisation's ability to generate credible estimates

ID	Recommendation	Difficulty to implement	Impact on capability
R1.2	Provide staff access and training to commercial parametric models	Medium	High
R1.3	The organisation should mandate a consistent approach for including cost and schedule risk within their cost estimates	Easy	High
R4.3	The organisation should develop a data dictionary for use in archiving historic costs and technical information	Easy	High
R3.1	The organisation should recommend an authoritative source for escalation rates (or develop their own authoritative source)	Easy	High
R1.4	The organisation should create an independent cost model verification and validation cell for the review of all costs being provided to management	Medium	High

Table 5.2 An example of Category 2 recommendations – designed to further mature the confidence in the cost engineering capability

ID	Recommendation	Difficulty to implement	Impact on capability
R3.2	Expose customers to the cost approach and methodologies	Medium	Medium
R1.6	Encourage staff to participate in professional costing organisation conferences and international conferences	Medium	Medium
R2.3	Ensure interfaces between the organisational cost analysis process and other analysis processes are clear and sufficient for the transfer of information	Easy	High
R1.1	Engage with stakeholders to fully understand the types of decisions with which they are using cost information to inform, and align costing outputs to them	Easy	High

With the recommendations in place for the transformation it is possible to consider their potential impact should the organisation decide to implement them, as shown in Figure 5.6.

It is also possible to provide a schedule for the improvement in capability maturity, provided that the recommendations are implemented, as shown in Figure 5.7.

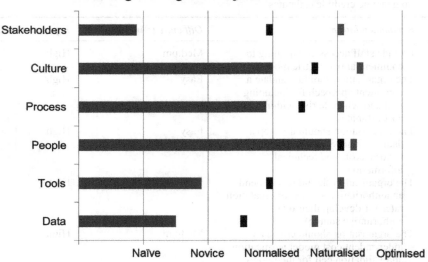

Figure 5.6 An example of potential migration of capability with the implementation of recommendations

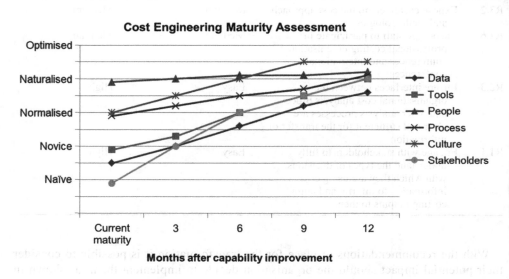

Figure 5.7 An example of the timeline for potential improvements

5.7 Cost Engineering Health Check implementation

When the prototype Cost Engineering Health Check was being researched, the cost maturity framework was implemented in an Excel spreadsheet to enable the easy and quick manipulation of the maturity questions and development of the analysis technique. Following a number of successful workshops and conferences, there seemed to be significant interest in this approach. The developer therefore considered a more long-term solution. Key requirements were the ability to allow collaborative input into the process from what might be a dispersed stakeholder community, and appropriate segregation and security protection of data and input from individual contributors, allied to transparency to enable the administrator to be able to accumulate a maturity benchmark across a number of anonymous databases for benchmarking against appropriate industries.

The suitable solution was the AWARD® system which provided a web-based, accessible, secure and collaborative framework for the health check implementation as seen in Figure 5.8.

5.8 AWARD® by Commerce Decisions Ltd

AWARD® by Commerce Decisions Limited, a subsidiary of QinetiQ, is used across the UK and increasingly in the international public sector and in defence procurement on strategic high risk and high value procurement projects. Strategic procurements involve multiple stakeholders, significant budgets and have a big impact on business performance. AWARD® is web based but delivered with a high level of assurance in terms of security, data integrity and business continuity. AWARD® provides a collaborative environment in which information can be presented – most typically bid documents and information that can be collected and analysed, most typically assessor scoring against sophisticated scoring models.

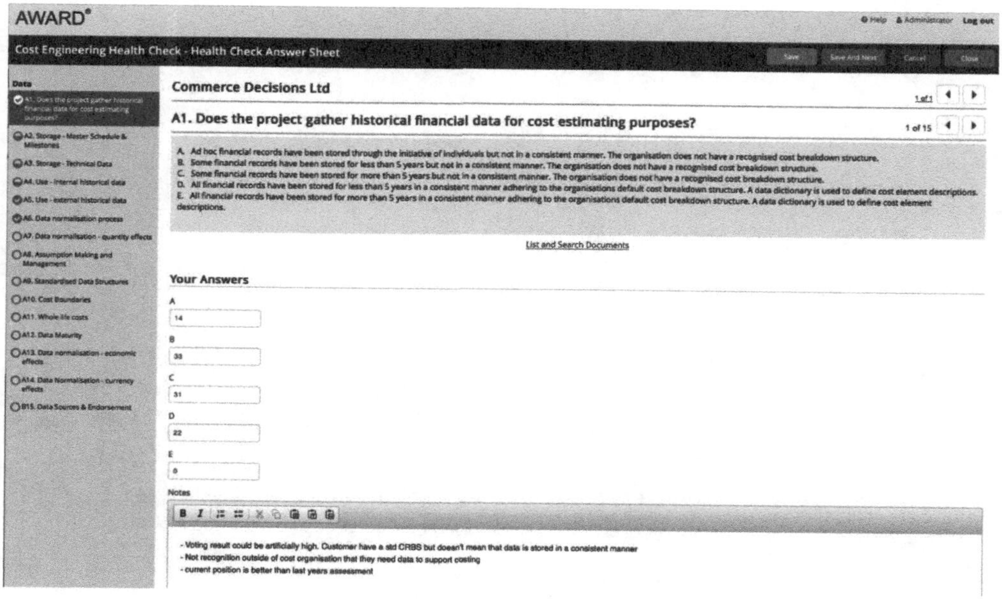

Figure 5.8 The Cost Engineering Health Check implemented in AWARD®

Commerce Decisions Limited also provides expert services to support both procurement and other related activities. Commerce Decisions configured AWARD® with the fixed cost maturity criteria and supported implementation and execution of the health check exercise. There is now an AWARD® Cost Health Check template that can be reused easily and securely across many more projects.

AWARD® is available in the UK via a number of routes, including the G-Cloud framework supported by the Government Procurement Service, and also in Australia and Canada.

6 Data gathering, normalisation and application

6.1 Introduction

Following the process of cost data collection, it is recognised in a mature cost engineering organisation that there is further manipulation required. To make it fit for the purpose of cost estimating there is a need for normalisation for currency and economic base year to produce a homogeneous data set. The critical aspect to this activity is maintaining complete transparency while conducting this normalisation. You need to be able to trace the outcome back to the original source information. A good example of this is the operating and support cost data capture exercise shown in Figure 6.1. During the manipulation of data the source data was stored in a Microsoft Access database to ensure that a third party could trace the output back to its origin in terms of the data source and the persons involved.

An experienced team will understand that it is typically necessary to manipulate, or normalise, all sourced data prior to being able to use it. The typical kind of attributes that sourced cost data must be normalised for includes:

- Attribution of overheads
- Outturn versus constant cost
- Quantity effects
- Fixed and variable
- Recurring versus non-recurring
- Currency
- Imperial to metric
- Questionnaire of method of allocation of costs (QMAC)
- Number of users
- Schedule durations

A mature organisation will have established processes on how data should be normalised, and these will be applied uniformly across the business. Typically, at the end of data manipulation there needs to be a book of anomalies. The book of anomalies will identify changes to the data since the last data gathering exercise; for example, it might highlight cost items which were previously directly attributable to projects which have now become overheads. This would account for a reduction in the costs that have been gathered in this annual data gathering exercise compared to the previous year. Other anomalies might highlight to the user of the data abnormal trends in the data or peculiarities in projects; for example, if a project had moved from the development phase to the manufacturing phase. The complete data set needs to be compared with the data set from the previous year and any trends identified. If there are any outliers from the trends that have been experienced in the past, then you should

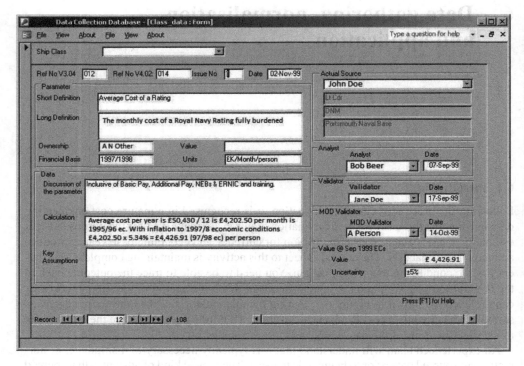

Figure 6.1 Example of an operating and support data collection database

investigate these rigorously and explain them. Once human error has been eliminated you should be able to document an explanation in the anomalies register.

It is important to differentiate between two phases of a cost model: the cost research and the software system, as seen in Figure 6.2. These two phases require complementary but different skill sets. Cost research relates to the data gathering, normalisation and creation of mathematical algorithms and cost estimating relationship (CER). The software system relates to the graphical user interface which is used by the cost analyst to apply the cost model or parametric model to a particular problem. This chapter deals with the former.

In terms of the cost research the important question is "How often should we update the model?" Generally there are two triggers that will prompt a requirement to conduct cost research:

- New data (requires current, accurate, complete data)
- Technical shift (introduction of new item of technology, manufacturing or design process)

This cost research requires cost analysts who are experts in data elicitation, manipulation and normalisation. It is important that such individuals have sufficient interpretation skills to help identify the elements against which the data must be manipulated and normalised.

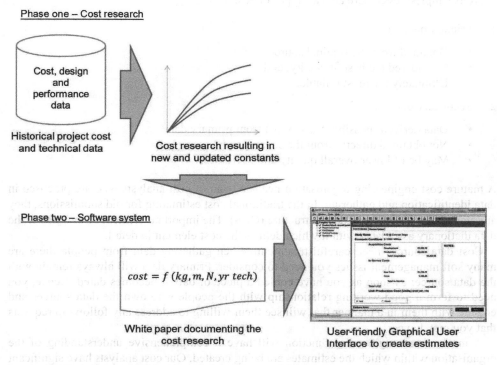

Phase one – Cost research

Cost, design and performance data

Historical project cost and technical data

Cost research resulting in new and updated constants

Phase two – Software system

$$cost = f\ (kg, m, N, yr\ tech)$$

White paper documenting the cost research

User-friendly Graphical User Interface to create estimates

Figure 6.2 Two-phase approach to generating a cost model

With regards to the software systems, the maintenance of the system is typically triggered by:

- The introduction of new operating system (Windows 27?);
- Updates in the underlying algorithms;
- Upgrades to the software or estimating capability function (new enhancements); or
- Simply periodic maintenance, such as fixing bugs.

The software system requires programmers who are expert in the field of programming with an understanding of the latest development techniques, languages and processes. QinetiQ has software standards such as TickIT and ISO9001 to maintain the quality of the product.

Data verification and validation of the system is of the utmost importance. There is little point in having new functionality in the software if the answer is no longer correct. You should have rigorous processes for cost model verification and validation.

As we teach students in the International Cost Estimating and Analysis Association (ICEAA) training course, the collection of cost data is the most time consuming and resource intensive part of creating a cost model. There is no amount of analysis that can compensate for poor cost data; therefore, the time spent sourcing, understanding and seeking cost data should be maximised.

At its simplest level there are two types of cost data:

1   Primary data are

- Obtained from the original source;
- Considered the best in quality; and
- Ultimately the most reliable.

2   Secondary data are

- Data derived (possibly 'sanitised') from primary data;
- Not obtained directly from the source; and
- May be of lower overall quality and usefulness.

A mature cost engineering organisation needs a team of cost analysts who are practised in data identification and gathering. In the traditional cost estimating for bid submissions, they are guided by the cost breakdown structure (CBS). The important element of the CBS is the data dictionary associated with it which defines the cost element in detail.

Cost data sources need careful treatment. When gathering data from people there are many soft management issues you need to consider. Primary data will always remain with the data source; as soon as you have copied a piece of data it becomes dated. Hence, you need to form a good working relationship with the people who own the data sources and engage with them in a manner that will see them willing to address any follow-up requests that you may have.

A mature cost engineering function will have a comprehensive understanding of the organisation within which the estimates are being created. Our cost analysts have significant experience in many organisations and experience of where to obtain cost information.

It is equally important to have a detailed understanding of the technical data associated with the project, system or service. To be able to derive the cost of your outputs, you will need to attribute overhead costs (for example headquarters, procurement, human resources and so forth) to those direct outputs. Without a good understanding of the project, system or service, you may attribute the overhead in an inappropriate manner.

When you gather financial and contextual data together, there are three principle categories of data when considered in terms of dimensions:

- Univariate – this is a single variable or element, for example, the cost of a car. We can collect cost data from a number of sources and calculate the average cost of cars.
- Bivariate – this is a set of data that consists of two variables, dependent and independent, for example the cost of ships (dependent variable) and the associated displacement of the ships (independent variable).
- Multivariate – this is a set of data that consists of more than two variables, a dependent and more than one independent, for example the cost of aircraft (dependent variable) and the associated mass when empty, year of manufacture, population unit power, manufacturer and so forth.

In cost forecasting, a mature cost organisation will understand the importance of Time Series data. Cost data in isolation is useful, but cost data that is time stamped is even more useful. Understanding that the costs occurred in 1990 or that the forecast cost will occur in 2035 is imperative.

Finally, a mature cost organisation will understand that not all contextual data can be quantified. This is particularly significant in the cost forecasting of services. It is often the case that qualitative information, for example the quality of the service, is gathered using a scale of very good, good, satisfactory, poor and very poor. The problem with qualitative data is that you are unable to use it in regression analysis; it's not possible to statistically test the relationship between the costs of services that are deemed to be good versus the cost of the same services provided by a poor supplier.

In such cases it will be necessary to code the independent variable, as you can then conduct mathematics on a Boolean scale, 1 to 5 or -2 to +2 with 0 becoming satisfactory.

6.2 Maturity considerations

6.2.1 Does the project gather historical financial data for cost estimating purposes?

Financial data is the lifeblood of any cost estimate. It is the starting point of any prediction of the cost of future projects, systems or services; a good knowledge base is essential [31]. It is highly unusual for a company to embark on a completely random venture or endeavour. Usually their offering has evolved from a previous offer, has been tested on the market or developed in some fashion and is highly likely to be related to the previous offering by magnitude, complexity or productivity [29]. Hence, if the previous offering has financial records, these are going to be extremely useful in generating an estimate of the cost of the next.

The type of data stored is generally important. This can be categorised as primary and secondary. Primary cost data is data that has been captured and sourced from the origin of the data, for example, time recording sheets that the engineers have completed or invoices for materials that the procurements organisation have paid. They are a direct record of the transactions.

Secondary sources are less authoritative. A secondary source will have been derived from a primary source but processed in some fashion; for example, the labour cost will have been drawn from the time records of the engineers, but will have been aggregated, combined with a labour rate, had overheads applied and so forth. The cost of raw material for a project will have been sourced from the invoices paid by the project but will have been summed together, perhaps had a procurement overhead applied, and might combine items from different batches of the end product.

For the estimating function, primary data is the holy grail of cost data, but we need to be realistic when an estimate is required and only secondary data is available to be used. Then it will be applied with the necessary caveats.

6.2.2 Does the project maintain a record of the master schedule and milestones?

For the purposes of cost estimating, the schedule of costs is important. Schedule of costs incurred can have a significant impact upon what those costs mean. Think for example about a 30-year programme, which is not untypical for large defence procurement and support programmes. Considering the all up cost of such a programme, expressed in, say, outturn figures, is likely to have limited value when estimating the cost of the next generation defence programme. The reason being is that the impact of escalation over such a time period will be significant; as a consequence, the cost should be appropriately normalised for inflation effects prior to it being used for any cost analysis. Without an understanding of the project schedule, the activities that were being conducted within each time period and the costs associated with those activities, it will be almost impossible to appropriately normalise the sourced cost data for the effects of escalation.

Additionally, the behaviour of a cost in relation to schedule variation is also an important consideration. If a cost is linked to the duration of a schedule, then it is likely that that cost is an overhead. From a cost engineering perspective, the activities within a schedule will be categorised as shown in Table 6.1.

A mature cost engineering organisation will consider and appreciate the difference between overhead related and task related activities, as shown in Figure 6.3.

When the term 'estimating' is used in general terms, it is in the context of cost estimating; however, there is no reason why schedule duration cannot be considered. Similar methodologies as those employed for generating cost estimates can also be applied to generate estimates for activity duration, thus informing a project schedule. In a similar fashion to cost estimating, all the same rigours must be placed around the collection of data, the use of tools, the behaviours of people and the application of process to ensure that a credible and defendable view on schedule is arrived at.

Table 6.1 Types of schedules related to cost

Name	Description	Schedule effect	Examples
Task related activities	This is the duration required by a resource to conduct a particular activity. It is a discrete activity that might be dependent on other activities but is solely required to take known inputs and process them to make outputs.	Fixed schedule	Writing a requirements document, testing a system or assembling a gearbox
Overhead related activities	This is the duration required by a resource to support a number of task related activities. It has a duration that is dependent on the activities that it supports.	Variable schedule	Project management, project control, risk management

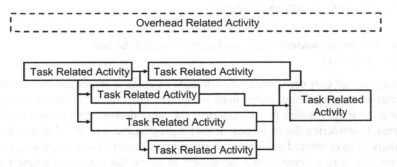

Figure 6.3 The relationship between cost influenced by overhead related activities and those which are task related

6.2.3 Does the project store technical information for the purposes of future cost estimates?

Normalised cost data is essential to all cost engineers, but cost data in isolation is meaningless. For a cost engineer to make sense of cost data, they need to have the associated technical and programmatic data. The most basic form of technical data is that which will enable the cost data to be stratified into information of a common type. That is, homogenous packages of data should be created. Hence the need for a formal product breakdown structure (PBS), work breakdown structure (WBS) and cost breakdown structure (CBS). The nodes within these structures need formal and agreed definitions to ensure that data across similar projects, equipment and work packages is collated uniformly in a manner that enables later comparison and analysis.

A typical way of ensuring this consistency is through the development of a data dictionary for each of the structures. A data dictionary simply provides an explanation as to what the cost associated with that node in the cost structure should relate to. At the most detailed level the accounting function will have established a data dictionary for the CBS. This is likely to have been agreed with the auditor; for example, in the UK MOD they adopt a questionnaire of method of allocation of costs (QMAC). This identifies the costs that are direct and indirect in detail. There is no random or arbitrary allocation of costs; if the cost is labour hours for a project manager, this is not considered on its merit: the accountants follow the rules and require a booking code and time sheets if it has been agreed to be direct cost, or the resources are allocated to an overhead general ledger if it has been agreed to be indirect. There is compromise to be had with respect to the degree of breakdown within the structure. The greater the degree of breakdown, the more specific the cost attribution against that node can be. The challenge then becomes the sheer number of nodes which makes comparison across different systems impractical or impossible as in some programmes not all nodes may be populated. This is where the experience and knowledge of the estimator comes to the fore, in helping to identify appropriate data structures.

Accountants will typically follow the generally accepted accounting principles (GAAP), which are the standard framework of guidance for financial accounting used in any particular country. These are generally known as accounting standards or standard accounting practices. They include the standards, conventions and rules that accountants follow in recording and summarising when preparing financial statements, for example the length of time to depreciate the cost of a laptop or computer. Although it is not necessary for a cost engineer to be an accountant, you need to understand the basic principles to be able to converse with accountants and obtain the cost information that you require.

In the same way there is a need to gather product costs together. A data dictionary can help to define the allocation. For example, in the aerospace industry a Reaction Control System is used to maintain the position of a satellite using thrusters. On different projects this can be referred to as a Reaction Control Systems, React. Cont. Syst., RCS and so forth. If a cost engineer is going to analyse the cost of this system across different projects, they need to be able to identify systems regardless of its title. Therefore a data dictionary might refer to the Reaction Control System as "the system of thrusters, pipes, valves, actuators and fuel tanks used to maintain the satellite in its correct attitude using thrust". With this definition all Reaction Control Systems, regardless of their title, should be included in any of the analyses.

It is important to gather the cost data in the appropriate format. Generally, analysis can only be performed on 'quantitative' data, for example binary, ordinal, and numeric data resulting from questions like multiple choice, rank order and averages. Questions that have textual outputs

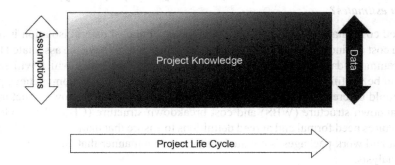

Figure 6.4 The migration of a project from the dependency on assumptions to the mature data

(qualitative data) need to be converted into numeric data before they can be used in any analysis. This can be achieved by linear or non-linear scales that equate to the qualitative output.

It is ideal to gather as much data as possible and as many different fields (or categories) of data as resources will permit. No amount of clever analysis can substitute for lack of data or poor quality data. It might seem fruitless gathering the number of wheels on the landing gear of an aircraft – it's highly unlikely to be a significant cost driver – but until you have tried to establish a statistical relationship between the numbers of wheels and cost, you are unable to say definitively.

It is possible to make assumptions in the absence of data. In the case of both technical and cost data this is an approach that is fraught with potential problems and should not be embarked upon without due care and consideration. A significant danger when making assumptions is that over the life of a project these can transform into accepted facts without ever having been appropriately tested (Figure 6.4). In such an example you then have a project built on very shaky foundations that is unlikely to be defendable and unlikely to withstand scrutiny.

When you are gathering historical data for the purposes of analysis, if you base the analysis on assumptions you are compounding errors. In the future you will then be making cost forecasts using a cost model that has potentially been estimated. This reinforces the need to spend significant resources gathering technical information. In many cases, the knowledge base you generate will be invaluable to the organisation in the future.

6.2.4 When estimating, does the project utilise historical data from the organisation's past projects?

The principal estimating techniques are parametric, analogous and analytical. All these techniques more or less depend upon historical cost and technical information. It is very rare for organisations to be forecasting the cost of completely new concepts; generally the product or service is an evolution from a product of service that they are familiar with. This makes good business sense and is low risk, and makes good acquisition sense as it is low risk. Even entirely new products or services are likely to be composed of elements of which the organisation has had prior experience. Consequently a mature cost engineering process will be able to call upon a large knowledge base of historical cost and technical data. In the extreme, when a product is entirely new to the organisation, there are still likely to be external organisations that may have costs that could be utilised (although getting access to this information may be challenging, and the insight that can be drawn from it may be significantly more limited than that if it were internally generated).

In the case of analogous estimating, or 'near neighbour' estimating, determine the projects that have been delivered previously or acquired previously by the organisation. Rank them in terms of size and complexity. For the new project it is then a relatively simple case to establish where the new project lies amongst the historical data.

For a parametric estimate, the historical knowledge base will already have been converted into parameters and cost estimating relationships that mathematically represent the knowledge base. To establish the new estimate, you need to populate the parameters to establish the cost forecast for the new projects.

Finally, the senior engineers responsible for generating an analytical estimate will have years of experience of past projects. In deriving the bottom-up estimate, they will use their knowledge of past projects to determine the likely resources required for a new project, assuming normal working practice. In other words, you won't get it right the first time.

Let us outline a rigorous approach to data management in a mature cost engineering organisation:

1   Ownership and confidentiality – data is owned by the company (except where specified otherwise under the terms and conditions applying to individual projects). All personal data is maintained for the purpose defined within the notification under the Data Protection Act. Project managers are responsible for maintaining the data protection of personal data specific to any project under their control.
2   Data access and retention – access to data is limited to those needing such access for work on any particular project. Each member of the staff is personally responsible for maintaining the confidentiality of the data to which they have access. Project managers determine who should have access to data.
3   Physical security – data is subject to physical security control appropriate to its nature. Physical access is determined on the same basis as data access.
4   Data – data may be held on local servers, personal workstations, laptop computers and other removable media such as CDs/DVDs and portable memory devices. Data held in servers are the responsibility of the IT manager. Security of data held on personal workstations, portable storage devices or removable media is the responsibility of the individual staff member operating the equipment.
5   Responsibilities – all staff (including associates and sub-contractors) have a personal responsibility to safeguard the integrity and confidentiality of the company's systems, data and physical facilities. Users of systems are responsible for ensuring that data and information to which they have authorised access is used only for the purpose provided and that the confidentiality and integrity of the data is maintained.

When considering the historical cost data from past projects, you need to analyse the information. The first analysis that any mature cost organisation will conduct will be to graph the data. There are numerous graphs that can be drawn, but some are more useful than others when it comes to analysing historical data. X-Y graphs or scatter graphs are helpful as they are able to indicate correlation between different data sets, for example plotting design or performance data as the independent variable against the cost or schedule as the dependent variable. This will provide an indication of the spread of the historical data and provide a first order indication as to whether or not a cost or schedule estimating relationship is likely to exist.

Statistics analysis provides a mechanism to characterise the data set. Typical characterisation of the data sets includes the measures of central tendency, such as the mean, median and mode. In a mature cost engineering organisation an appreciation of these terms would be understood and frequently utilised as follows:

- Mean – commonly known as the average, this is the total population divided by the number of samples, for example the total cost of a batch or lot of items divided by the number of items in that batch or lot.
- Median – commonly known as the 50% percentile, this is the middle items of a data set when ranked in order, for example when a Monte Carlo analysis has been conducted with 1,000 random numbers it will be the result of the 500th iteration.
- Mode – this is the most frequent data point; for example, when the data set is plotted as a histogram the mode is the tallest bar, which indicates the item of highest frequency within the population.

Once the centre of the data set has been determined for historical project information, the next useful and meaningful characterisation of the data set is the measure of dispersion between the data points within the data. Again, a mature cost engineering organisation will consider this in a number of ways; the range, variance and standard deviation are examples and would be considered as follows:

- Range – commonly known as the tolerance, this is the maximum historical value minus the minimum historical value; for example, the most expensive raw material less the cheapest raw material on a historical project will indicate the range of raw material costs.
- Variance – this is a measure of the deviation of the data set from the mean value; for example, the lower the variance indicates less dispersion from the mean and hence a tighter data set. It is the average squared distance of the data set from the mean.
- Standard deviation – this is the square root of the variance. This is a measure of the absolute distance of the data points from their mean.
- Coefficient of variation (CV) – this is the standard deviation divided by the mean. The coefficient of variation of less than 15% is desirable. Larger coefficient of variation indicates that the mean is a poor estimator and you need to examine the historical project data for outliers or stratify the data into several data sets.

6.2.5 Does the project consider historical data from outside the organisation?

When considering historical cost information, an organisation should not be introverted. In many large organisations the business strategy is to be the integration and design authority controlling the intellectual property and the clever aspects of the systems and platforms they market. Their business model seeks to maintain market dominance by keeping the intellectually challenging elements of their business in-house while outsourcing the seemingly mundane aspects to other companies. The details and manufacturing of the systems and equipment are left to other companies. For example, aircraft manufacturers will design the aircraft and integrate and test the final assembly, but they have suppliers for seats and galley equipment. Likewise, the car industry design and integrate their vehicles, but they have suppliers for seats and headlights. As a result, a large proportion of their costs are influenced by their partners' or sub-contractors' costs.

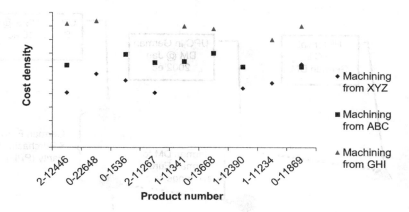

Figure 6.5 The productivity metric for different suppliers

In many organisations the task of negotiating the costs of sub-contractor services and products is left to the procurement department. But in a mature organisation the cost engineering function has a lot to offer in this area. Having a technical background is a huge benefit when considering the value for money of a proposal or quotation. An appreciation of the size, complexity and productivity of a sub-contractor is a genuine benefit when comparing the current proposal with the historical cost of analogous proposals from the same or similar organisations.

The application of a parametric model ([15]; Chapter 4) can make the normalisation of the historic data easier and will make the assessment time quicker. As you can observe in Figure 6.5, machined items from supplier XYZ are potentially cheaper than the other suppliers without consideration of the quality and delivery times.

6.2.6 Does the project normalise historical cost data?

Before you can make use of historical data, either internal or external data, it is necessary to normalise it. Once the data has been gathered it will be necessary to normalise the technical information for metric versus imperial. In the case of services, it will be necessary to normalise information; for example, resource hours data gathered over a period of months cannot be compared directly with resource hours data gathered over a period of years. In the case of cost data, it will be necessary to review the information and bring it to a common currency, economic base year, currency unit and so forth.

A mature cost engineer will appreciate the correct approach [12] to dealing with currency and inflation factors. It has been demonstrated that inflation rates for the country of origin need to be applied first and then the exchange rates (see Figure 6.6). These techniques need to be rigorously applied to ensure that the information used in cost forecasting techniques is normalised in a consistent process. It should be an integral part of the cost engineering training for an organisation.

A common problem is the application of the wrong index or the processing of the exchange rates and the index in the wrong way. Again, a mature cost engineering organisation will teach the correct process and recognise the need to differentiate between input or output indices, customer price index and retail price index, inflation and escalation, an index and a factor, and so forth.

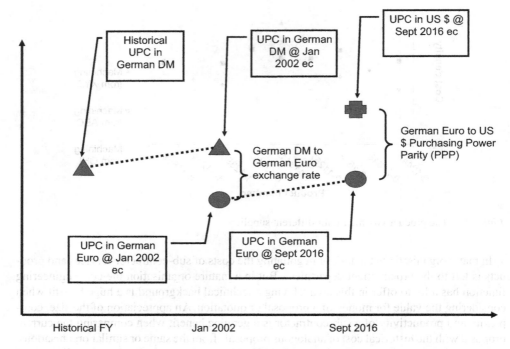

Figure 6.6 The correct approach to process historical cost data

6.2.7 Does the project normalise historical cost data for quantity effects?

The most common form of normalisation for cost data is the quantity effect. Commonly referred to as a learning curve, this is an important part of normalising recurring costs. It has been widely recognised in manufacturing that if a process is labour intensive, then the labour force will learn how to produce products quicker over a period of time. This might be as simple as an operative realising that they need to move a tool to make the process quicker for themselves, or it might be part of a time and motion works study. Regardless of the cause of the resource reduction, this phenomenon has been studied [11] and its impact on cost is widely recognised.

There are two common forms of the learning curve: the Crawford or Boeing curve where the output is a function of the cost of a unit, and the Wright or cumulative learning curve where the output is a function of the average unit cost of *n* units. The basic principle is that "every time the quantity produced is doubled, the time spent is reduced by the same percentage", as shown in Figure 6.7.

In a mature cost engineering organisation or project there will be recognition that recurring cost of manufacture cannot be compared directly when the item is manufactured in different batch sizes. The same item manufactured in a batch of 10 will not consume the same resources as the same item manufactured in a batch of 1,000. For this reason cost engineers will calculate the first theoretical piece or T_1 for a production line. This theoretical reference point can be used to make comparisons or to calculate the costs of different batches. Some organisations recognise that manufacturing does not approach a steady state until further into the production process and might agree to work on the assumption that a steady state is

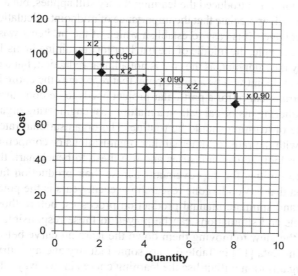

Figure 6.7 The effects of cost improvement or learning curves

reached at the 100th item, or T_{100}. The actual quantity value at which steady state is defined is typically a function of the learning rate and the margin of variance between one unit and the next that the organisation is willing to tolerate. Regardless of the agreed approach, the important issue is the normalisation of the recurring costs prior to any analysis of the raw data.

A mature cost engineering organisation will have a firm grasp of the concept of learning curve theory regardless of its local terminology. Learning curves are also known as cost improvement curves, quantity effect curves, experience curves, product improvement functions, learner curves and so forth. Since the original theory developed by T.P. Wright in 1936, numerous papers have been written and the concept has been developed and matured.

A mature cost engineering organisation will appreciate that the learning curve slope is a function of the industry and manufacturing process deployed in a particular creation of a product through its manufacturing process. The steeper the slope (70%–80%), typically the more manual the process; the shallower the slope (90%–100%), typically the more automated the process, until it becomes fully automated when no learning occurs. It will have a preferred reference point for its normalisation; many companies use T_1 but some have other preferences, in the aircraft industry the T_{100}, for example. Similarly, mature cost engineering organisations will understand that mixing unit learning and cumulative average learning is not a wise idea.

Cumulative average learning curve or Wright curve was the first application of the concept and is relatively straightforward to calculate. This was a development of the unit learning curve, also known as the Boeing curve or Crawford law. The two theories are similar and consider the cost saving observed when n units are produced; the principle difference is that cumulative average considers the average of the cost of the n units produced so far, while the unit learning curve considers the nth unit. When plotted on log-log graph paper, the slowly decaying curve becomes a straight line and the mathematics for a mature cost engineering organisation was obvious, even before the advent of computers.

When batches or lots are introduced the learning theory still applies, but a mature cost engineering organisation will appreciate that the importance of midpoint calculations and how these are challenging to conduct. It is easy to establish which of the 'n' items was in the middle of the lot or batch; for example, the middle of the batch or lot containing items 18 to 22 is 20. But this is not financially the midpoint, as the cost is not a linear reduction, but a decaying learning curve; therefore the midpoint will be a single point that represents the entire batch or lot.

Selecting the learning curve for a particular project needs to be done through the analysis of past projects. Gathering historical data in a mature cost engineering organisation and analysing it for the rate of learning should be routine. The organisational rates of learning can then be compared with the rates of other similar organisations or competitors. Alternatively the organisation can look across industries and use these to benchmark their efficiency, or to identify the opportunities for improvements across their production facilities and ways of working. An area that has undergone research in recent years is the potential opportunity to digitally model and simulate manual production processes, before those processes ever begin. These models and simulations can be played to those responsible for actioning the manual tasks with the view to moving them down the learning curve before production has even begun [14]. The data [13] in Table 6.2 are some industry average curves.

A mature cost organisation will utilise the learning curves in two ways: forward and backwards. Backwards is to apply learning curve theory to historical production data to determine the likely learning effect; forwards is to apply the same learning curve effect to analogous production projects with confidence and justification. During the backwards process the elimination of learning curve effect has the result of starting to generate a homogenous data set of historical data which is useful in comparing projects when currency and economic base years are also considered.

6.2.8 In the absence of data, does the project make rational assumptions?

When forecasting costs for new projects it is unlikely that all the information required to develop a cost estimate will be known. Consequently, in such situations it is important to give considerations to Assumptions (A), Dependencies (D), Opportunities (O), Risks (R), and Exclusions (E) to help bound the estimate and give something tangible against which to generate the estimate. QinetiQ calls the process of giving consideration to these things as an ADORE analysis. It is likely that an organisation's commercial department (and also a buying organisation) will mandate that the output of the ADORE analysis (the Assumptions, Dependencies, Opportunities, Risks, Exclusions) are made explicit in any formal offer of work being made by the organisation. For clarity they have been defined in Table 6.3.

A mature cost engineer or cost organisation will capture its ADORE analysis in a document; for example, in the UK MOD this would be a Cost Data and Assumptions List (CDAL)

Table 6.2 Possible learner rates

Military examples		Civilian examples	
Armoured personnel carrier	95%	Cars	85%
Helicopters	95%	Aircraft	80%
Radar	95%	Electric power generation	95%
Missile	70%	Integrated circuit	70%
Machine gun	95%	Handheld calculator	75%
Launch vehicle	85%	Steel production	80%

Table 6.3 The definitions of the ADORE analysis

Term	Definition
Assumptions	Assumptions are used to identify conditions which bound an offer or estimate. This definition also applies to a caveat.
Dependencies	Dependencies are used to identify customer supplied information, resource, equipment, etc. upon which a supplier relies to deliver a contract or service. Dependencies can be categorised as input or output dependencies.
Opportunities / Risks	Opportunities and Risks identify events that could occur that may impact deliverables; deviation from the baseline plan. Risk is modelled with opportunities where risk has a negative effect on output and an opportunity has a positive effect on output.
Exclusions	Exclusions are identified tasks or services which a supplier is not undertaking or intending to deliver.

or as part of a broader Master Data and Assumptions List (MDAL). As well as being a detailed technical, programmatic and schedule description, the purpose of the CDAL is to collect, integrate and coordinate technical, programmatic and schedule information necessary to estimate the costs of a program. It also ensures that cost projections developed by the analyst are based on a common definition of the system and the acquisition program. In the US DOD this document is typically referred to as the cost analysis requirement description, or CARD, and in NASA it's known as the cost analysis data requirement or CADRe.

There have been attempts to generate electronic versions of these documents. One project used the Dynamic Object Oriented Requirements System or DOORS system from Rational Software (currently owned by IBM) to treat the recording of the assumptions and data sources like a requirements document with tracking of changes and rigorous linking of data sources to the cost model; this is an example of a forward-thinking, mature cost engineering organisation that is actively engaged in attempting to undertake its costing in a more structured and efficient manner.

The format does not matter; neither does the length of the document nor where you store the information, as long as you do. The real key to the document is that recorded assumptions facilitate negotiations and dialogue. And document your estimate as you go rather than waiting until the end!

6.2.9 Does the project cost engineer collect historical project data against the organisation's standard CBS?

For a cost engineer, any financial data regarding their historical project, systems or services is desirable rather than none. It is impossible to produce a credible and justified cost estimate without data against which you can validate and verify your prediction. It is preferable for this information to be held electronically rather than in paper format, but cost engineers are not fussy and would be happy to scan or transcribe paper data into electronic data rather than have no data.

Ideally, this financial data will be structured in a fashion that is useful to a cost engineer, rather than an accountant. For example, in the American DOD the Mil Std 881 is used to structure the cost data together with the contextual information such as specifications, contracts, drawings and so forth. The European Space Agency (ESA) has an electronic system of tendering and proposals called ECOS, which requires financial and technical data to be populated for a compliant proposal. As such, cost data will be broken down into deliverable elements, systems, sub-systems and parts including the identification of any software. This is typically referred to as a product breakdown structure (PBS), equipment breakdown structure (EBS) or product tree (PT).

These deliverable elements will be broken down into a work breakdown structure (WBS). At the nodes of the WBS will be a work package that can be used to describe the inputs, outputs, activities, dependencies and so forth.

Finally, the WBS will have a cost breakdown structure (CBS) that identifies the resources within the organisation that will be used to deliver the work package (see Figure 6.8). The CBS will be recognised by the accountant as it deals with labour and non-labour elements. Typically, the labour elements will be the functions or departments with associated department numbers, for example drawing office, stress office, project management, structural engineering, electrical engineering, quality assurance and so forth. The non-labour will be purchased items and material; also sub-contracted items that are purchased or contracted

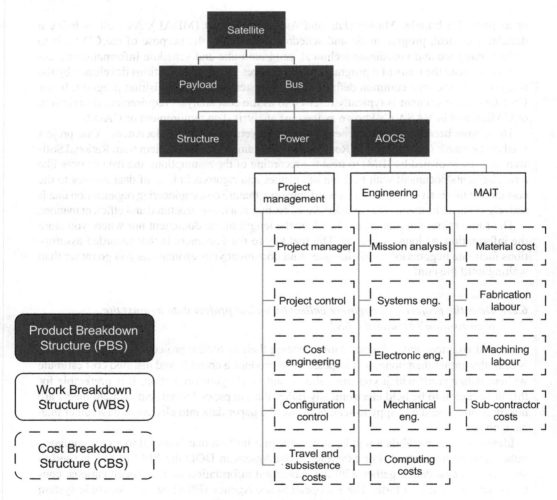

Figure 6.8 Relationship between the PBS, WBS and CBS with example products, work packages and functions

for this project or service, for example printing, computing, stationary, raw material, metal finishing and so forth. At the CBS level the accountant will determine the labour rates applicable to each labour category and the overheads associated with each labour and non-labour category.

In the ideal situation the cost engineer will have a data dictionary for the consistent application of costs to their cost elements. This ensures that costs are stored in a consistent manner with similar items grouped together.

6.2.10 Is there a cost boundary for the project?

When considering the whole life cost (WLC) of a project, it is easiest to consider that cost against a life cycle. Plotting the project from its conception to its disposal will ensure that all costs are considered. However, there is still a need to establish a boundary.

The most effective means of achieving this is with a stakeholder working group. During the development of the cost estimate it is good practice to expose all the stakeholders of the project or bid to the data sources that you are using and the boundary of the project or bid. The stakeholders could include, but are not necessarily limited to:

- Operators and maintainers
- Disposal team
- Engineering team
- Project management
- Quality assurance
- The customer
- Requirements manager
- Software developers and information / systems management

- Support staff
- Logistics team including transport and fuels
- Training and simulation
- Infrastructure team
- Procurement specialists and commercial team
- Trails and acceptance authority
- Safety authority

These stakeholders will be able to inform the cost engineers what other systems are influenced or have influence upon the product or service that is being estimated. For example, a Royal Navy destroyer is replenished at sea by a Royal Fleet Auxiliary (RFA), but should the RFA be included in the cost of the destroyer or not? A military jet has in-flight refuelling when on long sorties from a tanker aircraft – is the tanker aircraft part of the WLC?

Once these items have been identified, then the assumption regarding their inclusion can be captured in a Cost Data and Assumptions List (CDAL). The decision whether the cost is included or not should be made by the appropriate authority, but it can be informed by the question: If this product or service did not exist, would the service provided by this boundary element be required in part or in whole?

6.2.11 Does the project consider non-equipment costs?

Modern systems and platforms built from high technology hardware and software are miraculous pieces of engineering. Then we take these systems and integrate them together to form system of systems (SoS) [26]. However, they are only as good as the operators that use them and the operators are only as good as the training that they receive. Likewise, services are only provided when the service providers are trained to a high standard.

Hence, when a capability is delivered there is more to the capability than just the physical hardware. In Australia they consider Fundamental Inputs to Capability (FIC), in the US they consider Doctrine, Organizations, Training, Materiel, Leader Development, Facilities, Personnel or DOTMLFP and in the UK the MOD refers to these additional elements as Defence Lines of Development (DLoDs) and has a memory aid 'Tepid Oil', which is defined as follows:

- Training – the acquisition of the means to practise, develop and validate, within constraints, the practical application of a common military doctrine to deliver a military capability.
- Equipment – the acquisition of military platforms, systems and weapons (expendable and non-expendable, including updates to legacy systems) needed to outfit/equip an individual, group or organisation.
- Personnel – the timely acquisition of sufficient, capable and motivated personnel to deliver defence outputs, now and in the future.
- Information – the provision of a coherent development of data, information and knowledge requirements for capabilities and all processes designed to gather and handle data, information and knowledge. Data is defined as raw facts, without inherent meaning, used by humans and systems. Information is defined as data placed in context. Knowledge is information applied to a particular situation.
- (Concepts and) Doctrine – a concept is an expression of the capabilities that are likely to be used to accomplish an activity in the future. Doctrine is an expression of the principles by which military forces guide their actions and is a codification of how activity is conducted today. It is authoritative, but requires judgement in application.
- Organisation – relates to the operational and non-operational organisational relationships of people. It typically includes military force structures [50], MOD civilian organisational structures and defence contractors providing support.
- Infrastructure – the acquisition, development, management and disposal of all fixed, permanent buildings and structures, land, utilities and facility management services in support of defence capabilities. It includes estate development and structures that support military and civilian personnel.
- Logistics – the science of planning and carrying out the operational movement and maintenance of forces. In its most comprehensive sense, it relates to the aspects of military operations which deal with: the design and development, acquisition, storage, transport, distribution, maintenance, evacuation and disposition of materiel; the transport of personnel; the acquisition, construction, maintenance, operation and disposition of facilities; the acquisition or furnishing of services for medical and health support.

There is an additional overarching theme of **interoperability** that must be considered when any DLoD is being addressed. This is the ability of UK forces and, when appropriate, forces of partner and other nations to train, exercise and operate effectively together and with other governments' departments in the execution of assigned missions and tasks.

When estimating the WLC, in a mature cost engineering organisation all of these DLoD elements need to be considered and funding estimated.

6.2.12 When considering data, does the cost engineer consider data maturity?

How does a decision maker establish if the cost estimate that he or she is presented is a good estimate? One approach is to consider the tolerance of the estimate. That is why we present decision makers with a point estimate with an indication of the tolerance, for example £13,000 +/- £2,000. This enables them to appreciate the accuracy of the estimate, but it still does not help them to appreciate if the estimate is good.

Another approach is to consider a maturity model such as the Cost Engineering Health Check (CEHC). This will consider the health of the organisation, project, team or estimator. In the case of the Cost Engineering Health Check, the maturity is monitored against the Knowledge Based Estimating (KBE) building blocks of the Data, Tools, People and Process.

Should we want to provide an indication of the credibility of the data that has been used in the estimate, then this would provide a further level of confidence. The normal term used for this type of confidence is the 'Derivation of the Estimate'; in other words, from what is the estimate derived?

This can be very informative and can lead to some useful metrics. The assessment criteria for the cost data going into an estimate can be judged from the following questions:

1   What estimating method was used to establish the figure?
2   Is the data up to date, or when was it last refreshed?
3   Is the data accurate or close to the data source?
4   Is the data reliable, or has it been validated and verified?
5   Is the data understandable, or does it have a standard definition?

When judging a piece of data it is not the average of these questions that determines the overall maturity, but the elements of lowest maturity will establish the benchmark and will prompt action to improve the level of maturity.

The definitions in Table 6.4 below have been established by QinetiQ and applied to their cost estimates.

There are potentially many issues in data collection for a mature cost engineering organisation. For example, *availability*: Does the data easily exist? Is there a part of the organisation, such as finance, who are already gathering the data which you seek or will there need to be investment to gathering the data. If an investment is required, then it will be necessary to produce a business case to justify the expenditure in a data gathering project which some could perceive as wasteful. *Accessibility*: Are there commercial or security classifications which mean that, although the data exists, it is not accessible to the cost engineering organisation to utilise? Contractually, the data has been provided to the organisation for a purpose which does not permit the reuse of the data; it may be subject to a nondisclosure agreement or NDA. *Completeness*: Is the data representative of the whole project? If the project or service is partially completed, perhaps two-thirds of the way through a project, then the data is not usable, as you don't know the actual complete state of the project or service; it might be the final third when all the resources are consumed, and the expenditure can't be assumed to be linear. *Validity*: Is the data up to date? When was it last collected and how current is it to the proposed new project or service which you are likely to be estimating or forecasting? It is possible to cross-check the data with other known sources to validate the data. This might alleviate the issue of data collection from a validity perspective. Finally, *timeliness*: Is the data available when you need it? The mature cost engineering organisation will realise that gathering validated, complete, accessible, available data next year is of little use if the forecast or estimate is required by the end of the month.

Table 6.4 Cost data maturity assessment matrix

Maturity class	Assessment criteria				
	Estimating method	*Current – is the data up to date?*	*Accurate – is the data close to data sources?*	*Reliable – is the data validated and verified?*	*Understandable – is the data defined?*
Class 5	Rough order of magnitude (ROM) estimate or judgement from subject matter expert (SME)	Not reviewed and/or endorsed in the last 18 months	Provenance unknown	Single estimation methodology employed No assurance	The scope/boundary/ economic conditions relating to the data are not explicitly defined and assumptions concerning its definition are tenuous
Class 4	Analogy	Reviewed and endorsed in the last 18 months	Provenance incomplete Predominantly tertiary data sources	Single estimation methodology employed Project team assurance only	The scope/boundary/ economic conditions relating to the data are not explicitly defined but reasonable assumptions concerning the definition have been made
Class 3	Parametric	Reviewed and endorsed in the last 12 months	Provenance predominantly complete Predominantly secondary data sources	Multiple estimation methodologies employed No assurance	The scope/boundary/ economic conditions relating to the data are partially defined but understood by only a small number of individuals within the project team
Class 2	Activity-based estimating based on agreed schedule of work or bill of material	Reviewed and endorsed in the last 9 months	Provenance predominantly complete Hybrid primary and secondary data sources	Multiple estimation methodologies employed Project team assurance	The scope/boundary/ economic conditions relating to the data are defined and understood by all relevant stakeholders
Class 1	Supplier bid or actual cost	Reviewed and endorsed in the last 6 months	Provenance complete Predominantly primary data sources	Multiple estimation methodologies employed Independently assured	The scope/boundary/ economic conditions relating to the data are completely defined, understood by all relevant stakeholders and is mapped to the CRBS data dictionary

6.2.13 What is done in the project regarding escalation or inflation data following cost normalisation?

When a cost engineer normalises historical cost information for utilisation in statistical analysis, bringing the cost to a constant cost year is essential. Typically the cost information that is gathered in an accounting general ledger is the cost at the time of expenditure, for example labour direct booking and non-labour cost for purchased items, services and material. They are considered to be 'as-spent', 'outturn' or 'then-year' costs.

As shown in the figure below (Figure 6.9), to enable the costs of different units to be compared they need to be brought to constant cost, for example all 2008 constant costs. This would simulate a situation when all 20 units were manufactured in the year 2008, rather than 20 units manufactured over four years. This is achieved by extracting the appropriate level of inflation from the as-spent prices.

Once the prices are all normalised to constant 2008 economics, then further normalisation – such as quantity improvement, removing the profit or fee – can be considered prior to statistical analysis. By removing the effect of inflation it is possible to establish the constant price at 2008 economics date. A mature cost engineering organisation will train its staff, have procedures and fully understand the transition from:

- Then year to current year
- Current year to then year
- Constant year (20XX) to constant year (20YY)

A mature cost engineering organisation will understand that different terms are used internationally for these effects. Generally, inflation is recognised as the sustained level of price increase of a product, service or project in the economy. Deflation is the opposite effect, but is quite rare; most prices will increase. They will recognise that not all prices will rise at the same rate. When there are a variety of elements which have been added to generate a single price, for example material and labour, then it is common to generate a composite inflation index comprising the appropriate proportions of the material inflation rate and labour inflation rate to be applied to the overall price, as shown in Table 6.5.

It is important to a mature cost engineering organisation that the correct inflation rates are used from an authoritative source. It is common to find that a contracting authority will specify the inflation tables to be used in their contracting mechanism; it is also possible that they will sponsor an organisation to maintain and publish inflation rate tables on a monthly

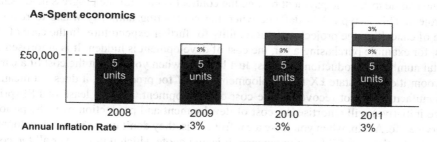

Figure 6.9 The importance of the inflation rates applied to constant prices to establish outturn prices

Table 6.5 Inflation rates applied individually and composite inflation rate calculation

	Price @ 2000 base year	Proportion of price	Annual inflation rate	Price @ 2001 year	Base
Composite material	£ 350	35%	7.50%	350 × 1.075 =	£ 376
Bonding resin	£ 100	10%	8.00%	100 × 1.080 =	£ 108
Management	£ 50	5%	6.00%	50 × 1.06 =	£ 53
Fabricator	£ 500	50%	5.00%	500 × 1.05 =	£ 525
Total	£ 1,000	100%			£ 1,062
Alternatively: Composite inflation rate = 0.35 × (7.5%) + 0.10 × (8.0%) + 0.05 × (6%) + 0.50 × (5.0%) =					6.23%
Total price of item =	£ 1,000	× composite rate 6.23%		=	£ 1,062

basis. The consumer price index (CPI) is an example of an inflation index which is common across nations and is based upon a common basket of items.

The inflation rate is the percentage change of the cost of a material or labour category over a period of time when escalation effect is considered. Conversely, to consider the deflation effect on costs, a deflation rate is applied.

The terms 'inflation' and 'escalation' are frequently used interchangeably in an immature cost engineering organisation. Inflation should only be referred to in the context of prices, while escalation should be discussed when costs are being reviewed.

In the context of cost estimating, once the effect of inflation has been removed from a time-phased historical set of cost data, then it will be normalised to a constant year. That constant year is recognised as the Base Year of the data. If a cost estimating relationship is generated for this data, then this will be the Base Year of that cost estimating relationship. It is possible to move from one Base Year to another Base Year through the application of indices. A mature cost engineering organisation will recognise that the profiling of costs or the time relationship is important when considering this economic effect. The period of time across which the project funds are spent is important; they need to consider the time that the costs are committed, the time they are contracted and the expenditure profile. A good example of this is shown in Table 6.6.

In the classic milestone payment regime the contract is paid for the progress made against the project. This is typical in defence when the contracting authority wants to retain the option of cancelling the project without liability for further expenditure. In the case of retail goods, for example purchasing a car, the cost of development is hidden. It is amortised over the total number of production vehicles. Just because when you look at the cost of a car in a showroom it doesn't state £X for development and £Y for production, it does not mean that the manufacturer is not recovering the cost of development. Finally, lease or PFI (private finance initiative) will amortise the cost of development and production over the period of the service life. Again, when you lease a car from Avis, they don't quote $X for development, $Y for production and $Z for maintenance; it is one quote which will recover all the cost in the supply chain. Naturally, Table 6.6 is very simplistic as it does not include the costs of funding the retail and lease options. There is a need in these options to borrow money, and

Table 6.6 Time phasing of costs

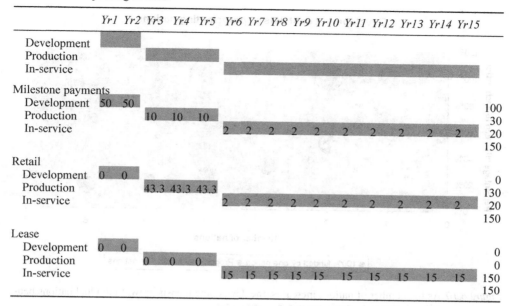

	Yr1	Yr2	Yr3	Yr4	Yr5	Yr6	Yr7	Yr8	Yr9	Yr10	Yr11	Yr12	Yr13	Yr14	Yr15	
Development																
Production																
In-service																
Milestone payments																
Development	50	50														100
Production			10	10	10											30
In-service						2	2	2	2	2	2	2	2	2	2	20
																150
Retail																
Development	0	0														0
Production			43.3	43.3	43.3											130
In-service						2	2	2	2	2	2	2	2	2	2	20
																150
Lease																
Development	0	0														0
Production			0	0	0											0
In-service						15	15	15	15	15	15	15	15	15	15	150
																150

the bank will want their return on this investment; hence these options, although resulting in the same service or product being received by the contracting authority, are likely to cost more in the long-term.

6.2.14 Does the cost engineer consider the influences of currency exchange rates?

Working with foreign nations has the advantage of acquiring skills and technologies that are not necessarily available in your home nation; however, it does have its drawbacks as well. In simple terms, if you fund the development of a project as a single nation, then 100% of the development budget falls to you. However, if the development work is split between two nations, then the effect is to increase the size of the development budget marginally due to communication, culture and time zone difficulties, but then as a funding nation it is only necessary to fund half of the money required. In theory, as seen in Figure 6.10, more nations will increase the development funding overall, but reduce the size of the funding requirement to any individual nation.

The added complexity is the need to deal with exchange rates and the fluctuation of the currency. This leads to a requirement to analyse trends within currency fluctuation. Consider Figure 6.11: there is a need to fund foreign currency for a four-year period in a project. As we approach this period we can establish the likely funds that will be required to convert into the foreign currency at the time. One solution is to hedge this currency or buy-forwards. This will guarantee the exchange rate at which we can buy our foreign currency. However, this is expensive and will add cost to the project as someone else is taking the risk of the currency changing and will require recompense for this action.

Alternatively we can consider the range of possible exchange rates that are possible and conduct a risk analysis to establish the appropriate confidence level. In this example there

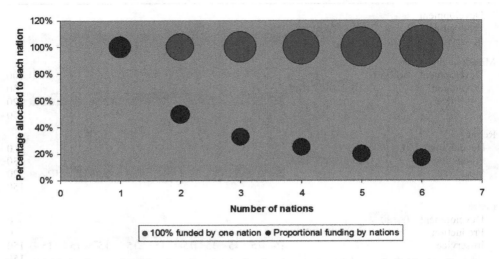

Figure 6.10 As the number of nations increases, the development costs grow. Individual nations benefit if they share equally the non-recurring costs.

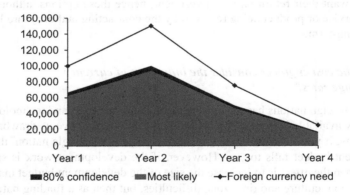

Figure 6.11 FOREX prediction is necessary in a mature cost estimating environment

is 80% confidence, thus providing an enhanced level of national funds to ensure with 80% confidence that when the time arrives there will be sufficient funds available.

6.2.15 Does the project have a stakeholder working group or equivalent?

The worst possible outcome for a cost engineer is the rejection of their estimate, analysis or forecast. This results in a lack of confidence in future work conducted and the whole cost organisation being discredited. Experience has shown that the most effective means of avoiding this situation is to manage the expectations of the customer for the task and all the other stakeholders that are likely to have a say in the adoption of outputs of the analysis. If their needs and requirements are clearly articulated at the start of the process and then regularly monitored throughout the task, the result of the task will not be a shock to them or a disappointment.

The most effective means of managing the expectations of the stakeholders is to conduct regular workshops. This simple but effective process will open a dialogue between the customer and the provider of the service. As a result, the decision maker will be provided with an explanation of the difficulties to obtain information, what has happened to the information and how the cost output has been derived.

7 Tool development and usage

7.1 Introduction

The *Oxford English Dictionary*'s definition of a tool is "a device or implement, especially one held in the hand, used to carry out a particular function". Tools augment us in the process of conducting our daily business and have evolved in sophistication to meet the ever more challenging demands of our technologically advancing society. In the instance of a cost engineering function, a tool can be considered to be a "calculator or mathematical model which makes the prediction of cost easier". They provide the means to quickly analyse data and the ability to embody cost estimating relationships such that estimates can be generated in a repeatable systematic fashion. The most common go-to tool for cost engineers is the ubiquitous Microsoft Excel spreadsheet. The ready access that most cost engineering professionals have to Excel, combined with its versatility, has resulted in its use being commonplace within most cost engineering functions. Despite its usefulness, the application of Excel does come in for some criticism within the cost engineering profession, mostly, though, because it is used inappropriately. The saying "a fool with a tool is still a fool" is especially true within cost engineering circles.

The cost engineering profession's relationship with Microsoft originally began with the spreadsheet program called Multiplan in 1982, but this eventually lost popularity to Lotus 1–2–3, which combined spreadsheet functionality with charting and some simple database functionality. Microsoft released the first version of Excel for Windows 2.0 in November 1987.

Since the time that spreadsheets first became available, cost engineers have developed numerous applications to support and make much easier the methodologies that they use within the domain of costing for data analysis and estimating. Approaches for which applications have been developed include, but are not limited to:

- Learning curves theory
- Exchange rate variations
- Database of historical information
- Cost aggregation tools
- Risk analysis capability

The level and sophistication of applications in a cost organisation will be varied, but how organisations approach such tools will be reflective of the maturity of its cost engineering function.

7.2 Maturity considerations

7.2.1 *Does the project train staff in the usage of cost engineering tools?*

The maturity of an organisation can be assessed through the importance it places on ensuring that its staff are appropriately trained to use the tools that they have at their disposal. Training in tool use can take the form of being tutor-led or through self-study such as working through exercise books, examples and/or e-learning [59]. A mature organisation is one that recognises that investment in training cost engineering staff in the use of cost estimating tools works on two levels: it is good for the business as a whole as it leads to the generation of higher quality estimates, but also it acts as an incentive for staff to remain in the organisation and hence strengthens organisational knowledge. Training in the use of cost engineering tools is of particular importance. A good chief cost engineer once told me, "a fool with a tool is still a fool", by which he meant unless you are educated in the utilisation of tools they are not going to enhance your capability. Why is this? Well, in the case of cost engineering tools it is necessary to implement them as the originator intended. When the cost research of the tool originator began to mature into a tool that was worth turning into a product, then that cost research had a particular approach or methodology at that time. The originator probably had an original idea that they considered to be sufficiently unique, and its application sufficiently valuable, that it was worth taking out of the research state and putting into production to enable third parties to benefit from that investment. Hence a cost engineering tool is brought to the market.

Now, when a tool is launched on the market, it is important that the core concepts and ideas are communicated to the recipients also. For this reason training is necessary, otherwise there are expectations from the senior management who have made an investment in the cost engineering tool that will not be fulfilled, communication will breakdown and the credibility of the tool will become lost. In a good, mature organisation the training is tailored to the requirements of the different audiences:

1   Executive level – short, concise, overview of the cost engineering tool and the application. This will ensure that the demand for the application of tools is realistic.
2   Management level – appreciation of the cost engineering tool and its usage with an understanding of the outputs of the tool.
3   User level – a detailed understanding of the cost engineering tool, its core concepts, application, and interpretation of inputs and outputs.

External training is desirable when a cost engineering organisation begins to embrace a tool set, but as the organisation matures it is possible that the organisation will begin to conduct its own tailored training. While the vendor of the tool set will understand the tool in significant detail, only the organisation itself will fully appreciate its application in the context of the organisation into which it is being deployed. Inevitably the organisation will indicate a level of maturity through the self-teaching of the tool set through super users. It is also important to learn by reading books relevant to the cost engineering topic [15] and around the topic area. It is conceivable that this level of understanding could develop into teaching third parties [22].

7.2.2 *Does the project maintain the cost engineering tools that it uses?*

Cost tools are seen as valuable when they are created, but the importance of maintaining and calibrating them is often either not recognised by an organisation or alternatively overlooked and forgotten. As a result, cost tools often fall into disrepair and eventually become redundant and hence worthless. Indeed, failure to maintain and calibrate tools results in a loss of organisational knowledge. It is worth recognising that calibration and maintenance are two separate activities. Maintenance is the activity of ensuring a cost tool will continue to function. For example, as the underlying operating system on which the tool is hosted migrates from Windows 95 to Windows XP through to Windows 7 and beyond, the cost model needs to be updated to remain functional. Such an update does not necessarily need to change the underlying tool functionality or improve the tool's estimating accuracy; it is just a necessary activity to ensure the tool remains useable.

Maintenance should also consider the opportunity to upgrade the cost tool, that is it should act to improve the tool functionality and/or accuracy. In such a case it is typically common practice to seek feedback from the community that is using the tool and to use this feedback to influence how the tools are upgraded. At training courses it is common to seek course and cost tool feedback, and in the interaction of a group training session it is easy to generate potential enhancements.

Calibration is the activity of ensuring the answer remains accurate [63]. It is the act of ensuring that the data components embodied within a tool such as the algorithms, inflation factors, exchange rates and so forth are current and up to date, and remain reflective of the systems for which they are being used to generate estimates. If a cost tool is a proprietary model from a third party, rather than having been developed in-house by the organisation using organisation-specific data, then it is important that the tool is calibrated against organisation-specific data and the organisation's productivity levels. This calibration might cover product or service calibration specific to the organisation for which you are working, but it will certainly include global calibration such as your labour rates and overheads.

Frequently calibration is seen as an overhead with little added value. However, this is not the case if it is approached as a learning exercise. A good example is the calibration of a proprietary cost model for a well-known electronics company. The cost engineer began the calibration of the electric weight and cost. He established results similar to those shown in Figure 7.1. As he expected working for a renowned world-beating electronics organisation, the results of their organisation were better than industry averages when plotting cost versus electronics weights. Their products were below the line.

However, when they started to consider the structural element of their electronic boxes, the packaging element, they were horrified to find that they were worse than the industry

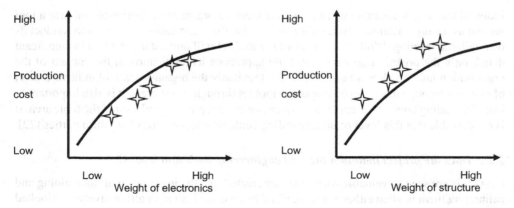

Figure 7.1 Understanding the organisation's productivity is essential in a mature cost engineering environment

average! Following a review of the input data and a check of the calibration information, it was determined that they were below the average industry line – not a good place to be. The calibration of the cost model did not determine the solution, but held up a warning flag to warrant an investigation. The subsequent investigation highlighted that when they recruited graduate employees, they took the best electronics graduates that they could find – they were the best in the world. However, when they had filled the electronics department, these same graduates were deployed to the structures department. As a result, there was no structural design expertise in the department. Following reorganisation and a recruitment campaign, a modular packaging scheme and commonality of bolt rather than custom and random sizes were introduced, and this resulted in a reduction of cost and weight. Calibration did not solve the fundamental problem, but it did highlight the need for an investigation.

It is worth considering how often a cost model needs to be updated. Some organisations will have an annual cycle of calibration, which is good. In reality calibration needs to be triggered by two events:

1   New cost data – for example, if the accounts department changes the relationship between direct and overheads, or process changes designed to make the organisation more productive.
2   New technical data – for example a technology shift, or the introduction of a new material such as composite in the aircraft industry.

7.2.3 Do the project stakeholders request estimates from cost engineering tools?

A recognition from project/organisational stakeholders in the value of the cost engineering function is evidenced by the demand stakeholders place upon the function for output. A cost engineering function that does not receive requests for estimates to support organisational or project decision making is likely a function that is not viewed particularly positively. Indeed, one would question why the organisation would continue to fund such a resource if it is not being used. Additionally, if stakeholders request estimates from the cost estimating function but don't actually then go on to use them, then this suggests again that there either is something wrong with the quality of output from the function, or, more perversely, that there is something inherently dysfunctional about the organisation's management and governance structure that would allow such a situation to occur. Either way, the cost engineering function should be seen as a key resource for the provision of context to aid any important organisational decision.

The project stakeholders can vary depending upon the type of estimate or forecast that is being generated. A good estimating function will have the tools that allow them to pro-actively respond to the needs of their stakeholders and provide output that is pitched at an appropriate level to ease understanding. Typical types of estimates that will be requested by stakeholders and the situations in which they may be requested are as follows:

•   Initial 'rough order of magnitude (ROM)' estimate

    •   New start or planning estimate
    •   Limited technical and performance data
    •   Estimate is normally completed using analogy, expert opinion or parametric
    •   Baseline estimate from which iterations are completed (based on alternative technical solutions)
    •   To support high level decisions

- Budget estimate
  - Normally required to obtain program funding such as the MOD Main Gate approval process
  - Estimate identifies funding profile by funding appropriation for each fiscal year
  - Time phased
  - Program requirements are moderately well defined
  - Estimate is completed using parametric, analogy or detailed bottom-up techniques
  - Budget estimate may contain cost elements beyond current need
  - Risk and contingencies are explicit and justified

- Proposal/bid
  - Competitive bid or proposal (contractor)
  - Source selection estimate (government's own most probable life cycle cost)
  - Well defined technical solution in existence
  - Normally completed using parametric techniques or detailed bottom-up techniques
  - Cost estimate typically in a prescribed format
  - Estimate may support yearly budget request

- Independent cost estimate (ICE)
  - Required to support program milestone decisions
  - Generally completed by a team of non-program personnel
  - ICE estimate is compared to other estimates
  - Cost delta between the two estimates may be defined as cost risk
  - Can result in a change to the program budget
  - Program requirements and processes are generally firm

- Point estimate
  - Measures or reflects a single number for the program

- Probabilistic estimate
  - Reflects a range of possible 'outcomes' or the probability of the estimate
  - Normally accomplished using risk simulation techniques

- Estimate at Completion (EAC)
  - Reflects the expected cost at the end of the program based on current progress
  - Terminology used in earned value management (EVM)

- Should cost estimate
  - Term usually used to describe the outcome of an ICE
  - A forecasted view of the expected cost based on current design, program and schedule inputs

- Would / could cost estimate
  - A variation of a 'should cost'
  - A 'what if' or alternative view of what a cost would be 'if' the program were to have taken a certain direction with changes

- Will cost estimate

  - A predicted cost with almost 100% certainty of being the final cost
  - Usually a cost quoted by a supplier

- Not to exceed (NTE)

  - A contracting term that implies that a cost will not exceed a certain maximum level

- Expert opinion / subject matter experts (SME) estimate

  - An individual's best 'guesstimate' or 'gut feel' based on experience

- Catalogue prices / vendor quotes

  - Current cost quoted by third-party suppliers

Each of these different types of estimates will require a diverse range of different tools and methodologies to generate. A mature organisation will recognise the importance of ensuring ready access to these tools for their cost engineers in anticipation of supporting the decision making process.

7.2.4 When producing an estimate, does the cost engineer use risk analysis tools?

At the core of this question is the realisation that estimating and forecasting cost is not a precise science. It's a bit like trying to forecast the weather: you assess all the data, look for patterns and then extrapolate into the future. The best that we are able to do as cost engineers is to bring some science to our profession rather than rely upon gut feelings. The only certainty regarding a deterministic, single point estimate is that it is extremely likely to be wrong. As soon as it's been published, if there is a change to the project or if a risk occurs, then the point estimate is incorrect or requires updating.

One of the most common applications of science to cost estimating in recent years has been the introduction of Monte Carlo analysis. This has provided the cost engineer with the opportunity to model the inherent uncertainty and risks associated with the systems that they are estimating. Monte Carlo analysis basically provides the means by which to model the uncertainty in the model inputs and run a large number of simulations considering likely possible permutations of cost, thus compiling a database of potential outcomes. Statistical analysis can then be applied to this database of potential outcomes to establish the level of confidence associated with any given point estimate. More typically, though, the output of the analysis will be used to provide an estimate at 10%, 50% and 90% confidence intervals.

A mature organisation realises that in terms of uncertainty the further into the future that costs are considered, the more uncertain the outcome will be. In terms of uncertainty, the default would be a funnel with the near-term uncertainty of costs being small, perhaps +/- 5% or 10%. When we try to predict into the future, the tolerance on the baseline costs becomes wider, perhaps +/- 50% or 100%, as shown in Figure 7.2 as a solid line.

However, the opposite is true when considering the risk. When the cost engineer seeks risks or problems that will cause a deviation from the baseline plan, it is easy to envisage many in the near-term while the future risks are harder to conceive. This observation looks like a trumpet too, but the opposite to the uncertainty trumpet as seen in Figure 7.2 in dashed lines.

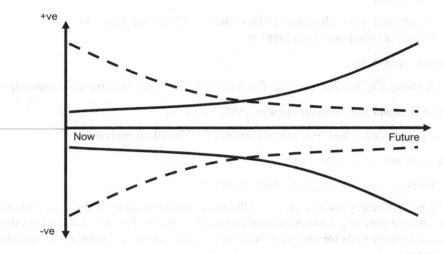

Figure 7.2 The relationship between risk and uncertainty

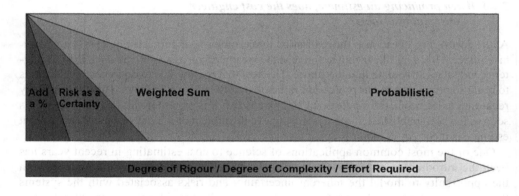

Figure 7.3 Varying degrees of complexity in risk analysis

As a result, we find the theoretic outcome in Figure 7.2 where uncertainty and risk cause an opposite emphasis on the deviation from the baseline resources, while the cumulative outcome is an increased effect on the budget of deviation from the most likely outcome.

Figure 7.3 summarises four approaches to the analysis of risk and uncertainty when considering the effort required. Let's consider them in detail together with their advantages and disadvantages.

Many organisations forgo any form of bottom-up risk analysis and instead add a flat percentage onto their baseline costs. For example, say the cost of a project is estimated at £50,000, then using the flat percentage method the organisation adds an additional 10% allowance for risk, or £5,000, bringing the total project cost to £55,000. The advantages and disadvantages of such an approach are shown in Table 7.1.

Circumstances when it would be appropriate to use a flat percentage are:

1   When an organisation does not want to invest in risk identification, risk analysis and risk management.

Table 7.1 Advantages and disadvantages of adding a percentage

Advantages	Disadvantages
• Quick – does not require a risk process • Cheap – does not require any investment	• Provides no insight onto the risks • Lacks credibility – how can you be certain that 10% is adequate? • In open book accounting this is difficult to defend • Limited scope for the transfer of risk to other parties

Table 7.2 Treatment of risks as a certainty

Risks	Impact
Unexpected requirements emerge	£5,000
Impact of incorrect data	£10,000
Specialist SME required	£5,600
Sum	£20,600

Table 7.3 Advantages and disadvantages of treating risk as a certainty

Advantages	Disadvantages
• Straightforward • Covered for all eventualities • Greater insight – requires an organisation to think about the actual risks that it faces • More evident when certain risks can be retired	• Leads to over inflated costs / prices • Can make you uncompetitive • Tie up funds on a project that aren't needed • More time consuming – requires an organisation to think about the actual risks that it faces

2   When an organisation is involved in highly repetitive business, and knows from experience that costs increase typically by a set percentage on every contract. Organisations require good quality historical evidence to use this as an explanation.

3   When an organisation will not be requested to justify their allowance for risk by their customers.

4   When an organisation does not foresee the need to transfer risk.

An alternative approach and only slightly more complicated is to treat risk as a certainty. This is the way a lot of organisations do things and is the most risk adverse way of dealing with potential risks and the simplest, i.e. you make the assumption that all your risks will occur and cost for all of them as if they were certain. It requires no complex mathematics to perform, as shown in Table 7.2.

So in this example an allowance of £20,600 would be made specifically for risk, in addition to normal costings. The advantages and disadvantages of this risk technique are captured in Table 7.3.

Circumstances when it would be appropriate to treat risks as a certainty are:

1   When an organisation has invested in risk identification but not risk analysis.

2   When an organisation wishes to be risk adverse, e.g. in high risk projects, or when doing so enables them to remain competitive.

3   When an organisation wishes to retire risk as a project progresses.

Weighted sum

Another approach would be to use a weighted sum of all the risks. This approach is predicated on the assumption that not all your risks will occur at the same time and hence you can have less in the risk budget than you would need if all your risks did occur. An example of the calculation is shown in Table 7.4. The advantages and disadvantages of the weighted sum approach is shown in Table 7.5.

Probabilistic modelling

This is an extension of the above but uses the statistically probabilistic Monte Carlo method. This is the most advanced method and allows you to do some pretty neat stuff. Not unsurprisingly, though, it is also the most complicated and requires the most understanding. It typically requires that you have specialist statistical software. For it to be absolutely effective you have to use it in combination with cost uncertainty, i.e. when putting together cost estimates for certain events (not risks), you get people to think in terms of three-point estimating, i.e. a minimum value, a most likely value and a maximum value. This is the technique that the MOD requires all its acquisition approaches to adopt. The advantages and disadvantages are listed in Table 7.6. The output looks like an S-curve as shown in Figure 7.4. The solid black line is a sum of all the most likely costs excluding any allowance for risk and cost uncertainty; it represents the most likely cost to conduct the baseline activities. Adding in cost uncertainty gives the dashed line; this represents the Monte Carlo aggregation of the baseline three-point estimate: the minimum, most likely and maximum. Adding in non-mitigated risks gives the double line curve; this represents the uncertainty in the baseline cost with the addition of a cost allowance for deviations from the baseline plan in terms of probability and

Table 7.4 Weighted sum calculation

Risks	Probability	Impact	Weighted Impact
Unexpected requirements emerge	20%	£5,000	£1,000
Impact of incorrect data	40%	£10,000	£4,000
Specialist SME required	10%	£5,600	£560
Weighted sum			£5,560

Table 7.5 Advantages and disadvantages of the weighted sum approach

Advantages	Disadvantages
• Greater insight – requires an organisation to think about the actual risks that it faces • Acts to reduce your overall risk budget (as compared with previous approach) • Less risk adverse but still means you are making some allowance for risk • Takes account of the uncertainty of a risk happening • Easy to understand calculation	• The weighted risk budget is less than the value of any risk meaning that if any risk did occur then you wouldn't have enough in the risk pot to deal with it. • The important thing here is that you really need a large number of risks to make it work and the weighted risk figure should exceed the value of any one individual risk. Any risks that are specifically large should be held outside the contract and articulated as a dependency within the contract documentation. • More time consuming – requires an organisation to think about the actual risks that it faces.

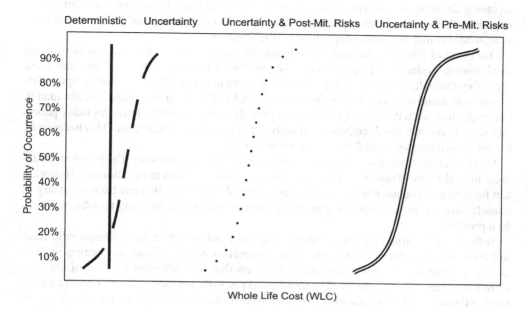

Figure 7.4 Relative outcomes of the Monte Carlo analysis

Table 7.6 Advantages and disadvantages of the probabilistic modelling approach

Advantages	Disadvantages
• Mathematically correct – the approach is not prone to errors • Greater insight – requires an organisation to think about the actual risks that it faces • Acts to reduce your overall risk budget (as compared with previous approach) • Less risk adverse but still means you are making some allowance for risk • Takes account of the uncertainty of a risk happening • Easy to understand calculation	• More time consuming – requires an organisation to think about the actual risks that it faces. • Buy in – all the stakeholders need to understand and be educated about the analysis approach so that they are able to act on the outcome. • Tools – there is a need to invest in specialist tools and training staff on the application and interpretation of the Monte Carlo systems.

cost impact of risks. Mitigating your risks takes you back to the dotted line; this represents the cost of the baseline uncertainty, plus the planned mitigation activities with an allowance for the residual cost risks that remain following mitigation activities. Each line gives you the percentage confidence you have that your costs will fall below that value, i.e. I can be 50% confident that my costs inclusive of risk and uncertainty will not exceed X amount. It is then management discretion as to how risky they want to be, i.e. are they willing to take on risk and work at the 30%, 40% etc. confidence level, or do they want to be risk adverse and work at the 80%, 90% or 100% confidence level. The choice is then theirs.

7.2.5 Does the project consider software estimating tools necessary?

The desire to acquire capability, rather than platforms, systems or equipment, has been driven to a large extent by the need to keep acquisition options open and flexible. Rather than replacing an aging or obsolete platform with the same – a plane for a plane – describing the requirements in terms of its capability encourages the consideration of different solutions, even solutions that have more capability for the same cost.

One result of this move to capabilities is the utilisation of increasing amounts of software in platforms, systems and equipment. It is possible to provide more flexibility and more capability through a software upgrade than a hardware upgrade. When the Hubble Space Telescope was found to have a flaw in its mirror, NASA did not rush to replace it or abandon it, but made changes to the imaging software to provide some capability. There are many papers that identify the increased application of software in aerospace and defence. This necessarily results in an increased need for software estimating.

Many estimators shy away from estimating and forecasting software. The problem would seem to be the lack of tangible or physical composition of the item to be estimated. Hardware can be seen and you are able to visualise the material and labour that has been necessary to manufacture and even design the item. With software the lack of anything tangible seems to be a problem.

Software cost estimating tools represent an easy solution to cost engineers who have difficulty in estimating software. The input parameters of the software estimating tools or models prompt the estimator with the cost drivers that will influence the cost of the software [51]. Hence you do not need to be an expert in software estimating to become a software estimator. You will need to employ the help of software systems engineers, designers or programmers to help you assess the inputs. To prevent your looking like a fool in front of a software expert, it will be worthwhile becoming very familiar with the terminology of software world: machine code, source code, SLOC, function points and so forth. But this is no different than moving to an industry where the acronyms and terminology are different.

Whether hardware or software, an estimate can be considered in terms of size, productivity and complexity. In the case of software, the size is the critical parameter. A mature organisation will recognise that if you are able to determine the size of the software consistently, then you will be able to have confidence in your cost estimate. Size can be measured in many ways depending upon the type of software and the maturity of the project. The most common methods of software sizing are source lines of code (SLOC), function points (FP), use case conversion points (UCCP), predictive object points (POPs) and estimating by analogy. Generally, SLOC is a developer's consideration of the software from the inside, the code, while function points, use case conversion points and predictive object points are all views of the software from the outside, the user's perspective. While the final delivered SLOC can be checked against the initial estimate of SLOC during the bid or proposal stages, the same cannot be true for the other methods. Even when the software has been delivered it is possible for different experts to count the function points, use case conversion points and predictive object points differently because they are subjective.

With all of these definitions it is important to ensure that you completely understand what is included and not included. A mature cost engineering organisation will have rules regarding comments or non-executable elements of the code and how their sizing approach will deal with them. This becomes more complex when considering linear, non-object-oriented cost compared to object-oriented code. The introduction of this type of code means that it is recursive and will ultimately generate a lot more machine code when compiled than traditional non-object-oriented code. This is when there is a realisation in a mature cost engineering organisation that to produce high quality software estimates you need specialist cost engineers to produce outputs that are justified and credible.

Table 7.7 The ESLOC calculations for four computer software configuration items

		SLOC	*Design*	*Code*	*Test*
CSCI Alpha	New	5,000	100%	100%	100%
CSCI Bravo	Minor adaption	25,000		10%	20%
CSCI Charlie	Reused	10,000			
CSCI Delta	Major modification	20,000	30%	40%	50%
	Total SLOC =	60,000			

			ESLOC
CSCI Alpha	ESLOC = 5,000 × (40% × 100%) + (30% × 100%) + (30% × 100%) =		5,000
CSCI Bravo	ESLOC = 25,000 × (40% × 0%) + (30% × 10%) + (30% × 20%) =		2,250
CSCI Charlie	ESLOC = 10,000 × (40% × 0%) + (30% × 0%) + (30% × 0%) =		0
CSCI Delta	ESLOC = 20,000 × (40% × 30%) + (30% × 40%) + (30% × 50%) =		7,800
		Total ESLOC =	15,050

A common approach to software sizing is to consider equivalent sources lines of code or ESLOC. This technique will consider the relative effort required to produce a new line of code compared to one that is modified or adapted. The technique suggests factors which can be used on the design, code and test attributes of a software project to convert all modified or adapted code into the equivalent of new lines, as shown in Table 7.7.

This is a useful technique for normalising the quantity of code to be developed and has been used successfully in COCOMO. In addition, it should be recognised that software code has a tendency to grow. This is mainly due to: under estimates of the code at the start of a project due to an immature understanding of the requirements, requirements creep during development and an overly optimistic view of the amount of reused code that materialises during development. Code growth can be particularly acute when there is a high reliance on commercial of the shelf, or COTS, software to satisfy some of the requirements when in reality it becomes apparent that the perceived COTS solution will not satisfy the requirements and that additional code will need to be developed.

Once the size of the software has been determined, a mature cost engineering organisation will populate a software cost model and adjust the project cost for complexity (language, operating environment, etc.) and productivity (development environment, processor capability, programme skills, tool chain, etc.).

When a mature cost engineering organisation approaches a software estimate, it will consider the type of software development process being employed. This does not necessarily have an effect on the cost estimate or forecast that will be generated, but it will have an effect on the profiling of the resources. The overall software development process is based upon the classic problem solving process. When confronted with a problem there are five steps to considering the solution, as follows:

1   Gather intelligence about the problem to be overcome;
2   Develop all alternative options to challenge the problem;
3   Select an alternative option using customer requirements to guide the selection;
4   Implement the solution;
5   Monitor the satisfaction of the solution against customer need and results.

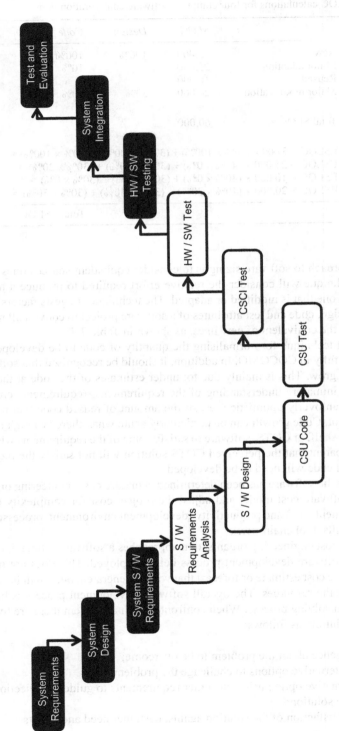

Figure 7.5 Traditional V diagram of systems engineering leading to waterfall software development

In essence, steps one to three are decision making processes, but all five steps are used as the basis of the software development process. The main software development processes that should be recognised are:

- Waterfall
- Incremental
- Spiral
- Evolutionary
- Agile

The traditional waterfall approach to software development follows the classical V diagram used in systems engineering, as shown in Figure 7.5.

A mature cost engineering organisation will profile the resources with the requirements and design staff initially deployed, leading to the programmers coding the computer software units (CSU), then the test and integration team resources finally leading to the specialist hardware (HW) and software (SW) integration team.

When the alternative software development processes are substituted for the waterfall approach, then the profiling of the resources is altered, as shown in Figure 7.6.

The most common measure of software development is man-months, which are frequently measured in the number of staff per month. This should not be confused with a schedule measured in months; the schedule for developing the software will be independent of the resources required.

Once the software has been developed, then a mature cost engineering organisation will consider the cost of deploying the software, which is analogous to hardware production and finally maintenance. The costs which can occur in the maintenance phase of the software life cycle will include:

- Corrective maintenance – the correction of bugs not identified during development testing.
- Adaptive maintenance – the adaption of the software to accommodate changes in the operating systems or other interfaces and feed systems.

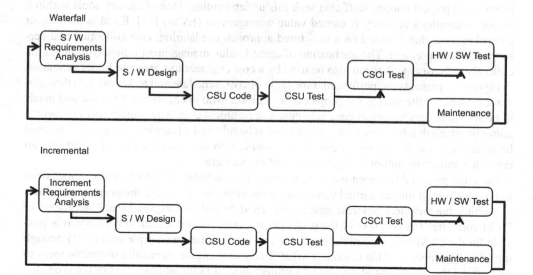

Figure 7.6 Alternative software development methods

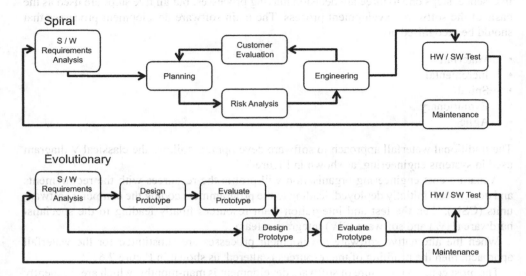

Figure 7.6 (Continued)

- Perfective maintenance – another source of requirements creep which occurs during this phase to extend the capability of the software beyond the originally conceived requirements.

7.2.6 Does the project use an earned value management (EVM) tool?

Cost engineers are dependent on technical, schedule and cost data to enable them to make the credible and justified predictions of the future cost of systems, equipment and services perhaps decades into the future. However, they are not unique in this desire for knowledge of projects; project control staff also seek this understanding. One of the key tools within a project controller's armoury is earned value management (EVM) [52]. EVM is the project control process that is based on a structured approach to planning, cost collection and performance measurement. The application of earned value management typically requires the collection of cost data that can also be used by a cost engineer too generate future estimates.

Figure 7.7 presents the perfect, mature cycle of cost, schedule and technical data throughout a project. At the start is the project cost engineer who needs to bid for work and needs to be able to access historical cost, schedule and technical data. The project cost engineer is going to establish a baseline cost against a bid schedule and a technical proposal. This must be cohesive in the three parts to enable the organisation to secure the project, otherwise no credible contracting authority is going to fund the venture.

Once the proposal has been won, the baseline cost, schedule and technical volumes need to be transformed into an earned value management system to enable the project controllers to monitor the technical progress against the schedule and cost expenditure. The process of EVM correlates the progress of the project cost, schedule and technical delivery. It is possible for the EVM system to make predictions of the Estimate at Completion (EAC) through the life of the project. This is exactly what future cost engineers require to enable them to understand the actual cost at the end of a project as well as the achievement of the project.

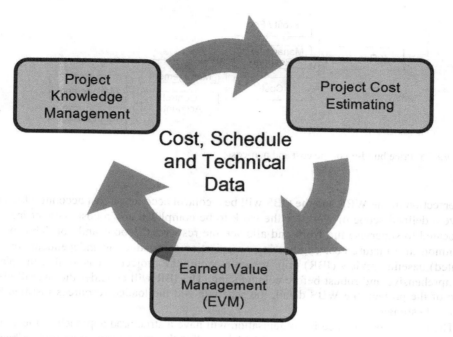

Figure 7.7 The flow of data through the tools at the hands of a mature project control function

At the completion of a project a mature organisation will conduct a closure process including a White Review to learn lessons about the project and ensure that any changes necessary to make the organisation more effective are captured. The final cost and schedules need to be captured in a knowledge base for future reference and utility in the generation of cost and schedule estimates for kindred projects in the future.

Many contracting authorities will mandate the application of EVM systems and EVM reporting on their projects to ensure that they remain an intelligent customer from the inception of the project to its completion [60]. Truly mature organisations will utilise the project control technique regardless of the customer requirement, realising that it provides an opportunity for process improvement.

A mature cost engineering organisation appreciates the benefits of EVM including the discipline of planning resources following the creation of work packages and scheduling. This would be indicated in standardized manner so that project control staff can be cycled through the organisation without loss of efficiency. There is a benefit of integrating cost and schedule metrics to the performance and progress of the technical work. When combined in this way it is possible to analyse performance metrics impartially.

A mature cost engineering organisation will recognise that the key to the successful implementation of an EVM process is a realistic fully resource loaded schedule. This time phased budget is the backbone of the EVM process and achieving this resource loaded schedule requires an upfront investment in the project. It will involve the definition of a comprehensive work breakdown structure (WBS) specific to the project. This will be combined with an organisation breakdown structure (OBS) which is consistent for the organisation. At the

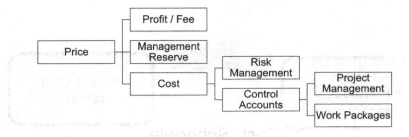

Figure 7.8 Price build-up of the cost and non-cost

intersection of the WBS and the OBS will be a control account or cost account which will have a defined scope of work for the work to be completed and a cost account manager allocated to supervise the work and allocate the resources (labour and non-labour). It is common in a mature cost engineering organisation to conduct an independent (or integrated) baseline review (IBR) prior to commencing the project to ensure that the plan is comprehensive and robust before commencing. The IBR will consider the overall objective of the project, the WBS detail, the schedule and the loaded resources justified by a basis of estimate.

The mature cost engineering organisation will have a structured approach to the generation of a price for the project. When EVM is applied the price needs to be broken back to ensure that management of the unallocated portion of the price is protected and managed in a controlled way. Figure 7.8 provides a general guidance.

The price is summed from the cost of the project, plus the management reserve and profit or fee. The management reserve is not provided to the project, but kept by the senior management and executives of the organisation as a central reserve to fund possible unknown-unknowns that could occur in this project. At the time of assessment it is recognized that there will be events that are currently unknown probability and unknown cost impact; there is potentially a relationship to the riskiness of the project measured by the risk register. The cost is the sum of the project management resources required and technical resources contained in the control accounts plus the risk management reserve. While the resources in the control accounts will fund the known planned activities and tasks, the risk management fund is for known-unknowns which is calculated using some form of numeric analysis of the risk register (see section 8.2.13). The risk management fund is to be used at the discretion of the project manager to resolve the risks and opportunities identified in the risk register should they mature.

A mature cost engineering organisation understands that EVM will be able to predict the Estimate at Completion (EAC), which is also termed the latest revised estimate or LRE. This is achieved through the application of EVM metrics which record the actual cost to date (ACWP) in the project plus the remaining work (BAC–BCWP) when considering the historical performance factors (CPI) as defined in Table 7.8.

The mature cost engineering will encourage its cost engineers to become competent in the application of EVM and encourage its use. A competent cost engineer will know that EAC is calculated as follows:

$$Estimate\ at\ Completion(EAC) = ACWP_{cum} + (BAC + BCWP_{cum})/CPI_{cum}$$

Table 7.8 The terms used in earned value management (EVM)

EVM term	Title	Source	Interpretation
EAC	Estimate at Completion	Result of EVM metrics calculation	The monitored prediction of project final cost
ACWP	Actual Cost of Work Performed	General ledger and finance organisation	The classic accountancy view of the project
BAC	Budget at Completion	Project control team's target cost outcome	The planned cost of the project when finished
BCWP	Budgeted Cost of Work Performed	Technical team's assessment of their progress	The earned value on useful work expressed in cost
BCWS	Budgeted Cost of Work Performed	Project management baseline plans	The planned value (PV) on the project for study

Where:

$ACWP_{cum}$ is the cumulative actual cost spent to date
BAC is the original planned cost of the work on completion
$BCWP_{cum}$ is the cumulative earned value of the work completed to date
CPI_{cum} is the cumulative cost performance index, defined below

The performance of a project can be measured by either an index or a variance as follows:

$$Schedule\ Performance\ Index\ (SPI) = \frac{BCWP}{BCWS}$$

$$Cost\ Performance\ Index\ (CPI) = \frac{BCWP}{ACWP}$$

Where:

CPI or SPI < 1.0 is unfavourable; work is costing more than planned or accomplished quicker than planned
CPI or SPI > 1.0 is favourable; work is costing less than planned or accomplished slower than planned

$$Schedule\ Variance\ (SV) = BCWP - BCWS$$

$$Cost\ Variance\ (CV) = BCWP - ACWP$$

Where:

SV or CV < 0 is unfavourable; an indication of behind schedule or over cost
SV or CV > 0 is favourable; an indication of ahead of schedule or under cost

7.2.7 Does the project have a tool requirement?

The cost model requirements are a vital part of the model development process. These should be developed in adherence to good systems engineering practices. Figure 7.9 highlights the typical process for model development, from the identification of requirements through to verification and validation.

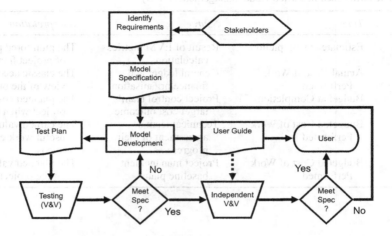

Figure 7.9 The flow process necessary for the development of a cost model on a mature organisation

The requirements document will record the requirements of all the stakeholders who will interface with the resulting cost model. Capturing such information will naturally require engagement with each of the stakeholder groups to understand their perspectives. Justifying the requirements is important so that the requirement is not biased. The stakeholders need to determine which are the key user requirements (KURs) to ensure that the emphasis and effort is not incorrectly focused. The remaining requirements need to be priorities, as shown in the requirements database in Figure 7.10, with a scale between 0 to 5. All stakeholders should be given an opportunity to endorse the requirement set prior to model build.

Examples of categories of requirements are:

- Key requirement
- Accuracy
- Analysis
- Cost elements
- Implementation
- Inputs
- Interfaces
- Miscellaneous
- Options
- Output
- Schedule
- Traceability
- Uncertainty/risk
- User friendly

From the requirements it is possible to articulate a model specification that will satisfy those requirements. The cost model specification identities the characteristics of the cost model to be developed and its functionality. Without appropriately drafted user and system require-ments documents it becomes difficult in the validation and verification stages to check that the model functions as required.

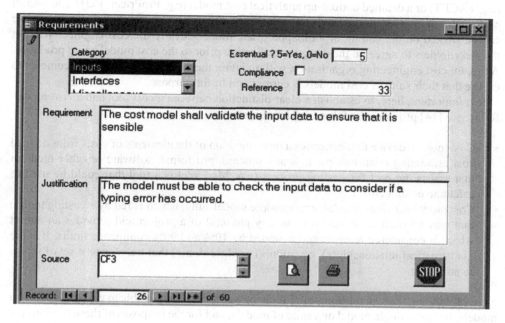

Figure 7.10 An example of a simple cost model requirements database in a mature cost engineering function

7.2.8 In the absence of a commercial solution to the cost tool requirements, was a tool design produced?

Where the decision is made to develop a new model, the following steps should form the basis of any model development process:

- Definition of requirement
- Drafting of a specification
- Model development
- Drafting of test plans and user guide
- Testing
- Validation and verification (V&V)
- Independent validation and verification (IV&V)
- Use

Too frequently cost engineers are too keen to open MS-Excel and start to write complex macros and VBA. This is seen as the sexy part of cost modelling and making progress in this area is seen as productivity. However, a mature organisation will recognise the need to design the functionality of the cost model prior to reaching for the software. A mature cost engineering function will assess the design of the overall functionality, what type of model, the inputs and outputs.

For example, will the model be a simulation model like an event based operating and support cost model (e.g. OSCAM) [47], or a parametric model like an early concept cost model (e.g. FACET) or a detailed bottom-up analytical cost model (e.g. ProPricer) [33]? The overall philosophy of the cost model needs to be designed otherwise a considerable amount of time can be wasted on the coding of an inappropriate model. Ideally the cost engineer will get the stakeholders to agree on the design specification prior to the cost model being produced. A mature cost engineering organisation will maintain their cost model design documents to ensure that their suite of cost models is current and fit for purpose.

It is important, here, to establish a clear distinction between a cost tool and a cost model. Reference [14] provides the following definitions:

- Cost tool – a device that generates a quantification of the elements of costs from defined cost estimating relationships. It is any process, pro-forma, software or other medium that assists the cost forecasting process (e.g. Ms-Excel is a tool that could be used to calculate or sum costs).
- Cost model – a single model, or a multiple model suite, which is fed by a costing tool(s) that may be used to obtain costs for any phase(s) of a project and provides an output which is considered realistic and bounded by 10% and 90% confidence limits. It is the mathematical relationship(s), equation(s) or algorithm(s) that transforms a set of inputs to an output.

Notwithstanding these definitions, the following sections are applicable to cost tools and cost models, be that a single model or a suite of models, and for the purposes of these sections the terms 'tool' and 'model' are interchangeable.

The contents of the cost model design specification will ideally cover:

- Model requirements

    - Rationale/background
    - Affected project

- Operating system requirements
- Model input requirements

    - Source data
    - Options to be considered
    - Model structure

- Model linkages
- Output requirements
- Boundaries/constraints

A mature cost engineering organisation will appreciate that a cost model will utilise fixed and variable relationships while understanding their application and usage. It will also differentiate between rate, factors and ratios appreciating that:

- A rate is a cost per technical parameter; for example, the cost per flying hour;
- A factor is a cost per cost; for example, the cost of design management is 10% of the cost of the engineering work package;
- A ratio is a parameter per parameter; for example, eight members of staff is the optimum size of a team to manage.

7.2.9 Does the project cost engineer maintain a validation and verification log book?

Cost models are used within the cost engineering departments to support major projects, and the integrity of the output of these models is relied upon to make key business decisions. However, despite the best intentions of model developers and parametricians, models can still be prone to errors. Quite often the individuals developing models have not been specifically trained in best practice model development techniques and consequently may not apply or not be aware of methodologies or techniques to reduce the risk of errors. Undetected, these errors can seriously impair the output and ultimately the business decisions made based upon these cost models.

A mature cost engineering function will be utilised by the organisation to endorse project costing, and more importantly its outputs will be used in support of associated business cases. Using an approved methodology for validation and verification (V&V) of all tools and models ensures that tasks are performed consistently across the organisation, department and individuals.

The objectives of undertaking an independent review of a cost model are to ensure that:

* The model achieves the specification and the purpose it was designed to meet;
* The model correctly interprets the data extracted from the Cost Data Assumptions List (CDAL) and accurately reflects the instructions contained in the Model User Guide;
* The model performs accurately under various scenarios;
* The model meets the user's requirements for flexibility, reporting and ease of use; and
* The data on which the model is based is accurate, and from documented and valid sources.

The ISPA handbook pages 1–13 [48] states that "Parametric models should be calibrated and validated before they are used to develop estimates". It continues to define the processes of validation and verification and calibration based upon multiple years of cost estimating experience and parametric knowledge.

Broadly the relationship between V&V and calibration can be shown in Figure 7.11.

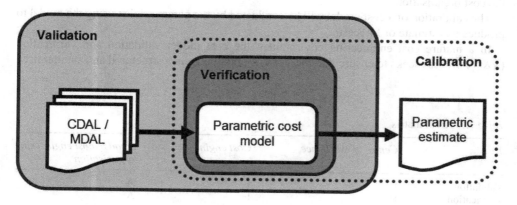

Figure 7.11 The relationship between cost model calibration and verification and validation

Validation is "the process, or act, of demonstrating the model's ability to function as a credible estimating tool [and provide outputs that are fit for purpose]. Validation ensures:

*   The model is a good predictor of costs;
*   Estimating system policies and procedures are established and enforced;
*   [Outputs are produced by] key personnel [who] have proper experience and are adequately trained" [48]. (pp. 1–13)

Verification is the process of ensuring that the cost model reproduces the cost research and cost estimating relationships (CER) accurately without errors.

Calibration is the process, or act, of benchmarking a commercial cost model developed from industry typical data to replicate the cost footprint of a specific organisation [30].

Calibration is dependent on the nature of the cost model. When the model is a bespoke model based upon a specific organisation's own historical data, then they can be considered to be self-calibrating. When the parametric model is a commercial tool with the ability to be calibrated, then calibration can be conducted to replicate the suppliers' output.

When the cost model is going to be used to assess a specific supplier quotation or single source contract, then the model must be calibrated to that supplier. When the parametric cost model is going to be used for an independent cost estimate (ICE) budget setting activity prior to any supplier competition, then an un-calibrated parametric model will generate an appropriate industry average parametric estimate [57].

A RACI analysis determines who is:

*   Responsible = multiple staff who will conduct the work
*   Accountable = single members of staff who are ultimately answerable
*   Communicated = two-way information flow
*   Informed = one-way information flow

These definitions have been used to define the RACI matrix shown in Table 7.9.

In a mature cost engineering organisation the verification testing of cost models will be conducted centrally by a centre of excellence. This is a cycle of testing that is repeated on an annual basis as a minimum. The validation activities can be conducted by any member of the cost organisation.

The calibration of a cost model will be conducted by the parametrician using the model to produce an estimate or forecast.

In a mature cost engineering environment the cost model validation and verification (V&V) process seeks to ensure that the V&V is undertaken in a structured and standardised

Table 7.9 RACI matrix

Task	Centre of excellence	Cost engineer	Head of cost engineering organisation
Validation	R	I	A
Verification	R	I	A
Calibration	C	R & A	

manner, using tried and tested procedures, producing a standard set of auditable outputs. This process defines:

- The scope of work to be undertaken, and deliverables produced, for the different types of parametric models and estimates;
- The structure and experience of the teams required to carry out this work;
- The procedures and checklists to be followed; and
- The documentation to be produced as part of the process.

7.1.10 Is there a cost database tool?

It is recommended that a cost engineer spend 75% to 80% of the task time gathering data. This process can be accelerated through the application of a cost portal or cost database. This database will ideally be electronic to support the control of the information and also to facilitate sharing. Hence an electronic database, rather than a paper-based system, is the sign of a mature cost engineering organisation.

An enterprise-wide system with password protection is highly desirable to protect commercially sensitive information. This should contain both suppliers' costs as well as in-house actual costs for a variety of products and services which the organisation delivers.

The further forward in the future we want to make cost projections, the further into the past that we need to go to understand the trend in costs with time. Consequently, the longer the initiative to collect and store financial data needs in a database, the more likely that that data will be of use to estimators. Emphasis should be placed on capturing as many of the different types of product that are relevant to the organisation as is possible, in addition to different types of projects. There is limited knowledge that can be learnt from multiple entries of the same information.

The database in a mature organisation will have a relational linkage between cost and its associated technical information. The technical information will provide context for the cost data and enable the development of parametric models and cost estimating relationships. In the ideal situation the cost and technical information will automatically be data mined from existing management information systems (MIS) to save time and effort.

Due to the application of software systems, the mature cost engineering organisation will hold and present the data in a consistent manner.

7.2.11 Does the project consider a statistical tool essential to the function?

Data is essential to a cost engineer; when there is little time to do an estimate, having the correct data at hand for an analogous quick judgement is vital. The value of this data is increased if it has been normalised. Normalisation usually means the processing of the data into a homogenous data set, for example, it is all in the same currency, year of economics, metric and so forth. When time is critical, the application of these processes is time consuming.

A mature cost engineering organisation will utilise regression analysis to describe the goodness of fit of a mathematical equation between two sets of numbers. Regression analysis is a statistical process to determine the relationship between two variables. For example Figure 7.12, on the left, is a plot of data. But on the right is the same data with regression analysis applied.

When the independent variable is a technical parameter and the dependent variable is a cost, then we recognise a cost estimating relationship or a cost response curve.

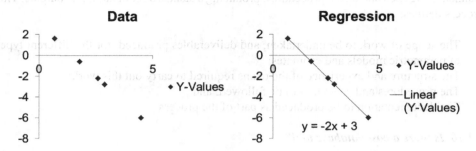

Figure 7.12 Regression analysis of data

Once the data set is normalised, then it is possible to apply more science than simple analogous ranking based perhaps on an assessment of historical project scope. The application of statistical tools provides the mature cost organisation with the possibility of generating cost estimating relationships. The application of the tools will enable more complex non-linear relationships to be considered for the prediction of future equipment, platforms and services.

In a mature cost engineering environment, the cost engineer has access to a number of statistical tools that they are able to utilise to generate cost estimating relationships (CER) quickly and easily from normalised data. They have been trained on these tools and the licenses are paid annually.

First, the mature cost engineering organisation will appreciate the difference between correlation and causation as follows:

• Correlation is the statistical proof of a relationship between two sets of data, but it does not mean they prove cause and effect. For example, there might be a statistical relationship between the number of layers of paint on a ship and its age, but this does not prove that aging causes paint.
• Causation is the statistical proof of a relationship between two sets of data that prove cause and effect. For example, there will be a statistical relationship between the age of a ship and the level of corrosion.

A mature cost engineering organisation will appreciate that various regression models exist including:

• Constants – where the dependent parameter does not vary against the independent variable.
• Linear – where the dependent parameter varies as a ratio against the independent variable.
• Non-linear – where the dependent variable varies not as a ratio (for example a power, log or exponent) against the independent variable.

The simplest relationship and the place to start is always the linear relationship. This has the form:

$$y = a + bx$$

Where:

Y = a technical or design characteristic
X = the cost
a and b = constants

A mature cost engineering organisation will recognise that this equation is only correct if the equation is a perfect fit. The more precise form is:

$$y = a + bx + \varepsilon$$

Where:

ε = the residual or inaccuracy of the linear relationship

For the relationship to be a true linear relationship there are two aspects that need to hold true for the residual:

1　The plot of the residual against the X variable should be a normal distribution with a mean of zero.
2　When plotting the residual against the X variables there should be a scatter graph; that is there should be no relationship and independence.

A mature cost engineering organisation will appreciate the statistical techniques that are useful to a cost engineer in creating a cost estimating relationship, particularly the analysis of variance in the:

- Regression sum of squares (SSR)
- Error sum of squares (SSE)
- Total sum of squares (SST)

In addition to the above, the organisation will appreciate the uncertainty surrounding an estimate in terms of:

- the estimated regression coefficient (SE); and
- standard error of the regression equation (SEE).

When the SEE is divided by the mean, then the coefficient of variation (CV) is calculated, which can be used as an indicator of the associated percent error. Generally a percentage SEE of less than 15% is considered to be acceptable.

The next regression concept that a mature cost engineering organisation will appreciate is the t and F tests. The t test will result in a measure of the independent variables that is a good predictor and will tell the cost engineer if they are statistically significant, while the F statistic will provide a measure of the overall goodness of fit and the statistical significance of the regression model overall.

Most cost engineering organisations will consider the R^2 as a predictor of the correlation between the independent and dependent variables. Indeed, the R^2 can be used to indicate the closeness of fit of the regression, but this should not be used as the only indicator and the t and F test should be considered.

The mature cost engineering organisation can measure how precise a regression analysis is to the data set by employing the confidence intervals and prediction intervals. The former will be used to quantify the uncertainty around the estimate of the average cost and the latter the uncertainty around the estimated cost.

The mature cost engineering organisation will be familiar with the regression analysis tools for example MS-Excel. The ordinary least square (OLS) method of regression analysis will be applied to data sets when developing cost estimating relationships (CER) and schedule estimating relationships (SER). These will take the form of both linear and non-linear relationships as appropriate. The individuals will appreciate the LINEST (known-y's, known-x's, constant, statistics) function in MS-Excel and the Data Analysis Tool Pak. The mature cost engineering organisation will appreciate that the non-linear data can be transformed into a linear cost model for OLS analysis using appropriate mathematical transformations as demonstrated in Figure 7.13.

From single variable regression the mature cost engineering organisation will develop multivariate relationships through the analysis of the residuals to determine the next significant variable able to mathematically describe the error term in the modelling. When using multiple independent variables there is a potential problem with multicollinearity, when two

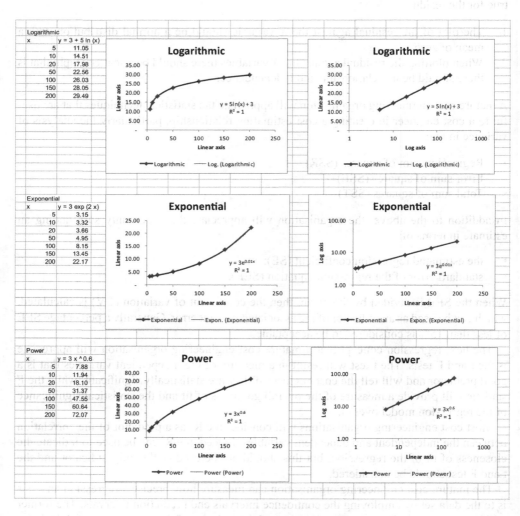

Figure 7.13 The non-linear relationships and the mathematical transformations to create a straight line

independent variables are highly correlated. In this case it is natural to remove one variable as it is inferred by the inclusion of the other variable.

7.2.12 When utilising a commercial cost model to generate costs, is the cost model calibrated?

The time and effort required to gather cost and technical data, normalise it, apply statistical tools and then socialise the resulting bespoke cost model and gain buy-in from peers and customers is a considerable investment. An alternative for a mature cost engineering organisation is the acquisition of a commercial cost model.

Commercial cost models by their very nature are generic. The developers of commercial cost models need them to appeal to a wide variety of customers to enable them to be commercially viable. If the cost model is only able to estimate the cost of right hand aero engine for commercial aircraft with five wheels or less, then the market is going to be limited! This effect means that while the vendor of commercial models will be able to assure the verification of their cost model and support the validation, they will need to be calibrated to provide confidence in their outputs.

A mature cost engineering organisation has a programme of continuous cost model calibration against the organisation historical actual costs and schedules. It will recognise that calibration against estimates is highly likely to compound errors in the original estimate when applying the commercial cost model to future systems, equipment or services.

At the very least the mature cost engineering function will realise that commercial cost models that are not calibrated can at best be relied upon to generate 'should cost' estimates rather than generate cost estimates that are tailored to the organisation in which they work.

7.2.13 What is done in the project with regards to multiple cost estimating methodologies?

The aim of cost modelling for a decision maker is to provide confidence. At a project decision point or project hurdle, for example initial or Main Gate or First or Second Pass, cost modelling is to provide the decision makers with robust costs which they are able to depend upon. Frequently these decision points will require an independent cost estimate (ICE) or a value for money (VfM) benchmark as a comparator for the decision maker.

Confidence with these figures is provided by the application of multiple cost methodologies. To provide confidence in a cost forecast it is recommended to apply more than one cost forecasting methodology. A single methodology output provides an estimate from one perspective. Approaching the same problem from two or more different perspectives and arriving at a similar answer gives greater weight that the estimate is appropriate. The application of multiple estimation methodologies will help garner stakeholder endorsement of the estimate. It also reduces the opportunity for another engineer coming along and attempting to undermine your estimate by approaching the problem in a different manner than you and obtaining a different answer.

Generally, the three methodologies in cost estimating that are recognised are analogous, parametric and analytical, defined as follows:

- Analogous approach – this involves comparing the item to be costed with a near neighbour or similar item whose cost is known.

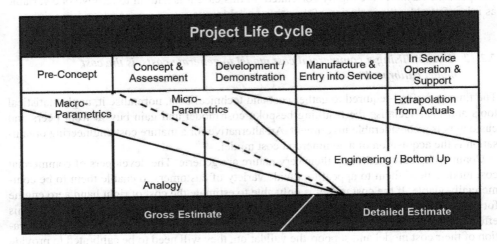

Figure 7.14 Cost estimating methods are applicable at different times in a project life cycle

- Parametric approach – this involves the application of mathematical algorithms that represent how the cost of item varies with certain key parameters based on a statistically significant population of historical items.
- Analytical approach – this involves the aggregation of detailed low level project costs as defined by a cost resource breakdown structure (CRBS).

It is good practice to use multiple costing methodologies [34] in order to build confidence in a cost forecast at different phases of the project life cycle, as shown in Figure 7.14. If different modelling methods provide overlapping cost forecasts, then it is possible to have confidence in the output. Conversely, a significant divergence between results will mean that it is difficult to have any confidence in any single result without reconciliation of the differences.

In a mature cost engineering organisation there will be a policy of using multiple estimating method and models. What is more, the decision makers will expect it and the cost engineering senior management will have a policy to train, develop, utilise and populate multiple cost models.

There will be a realisation that the methodologies require different types of tools. This can cause problems with training and consistency of assumptions through the life of a project. Ideally the mature cost engineering organisation will appreciate through life cost estimating when a single framework is used to provide a human interface to the cost estimating methodology [53].

7.2.14 *Does the cost engineer organisation have an analytical tool for aggregating man hours?*

The basis of an analytical cost estimate approach is a bottom-up exercise. Sometimes referred to as grass roots or detailed estimating, this technique requires the manipulation of a lot of data. The process of analytical estimating is a simple one which consumes a significant amount of time and resources:

- Plan the cost estimate as if it was a project.
- Establish the product or equipment breakdown structure (PBS).

- Establish the make or buy philosophy for each product or equipment.
- Append a work breakdown structure (WBS) to each item to be designed and made to identify the work packages (WP).
- For each WP determine the work package leader or manager who is going to be responsible for the delivery of the WP.
- To each WP leader issue:

  - A risk form – to register any risks including the probability and impact, trigger and mitigation plans;
  - A work package description (WPD) – to include the WP inputs, outputs, dependencies, assumptions, exclusions, activities; and
  - Estimated cost works plan (ECWP) – to forecast the labour and non-labour resource required to execute the WPD time phase, clearly identifying the organisation breakdown structure and authorised through signature.

- When the documents are returned to the cost engineering department they need to be scrutinised for duplication and omissions. They also need to be rationalised against previous cost estimates and challenged where appropriate.
- Finally, the ECWPs need to be entered into a cost aggregation tool and added up.

The cost aggregation tool can be a simple MS-Excel spreadsheet but the manipulation of the data can be complex. The accounting department will require the information summed against function, the HR department will require a departmental head count, the project control function will want work package totals, and procurement will need the non-labour element and so forth. What will start as a simple spreadsheet will very quickly become a huge beast [64].

A mature cost engineering department will have been trained in a cost aggregation tool including currency conversion, economic conversion, learning rate calculations, and so forth, which have been validated and verified.

7.2.15 Does the cost engineering organisation have access to risk management tools?

The ability to conduct Monte Carlo analysis to statistically aggregate uncertainty and risk has been a requirement for a mature cost engineering function for a considerable time. However, there is a need for this uncertainty and risk information to be validated, otherwise the analysis is simply an analysis of flawed information. The first step of any risk register audit needs to be the establishment of the ground rules: what is in the baseline, what is a risk and what is uncertainty. Simple definitions are included in Table 7.10.

The baseline is the estimate for the work that is to be conducted in order to provide the service, equipment or project. It is the resources, labour and non-labour, consumed during

Table 7.10 Risk and uncertainty terms

Term	Technique	Probability	Impact
Baseline activity "Baseline"	Deterministic	100%	Absolute
Uncertainty "uncertainty"	Three-point estimate (3PE)	100%	Distribution
Risk "Risk"	Probability and impact	<100%	Distribution
Mitigation activity "Mitigation"	Uncertainty	100%	Distribution

normal working practice when conducting this work. There is a 100% chance that this work will be conducted as it is specified in the work package descriptions as required to conclude the contract. The estimate of the resources represents the most likely level of effort needed to produce the work.

However, producing a service, equipment or project is not a precise science, and however repetitive an activity might be, unless it's completely automatic, there is an opportunity for human error. This results in uncertainty about the estimate and can be accommodated through the adoption of a three-point estimate of resources: a maximum, a most likely and a minimum. Considering the track record of an activity, it should be possible to determine the tolerance on the estimate and justify the three-point estimate which is offered.

There is risk, defined in terms of probability and impact. A risk is a potential deviation from the baseline set of activities which have been specified. As a result, the probability must be less than 100%, otherwise it would be a planned activity and part of the baseline. The risks are less than 100% likely to occur, but should they occur then they will have an impact which the project manager will need to mitigate. The impact can be defined as a three-point estimate like uncertainty, with a minimum, a most likely and a maximum, but in this case the probability is not 100% but less, for example 50%.

It is possible to mitigate the probability of the risk occurring or impact of risk when it occurs. This is termed a mitigation action. The project manager needs to make a business decision whether to invest in a mitigation action. They need to weigh up the consequences of doing nothing and seeing if the risk occurs and the impact versus investing resources to reduce the probability and the impact. If they decide to take a mitigation action, then this becomes part of the baseline plan as it will occur (100% probability) and project manager needs to allocate resources to the mitigation action; as a consequence the risk will be reappraised in light of this mitigation and the probability and impact reassessed.

A mature cost engineering function will have complete knowledge of these issues and access to the risk registers of the projects it is working with. In addition to access to risk register tools, it will have a culture of training that ensures that the staff are competent and knowledgeable regarding the uncertainty and risks in their projects.

8 People's skills, professionalism and knowledge

8.1 Introduction

I have the job of supporting numerous customers who are both government procurement agencies and prime industry suppliers. The common theme that I see is cost engineers are typically underfunded, not appreciated and their capabilities not recognised. Incredible though it would seem in this age of cost reductions and increased profit margins, the cost engineer is under threat [24].

Now, we are somewhat to blame. When there is a design review or project meeting, who fronts up the presentations? The project manager. The design manager and systems engineers are right behind him queuing to get onto the stage and demonstrate their engineering skill and ingenuity at solving the latest technical problems. They are proud of their work and forward in their desire to demonstrate their skills. But where is the cost engineer? Sure the costs usually get an airing, the costs are reviewed and even the whole life cost could be considered. The cost engineer or estimator is working on the next task, bidding for the next job or assessing the cost risks of the next phase of the project.

Consequently, when budget time comes around, cost savings are made in the non-core areas of the business, including the little known cost engineering function. Typically, these departments are not high profile and are reactive rather than proactive. As such, when budgets are tight this is an easy area for budget cuts. However, if correctly utilised this department can demonstrate areas for cost savings and opportunities for growing profitable work. Generally, cost engineers face a lot of responsibilities and face significant challenges (Figure 8.1) but typically remain committed to their jobs.

We need to recognise the need to publicise our capabilities to internal and external audiences. We need to present to customers the benefits of cost engineering, estimating or cost forecasting departments.

Start by establishing your credibility: Why should a customer listen to you? What have you achieved for the organisation? State the benefits of the cost engineering department. Emphasise that to ensure that bids and projects are credible, justified and sustainable, the cost estimate needs to be realistic at the start. This is crucial to the survival of an organisation or company. Be honest: this is a recruitment campaign for cost engineering.

Explaining the need for cost engineering, Figure 8.2 shows the diversity of tasks that a mature cost engineering organisation needs to satisfy. The cost engineer is service orientated, focused on providing the needs of the customer and projects, operating under challenging circumstances often with the odds stacked strongly against them.

It is also worth introducing the idea that a mature cost engineering organisation is the 'gate keeper' when it comes to cost estimates. Commercially it is good practice to stop unauthorised costs from leaking out from the organisation or company. It is shrewd during potentially

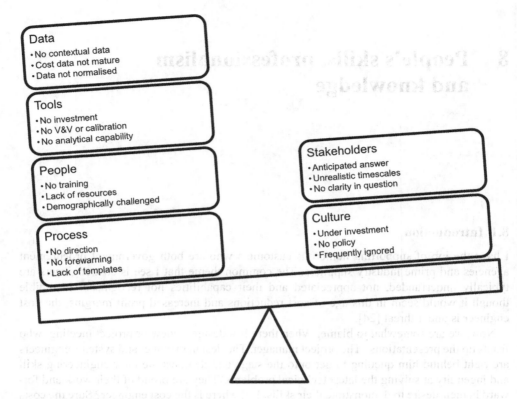

Data
- No contextual data
- Cost data not mature
- Data not normalised

Tools
- No investment
- No V&V or calibration
- No analytical capability

People
- No training
- Lack of resources
- Demographically challenged

Process
- No direction
- No forewarning
- Lack of templates

Stakeholders
- Anticipated answer
- Unrealistic timescales
- No clarity in question

Culture
- Under investment
- No policy
- Frequently ignored

Figure 8.1 Challenges faced by cost engineers

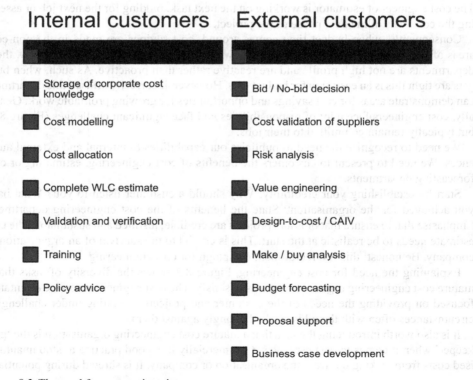

Internal customers

- Storage of corporate cost knowledge
- Cost modelling
- Cost allocation
- Complete WLC estimate
- Validation and verification
- Training
- Policy advice

External customers

- Bid / No-bid decision
- Cost validation of suppliers
- Risk analysis
- Value engineering
- Design-to-cost / CAIV
- Make / buy analysis
- Budget forecasting
- Proposal support
- Business case development

Figure 8.2 The need for cost engineering

competitive bidding situations that the only authoritative single source of truth is maintained by cost engineering and iterations of their proposal costs reconciled. It should appeal to senior stakeholders that the cost engineering function should become the focal point for all costs.

To be effective, a mature cost engineering organisation must have the following skills and resources:

- Experience
- Cost data
- Cost models
- Processes and procedures

What experience is required by a cost engineer to be able to perform his or her job? The experience is varied and broad; therefore these people are not easy to acquire. Figure 8.3 provides a diagram of the experiences required by cost engineers. Cost engineers must be all things to all people in the engineering and business worlds. They must be experienced in the domain in which they function, e.g. automotive, aerospace, defence. They must have a working knowledge of mathematical and statistical analysis techniques including risk modelling, have a knowledge of various different types of engineering disciplines, and knowledge and

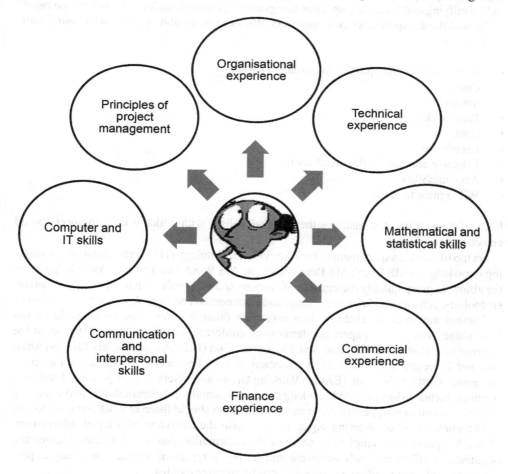

Figure 8.3 The experience of a cost engineer

experience of accounting practices. They must be experienced report writers, and exhibit excellent interpersonal and communication skills, both written and oral, with the ability to present complex analysis to the business in a non-technical manner. They must be self-motivated and have experience working both on their own initiative and as part of a team. The best cost engineers are those individuals who demonstrate an ability to persuade and influence people outside their own immediate area of specialism and provide leadership qualities to help their organisations articulate the questions that they wish their costs estimates to answer. They should be innovative in their approach to problem solving, with the ability to challenge existing methodologies and procedures, recommending solutions using new ideas and technology. They should be able to develop new capabilities, integrate into new environments and understand new domains quickly, reacting positively to change, and have a proactive outlook and a desire to delight their customers throughout an engagement.

In order to gather all the information necessary to achieve a credible and justifiable cost estimate, cost engineers need to be able to converse with many different functions in the organisation in a manner that garners them sufficient respect to get their job done. Cost engineers must exhibit commercial awareness and also need to have project management experience/capability, as generating a cost estimate is like running a small project in its own right, needing the ability to plan, schedule and monitor their own progress on the cost estimating tasking, and identifying and escalating up when things don't go to plan, which can often be the case.

Beyond these experiences cost engineers also need to exhibit specific behavioural traits [36] such as:

- An interest in, and aptitude for, problem solving
- Commitment
- Integrity
- Teamwork
- Care
- Excellence
- Effective communication at all levels
- Accountability
- Willingness to learn

Each of these traits demonstrates the professionalism with which a cost engineer should consider their work.

On top of this we expect them to be information technology (IT) literate, including a working knowledge of MS Excel, MS PowerPoint and MS Word, and also have knowledge of, or the ability to grasp quickly the concept of, various analysis tools such as Monte Carlo analysis toolsets, schedule and risk modelling, and commercial and bespoke parametric toolsets.

Another way to ensure that functions cooperate, other than demonstrating experience and knowledge, is to present papers at international conferences, such as the conferences of the International Cost Estimating and Analysis Association (ICEAA), the Society for Cost Analysis and Forecasting (SCAF), the Association of Cost Engineers (ACostE), the European Aerospace Cost Engineering (EACE) Working Group and others. Papers presented and conferences attended demonstrate knowledge and understanding. If international audiences are willing to listen to you, perhaps your own organisation should listen to what you have to say.

The mature cost engineering organisation is also the custodian of a lot of information. Figure 8.4 provides a template of some of the information that a mature cost engineering organisation will be routinely gathering and storing. It represents the data necessary to produce a credible and justified estimate and can be an extensive list.

Figure 8.4 The data sources of a cost engineer; meeting the needs

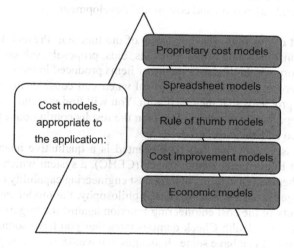

Figure 8.5 Modelling capability

Another capability a cost engineer needs is having the ability to model the project in terms of the cost outcome. This could necessitate the use of parametric, analogous and analytical (detailed estimating) models. A mature cost engineer needs to be well skilled in the utilisation and functionality of a spreadsheet. They have a capability to produce cost estimating relationships (CERs) and simple models. They understand the need for cost normalisation and are able to apply it. They can explain the principles and communicate the theory of cost improvement curves (Boeing, Wright and Crawford). They can appropriately use and explain escalation, inflation, discounted cash flow, net present value, and so forth. These members of staff are essential to the business (Figure 8.5).

Finally, they understand important company-specific processes for bidding, risk identification and price generation, and the procedures for presenting the price to the ultimate customer in a way that the customer will be satisfied. In other words, they interpret the customer's internal requirements or the external customer's ITT or RFP.

A mature cost engineer should be able to qualitatively analyse or determine their value for money. The cost engineering department is very economical when you consider the size of the budget and the size of the problems that they deal with. It might be appropriate to discuss the funding of the cost engineering function via mechanisms such as: direct versus overhead cost recovery.

The arguments for funding the cost engineer directly or indirectly are thus:

Direct cost recovery:

- Function is not independent; it needs the project, which could exert influence on the cost estimate
- Focused on one project
- Possible distractions of other tasks

Overhead cost recovery:

- Independent in order to provide management with cost estimates
- Time to perform cost data gathering
- Resources to fund calibration and cost model development

Give an assessment of the value for the money of the function. Present a graph of the cost of the function against the value of the estimates, bids, proposals, sub-contractors assessed, procurements support, whole life costs and other items produced in the same time scale. The cost engineering department is very economical when you consider the size of the budget and the size of the problems that they deal with. You will find that the resources going into the cost engineering function should be less than the results coming out of the organisation, otherwise there is no added value.

An alternative assessment that can be presented is a qualitative analysis. QinetiQ has developed the Cost Engineering Health Check (CEHC), a system which organisations can use to benchmark themselves in terms of their cost engineering capability (Figure 8.6). Based upon the Knowledge Based Estimating (KBE) philosophy, the model can be used to demonstrate the capability of the cost engineering function against the targets that they have set.

The Cost Engineering Health Check demonstrates that you have some capability, it is a worthwhile function and you have some challenges and weaknesses, due perhaps to funding constraints or resource problems. It is possible that you do not have responsibilities for all the process areas. It is possible that you have some capability even though you are not targeted with that responsibility!

Demonstrating that the cost engineering department is worthy of support can be achieved through qualifications and accreditation. If the cost engineering department is presenting papers in an international forum, then maybe the organisation should listen to them. Show the qualifications of the existing staff, NVQ ACostE or ICEAA certificates, incorporated, chartered or other qualifications. Professional memberships, Association of Cost Engineers (ACostE), Association of Project Management (APM) and other appropriate bodies will also demonstrate your worth.

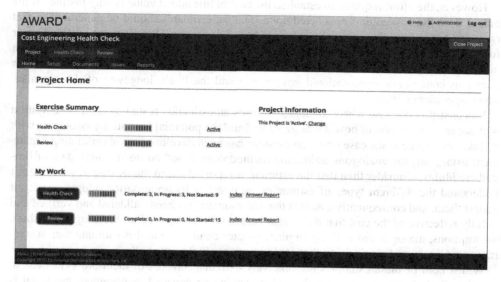

Figure 8.6 Cost engineering capability improvement model

Emphasise what a cost engineer brings in terms of:

- Constant culture
- Constant processes
- Constant output
- Confidence in the cost output results
- Uniform approach to cost and schedule estimating
- Retention of corporate cost knowledge
- Focus on cost initiatives
- Professional body of qualified engineers

What have you got to lose? Sell cost engineering to your peers and senior management – you're worth it!

8.2 Maturity considerations

8.2.1 What is the nature of the senior management's involvement in cost engineering?

In a mature cost engineering organisation, knowing the cost of the hardware, software and services that you deliver is critical to your ability to determine their price. When a manufacturing organisation takes raw material and manipulates it, then they are adding value to that raw material in the end item. The raw material and added value represents the cost of producing this item. When a software organisation designs, codes and tests a new application, it is adding value to the operating system upon which it operates. Finally, when an organisation provides a service to an individual or customer organisation which is appreciated, then this too is the basis for commerce.

However, the effort required to establish the cost of this added value is only justified if the output from the cost engineers is acted upon. That is, estimates should be generated so that management can use them to make evidence-based decisions. There is no use estimating or forecasting the cost of hardware, software or service within your organisation if the decision makers don't value it or recognise it, or even use it. Such a situation should act to raise wider questions concerning organisational governance and the likely longevity of the organisation's operational future.

Worse still is the case where management uses an estimate created by their organisation without an appreciation of how it was generated and the potential limitations associated with it. Take, for example, the case where an estimate has been developed by an estimating department using, say, the analogous estimating methodology based on open source data of limited credibility. Consider then that the estimate is reported out to management, who doesn't understand the different types of estimating approaches its organisation adopts or why it adopts them, and consequently assumes that the estimate has been validated and verified and is fully reflective of the cost that their organisation will be exposed to. Working under these assumptions, management is likely to place greater confidence in this estimate than it warrants, and hence make a decision that could be seriously flawed.

Whilst both of these examples are relatively extreme, flavours of them are evidenced in practice. Both, however, can be addressed by having an engaged management team that is aware of the need to make evidenced-based decisions and is fully supportive of the need for organisational estimates to be generated by an internal estimating function that it has guided in terms of the type of cost information that they require to inform their decision making process. As such, management should act to ensure that there is a written policy to have a cost organisation. If it does not exist, then the cost organisation should instigate its production and promote the existence of it. The executive board needs to buy into the policy to have a cost organisation and invest in it. They need to ensure that there is proper investment in training, tools and staff, and then they need to demand the best cost estimates and forecasts for this investment.

From an executive board perspective the policy should consider the funding of the cost organisation. It can be a direct cost or an overhead to the company; both sources of funding have pros and cons as shown in Table 8.1.

Similarly, management should be briefed on the various different types of techniques being employed by the estimating function, and the potential limitations associated with the estimates that are being offered. Ideally management should request that all cost information

Table 8.1 Advantages and disadvantages of the funding of a cost engineering function

	Advantages	Disadvantages
Direct cost	• The cost of the cost estimating is recovered through the project	• The project manager will fund the cost engineer and have influence on their outputs • Focus on one project • Possible distraction of other tasks
Indirect cost	• The cost estimating organisation is independent of any project influences • Can provide independent advice to the executive board • Time to perform cost data gathering • Resources to fund cost research, calibration and cost model development	• The cost of the cost estimating organisation increases the company's overheads

be reported to them in a consistent format, and have been developed in a consistent manner so that they can make decisions on an equitable basis.

At a lower level of maturity, the individual projects must adhere to the corporate policy. If they wish not to utilise the cost estimating organisation within their project, then they need to justify this decision within their project management plan and raise this as a point of exception at their project review meetings. Any approach that is adopted should then be rigorously reviewed to ensure that it still meets the quality standards demanded by the business. The executive board should treat estimates that have been generated in a manner that has deviated from corporate policy with greater scepticism than those that have adhered to the corporate policy.

Significantly, management also has a bearing on how other stakeholders interact with the cost estimating process. A management team that is strongly engaged with the process will likely see the generation of higher quality estimates than when management are not engaged. The organisation takes its lead from senior management and if stakeholders know that management supports the process and interrogate its output in a formal manner, then they are more likely to participate and provide quality information in the first instance.

8.2.2 What is the project's senior management's view of the cost information they are provided?

The senior management team within a project is considered to be the project manager and design manager. The project manager is responsible for the project direction, expenditure, schedule and progress. In addition, the design manager is technically the most senior member of staff, with responsibility for the technical deliverables, interpretation and solving the technical problems, and technical assurance and quality of the deliverables. The senior management team typically reports to the executive board on the profitability, progress and problems of the project. Within this is a need to appreciate the cost of the project in terms of the cost of the baseline programme of work, future work and the implications of schedule and cost risk analysis caused by the probability of a deviation from the baseline plan.

In this era we work flexible times and work from home in many industries. We have personal objectives and we trust individuals to perform their allotted task safely without supervision. Without significant staff decision, senior management are left to make critical decisions based upon the best quality information available. This should include the cost information.

Is information being presented to the project's senior management in a manner so that they can understand it? Are graphs used to ease understanding of the key messages? There are various different graphical types that a cost engineer should be competent in using, and they should understand how these can be used to report the relevant information to management.

Is all the information that they are provided with useable? Similarly, are they provided with a complete view of the costs or do they need to look to other sources before they can get a comprehensive picture of the costs in their projects? Do they have confidence in the information they are provided with? Or do they receive it but then use their own information anyway? Do they see themselves as being a key part of the validation activity, taking a proactive role in questioning the underlying assumptions and methodologies?

Are they overwhelmed with superfluous detail to the point that they cannot see the forest for the trees? It is the role of the cost engineer to understand the level of cost information that it is appropriate to report to PMs to help them make the decisions that they need to make. There shouldn't be too much detail, nor should there be too little. There should be just the right amount of detail that addresses the questions being asked. The detail should be available should they wish to see it and satisfy themselves that the costing was robust.

Senior project staff can depend upon their own ability to estimate cost or take guidance from cost estimating professionals. There needs to be an agreement regarding the cost information required by the senior management team, its format, content and appropriate level of accuracy.

The project manager uses this cost information to inform bids, contract variations, estimates to completion (EAC) and other cost-related project activities. The design manager calls upon the skill of the cost engineer to support technical trade-offs when considering alternative technologies and balancing the benefit of different design solutions. The mature cost engineer is proactive with regards to the identification of project specific cost drivers. They will work together for the financial benefit of the project when considering business decisions.

8.2.3   What is the project's external customer's view of the cost information they are provided?

The internal senior management is a relatively easy customer regarding the 'selling' of cost information as the cost engineer can be completely open with regards to the sources and assumptions made [27]. Gaining the respect of the external customer is more difficult for a cost engineer. Commercial interests can be a large hurdle for cost engineers as their ability to form a trusting relationship is hindered by the natural commercial need to control the flow of information presented to the customer.

The cost engineer needs to explore opportunities to influence the external customer with thoughtful leadership. Presenting at conferences and workshops provide an opportunity for the mature cost engineering organisation to demonstrate their cost engineering skills outside of the confines of a contractual deliverable. There presentations are enhanced if they are given jointly with the customer.

The cost engineer (and senior management) should explore what level of data can be released to the customer to provide confidence that the costing was conducted in an appropriate manner. The cost engineer may explore opportunities with a customer/client for the adoption of common cost estimating practices/methodologies leading to the endorsement of the costing process and hence limiting the amount of scrutiny that needs to be placed on any of the figures submitted.

Part of this relationship with the external customer should be monitored through quality questionnaires with the customer to ask them for their feedback. Only through proactive interaction with its external customer will an organisation be able to assess and plan current and future improvements to the service that is provided.

The other means of assessing the state of this relationship is to consider the extent to which the external customer uses the cost estimating information provided to them.

Do the customers continually see the cost of their projects rising beyond the initial forecasts, thus giving them limited confidence in the numbers being provided to them? Similarly, do they feel that they are being provided with a constantly negative picture, tying up financial resources in areas where they are not needed? Do external customers typical make systematic adjustments to the estimates provided to them to account for these biases (optimism bias)?

8.2.4   How well informed is the project regarding cost information of its main suppliers?

When considering a details analytic estimate, it is possible to consider labour and non-labour elements. The non-labour cost elements will have various degrees of maturity; the most mature will be commercially committing supplier quotations. However, this does raise the question: "How good are these supplier estimates?" When a cost engineer takes a supplier's quotation and includes it as a non-labour element in their estimate against a bill of material (BOM), they need to consider the level of uncertainty in that estimate and risks which might occur. Part of the uncertainty will be caused by the level of accuracy of the specifications or requirements provided to the supplier, but a significant part of their assessment will relate to the cost engineering process used by the supplier.

Ideally, the standard of the cost engineering process used by a supplier should complement that used by the cost engineer's organisation. There are various means to determine the supplier's cost engineering process including quality audits, visits to suppliers, questionnaires and so forth [61]. The important concept is to realise that the quotations provided are commercially sensitive and this exercise is best conducted outside of a period when you are requesting a quotation. Be aware that regardless of the supplier's process being assessed as excellent or poor, it is the unbiased accuracy of the assessment that is critical. If the assessment results in a poor ranking, the cost engineer can compensate their estimate with a risk or large uncertainty boundary, thus reducing the risk to their organisation in a structured and logical manner, rather than accepting that the costs of the supplier's goods are accurate.

It is to be hoped that a good supplier is proactive in offering the basis of estimate (BOE) to their customer including assumptions, data source and description of their estimating process. This would encourage the cost engineer's organisation to utilise their cost estimates and goods and services in the future.

An example of an organisation taking greater interest in its supplier's costs is the UK MOD with the introduction of its Single Source Pricing Regulations in 2015. These enshrine in law regulations with respect to pricing and transparency provisions for qualifying defence contracts and qualifying sub-contracts. They allow the UK MOD to impose civil penalties on organisations if they fail to comply with the transparency requirements. These regulations replaced a previous framework entitled the 'Yellow Book', which was little more than a guide as to how transparent an organisation needed to be, and consequently organisations often failed to comply with it. These transparency regulations give the UK MOD greater insight into what and how they are being charged and thus offer them up the opportunity to strengthen their negotiating position and reduce costs.

8.2.5 How well does the cost engineer understand their project and the way that it functions?

Typically, people do not enter the field of cost estimating as a career choice. You don't find a career advisor in a school or university saying, "Well your psychological profile suggests that your future lies in cost estimating." By far the majority of cost engineers had a career in another field first and then fell into cost estimating as a career alternative. As such, the majority of cost engineers have a bias towards hardware or software, manufacturing or support and so forth.

The modern cost engineer needs to be educated in the whole life of a product or service. It is no longer acceptable to only understand an element such as manufacturing; they need to appreciate the whole life and the costs associated with the whole life. If you consider the WLC of a car, you might consider its journey through life as:

1   Non-recurring research, design, test and evaluation
2   Recurring manufacture
3   Showroom facilities, marketing, advertising and sales
4   Legal cost associated with insurance, road tax, VAT

5   Maintenance and MOT
6   Fuel
7   Breakdown cover
8   Environmental disposal and scrap

A cost engineer needs to be able to visualise and consider all the aspects associated with the product they are cost estimating through life. A good process is to draw the life cycle and consider the cost associated with each element, as shown in Figure 8.7.

For example, the view could be taken that, as a cost engineer specialising in cost estimating/forecasting within a manufacturing environment, I have no need to understand the costs of operating or maintaining the equipment when it is in service, or my organisation's liability to the equipment when it is in service. As such, I could recommend a manufacturing approach that reduces the cost to produce the item. There have been examples of such situations in the past resulting in unexpected increased cost downstream for the organisation. The implications of design decisions on the whole life cost of a product is coming in for increasing levels of examination, and any competent cost engineer will give consideration to the whole life cost when creating their estimates [62]. In addition, they need to be able to converse with subject matter experts (SME) in their own language. A SME is unlikely to give you time if you are unable to understand the product that they are producing. It is important to be able to converse with them and understand when they are exaggerating or underestimating the tasks to be conducted. The mature cost engineer should be current, not just with up-to-date cost estimating techniques, but with new technologies, manufacturing processes, software, procurement philosophies and so forth.

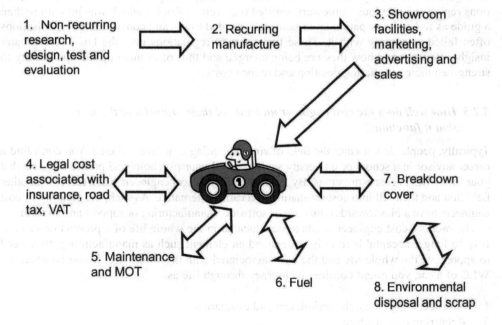

Figure 8.7 Life cycle of a car

Similarly, a mature cost engineer needs to be able to understand the project environment, the various different decisions that must be undertaken within a project and how the cost information that they will generate is required to help inform these decisions. This helps them understand what level of information needs to be reported to whom and when it needs to be reported. To facilitate their understanding of the project environment is useful if the cost engineer is familiar with the project management approach that is being used to plan, execute and control the project. Consequently, some form of project management awareness qualification is desirable. Within the UK these typically are qualifications such as the Association of Project Management (APM), PRINCE 2 (Foundation or Practitioner), MSP (Foundation or Practitioner) and the OGC Management of Risk (Foundation or Practitioner).

8.2.6 Does the cost engineer have an appreciation of maths and statistics relevant to cost engineering?

Some people refer to estimating as an art. Historically this might have been the case, but today the average professional cost engineer applies a considerable amount of science to what might otherwise be considered a guess. The strength of a professional cost estimate is having a basis of estimate (BOE). This provides the differentiation between a guess and a credible and justified cost estimate. The BOE has the ability to place the cost estimate in context and tell the story which has a natural and predictable conclusion: "Therefore the cost is in the range £X to £Y."

Part of the BOE will be taking historical information and interpreting it. This interpretation requires normalisation of the cost and non-cost data and the extrapolation of the normalised data into the future. This activity requires knowledge and understanding of statistics and mathematics, but not just theory, this includes knowledge about the application [54]. A fixed price supplies quotation requires inflation factors (the application of compounded percentages) to bring it to the budget required in three years' time, but what compounded percentage is required for the firm price?

Regression analysis is applied to historical normalised data to predict into the future. The cost engineer needs to have the mathematical skills necessary to apply regression and recognise when the resulting cost estimating relationship (CER) is valid. A pure statistician might look at Figure 8.8 and be content with the outcome – the R-square is good!

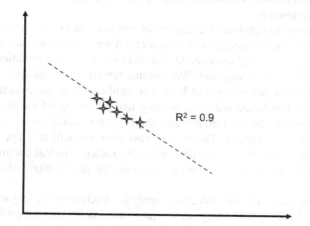

$R^2 = 0.9$

Figure 8.8 Statistically superior

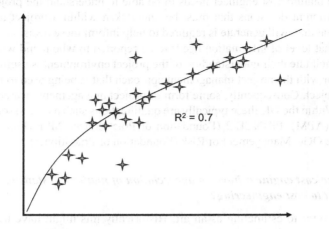

$R^2 = 0.7$

Figure 8.9 Superior CER

But when a cost engineer for a mature cost engineering organisation looks at the axis and real-ises that this CER is predicting that cost reduces when the volume or surface area increases, they might just pause and gather more data. The outcome might not be statistically superior, but the interpretation of the CER and engineering hypothesis might be easier to justify as a BOE, as in Figure 8.9.

Whilst statistical analysis forms the backbone of many cost estimating methodologies, acknowledgement must be made back to the environment in which the cost engineer is oper-ating. Data sets within the costing world are typically quite small relative to other fields that use statistical analysis. Data sets are often incomplete or missing important meta data. As a consequence, a cost engineer must be pragmatic in their application of statistical approaches whilst trying not to undermine the validity of the adopted approaches. This is a fine line to walk and requires the estimator to exercise discretion which in turn demands a thorough understanding of the underlying statistical analysis approaches. Whilst perfectionism is an admiral trait, a perfectionist statistician would probably end up being driven insane working within the costing domain.

There are many cost organisation conferences and courses available for cost engineers to learn or improve the mathematical skills necessary. It's never too late to learn.

A mature cost engineer will understand that there is a lot of mathematics that will bring a little bit of science to cost forecasting. Without mathematics and statistics, our cost estimate is just another opinion and a guess at best. The application of mathematics and statistics in the background, combined with engineering understanding of the problem being con-sidered and business acumen to understand the problem, results in a cost estimate which is a more credible and rigorous. The mature cost engineer will rely upon probability and statistics to underpin a lot of its forecasts, just as the meteorological community relies upon them too. The probability of rain is no longer forecast on the basis of cattle standing or lying in a field!

Statistics is the study of the collection, analysis, interpretation, organisation and pres-entation of data. Looking at history, it considers the likelihood and probability of events occurring based upon known information. Probability is the measure of the likeliness that an event will occur. A branch of probability is known as stochastic modelling and considers changing probability over time. Thus statistics is applied to look backwards and probability is applied to forecast in cost engineering.

As a study of the past, statistics has two elements:

* Descriptive statistics, which is a field of statistics which focuses on defining the historical data, for example mean, median and mode; and
* Inferential statistics, which is the field of statistics that considers the testing of hypotheses and inferences.

Generally, in cost engineering statistics is used to generate cost estimating relationships, leading to cost models and parametrics [55], while probability is used to quantify uncertainty and risk that reside in those cost estimates.

A mature cost engineer will appreciate the differences between, and use accordingly, mathematical terms when referring to a population or sample, where a sample is a subset of the population.

* Mean = the sum divided by the count of the sample.
* Median = the number between the higher half of the sample and the lower half of the sample; the middle number in an ordered sample.
* Mode = the number which appears most often in a sample, for example the peak (representing the most likely) in a triangular probability distribution function.
* Range = the difference between the maximum and the minimum value in the sample.
* Skew = when the distribution of the sample is not symmetrical, then the median and mean are not equal, hence the distribution is skewed. For example, the uncertainty in a three-point estimate is usually skewed to the right as there is more likelihood of overspend (the maximum) than underspend (the minimum).
* Variance = the measure of how far a set of numbers is spread apart, for example, if the variance is zero then the values are identical.
* Standard deviation = is the measure of the amount of variation or dispersion of a sample, for example, if it is close to zero then there is very little dispersion. Standard deviation is the square root of the variance.

A mature cost engineer will appreciate that a scatter plot or X-Y plot is a wonderful means of visualising data for a cost engineer. It is possible to plot dependent variables, for example cost, against a host of independent variables, such as:

* Cost versus time
* Cost versus technical parameters
* Cost versus cost

When the data has been plotted, the cost engineer is looking for correlations between the independent and dependent variables. If the plot looks like a good correlation, then the statistical test R^2, also known as the coefficient of determination, will be trending towards one. There is no absolute value of R^2 that should be adhered too, as a mature cost engineer will know the R^2 is only an indicator that there is a relationship between two variables and only by considering the F and t statistics will the statistical significance of the relationship be tested.

The coefficient of variation (CV) is defined as the standard deviation divided by the mean. It can be useful in cost engineering as a measure without units which can be used to compare different distributions. Ideally, in cost engineering it is desirable to have a CV of less than 15%; if the CV is greater, then there should be a recognition that outliers might be present in the sample.

In the first instance there is a need to consider only one variable, but ultimately multiple variables can be applied. To get the line of best fit for a data set there is a need to consider the function which fits the data. Once the data has been plotted there are a number of function types to select:

- Linear function
- Power functions
- Exponential function
- Logarithmic functions

A mature cost engineer will conduct data validation on the homogenous data set once it has been normalised. The objective of this work is to identify any anomalies within the data set normally referred to as outliers. Normally 99.7% of all data would be expected to be within three standard deviations. It therefore follows that if a data point is more than three standard deviations from the mean, it is likely to be an outlier and better modelled as part of another data set (see Figure 8.10).

A mature cost engineer will appreciate that when a sample of data can be described mathematically using central tendency, standard deviation and so forth, then these distributions have many applications in the work that they generate, as shown in Table 8.2.

The mature cost engineer will understand that distributions play an important part in statistical analysis and hypothesis testing. Two hypothesis tests are the null hypothesis test, which is assumed to be true unless it can be proved untrue, and alternative hypothesis, which is only accepted when there is enough evidence to reject a null hypothesis. A mature cost engineer will appreciate that a hypothesis in statistics can be a one-tail or two-tail test. A one-tail test speculates that there is a direction of difference in the alternative hypothesis, for example the productivity of German industry is greater than European

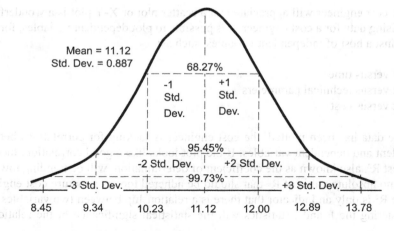

Figure 8.10 Considering the population and outliers through standard deviation

Table 8.2 Common types of distributions and their usage

Distributions	Usage in cost engineering
Normal	Regression analysis
	Cost distribution
	Risk distribution
Student t	Regression analysis
	Hypothesis testing
	Confidence intervals
Lognormal	Cost distribution
	Risk distribution
F	Regression analysis
Triangular	Risk probability distribution
Uniform	Risk probability distribution
Bernoulli	Risk analysis
Beta	Risk probability distribution

productivity, while the two-tail test does not speculate on the direction of the difference, just that it is different, for example the productivity of Europe is different to America.

There should be a good level of understanding regarding test statistics associated with statistical tests to understand if a hypothesis can be accepted or rejected, for example t-test and p-tests. Only through the application of descriptive statistics is it possible to describe and compare data using central tendency and dispersion. Only through the application of inferential statistics is it possible to test sample groups for differences in mean, variance and so forth using confidence intervals to rate the uncertainty.

8.2.7 What level of commercial awareness does the project cost engineer have?

Commercial staff generally enjoy the challenge of writing a good contract with the terms and conditions that legally favour their organisation. They will venture into the realms of pricing, provided the mathematics is not too complex, but generally they would admit that numbers are not their strength. Meanwhile, cost engineers enjoy the challenge of manipulating numbers and playing with spreadsheets. Ask them to read a contract and they will find numerous reasons why it can wait until tomorrow. Give a cost engineer a column of figures and they will normalise, manipulate and post process them until the answer is 42!

These might be broad generalisations, but they explain why some cost engineers struggle to appreciate the commercial aspects of their job.

The commercial awareness is not limited to the contract with the customer. The same rules apply when dealing with sub-contractors. A good cost engineer needs to understand and be able to interpret the implications of a supplier's commercial terms and conditions to enable them to deal with them properly in their estimate. If the supplier demands payment in advance, this will influence the annual cash flow; if the sub-contractor is demanding milestone payments or stage payments, this will provide another cash flow profile.

More complex payment plans such as performance based contracting (PBC), incentive payments against key performance indicators (KPI), partial achievement or other profit sharing contractual arrangements can be challenging and require the combined skills of contract managers, the purchasing department and cost engineers to calculate [45].

A mature cost engineer will have a good understanding of the commercial issues. They will appreciate the contracting is about offering and accepting a fair deal for the buyer or customer when offered by the seller or contractor. A fair deal means that both parties conclude their business feeling satisfied and prepared to conduct another deal another day. The cost engineer will appreciate the different types of contracting mechanisms and their effect on the price.

Some common commercial terms will be commonplace in a mature cost engineering organisation, such as:

- Cost – the value of resources consumed when providing hardware, software or services
- Profit or fee – the money earned in excess of any costs
- Margin – the profit expressed as a percentage (possibly of cost or price)
- Revenue – the price or cost plus profit

The margin can be calculated on either the cost or price, for example, if the cost of an item is £100m and the price paid is £110m, then the profit will be £10m. Now, as a margin based on cost (also known as return on cost or ROC), this is £10m / £100m equal to 10% margin. However, if the margin is calculated on the price (also known as return on sales or ROS), this is £10m / £110m equal to 9.09% margin.

The principle contracting mechanisms that will be recognised by a mature cost engineer are:

- Fixed price
- Cost plus

The focus here is either on the cost being paid in full or the price being paid in full. In both contracting mechanisms the cost is the consumption of resources required to provide the hardware, software or service. In addition to this element there is a fee or profit to be considered. This is added to the cost to determine the price. Now, a mature cost engineer will appreciate that a fixed price contracting mechanism will focus on the full payment of the price agreed, without reference to the cost. In this instance, if the cost is less than the price agreed, then there is a profit to be made; unfortunately, if the cost is greater than the price, then this will result in no profit or even a loss situation. In these contracts the supplier holds the risk and the customer has no risk. The mature cost engineer will understand that as a consequence of this potential loss the supplier will include a risk contingency and the customer will pay more. In the case of a cost plus or cost reimbursement contracting mechanism, the focus is on the cost. The customer will pay in full the costs; the profit is calculated on top of this cost to generate a price. In these contracts the customer holds the risk and the supplier has no risk. The mature cost engineer will understand that the customer will need to hold a risk contingency budget to accommodate any increase in cost from the supplier.

Regardless of the contracting mechanism identified by the commercial team, a mature cost engineer will recognise that the cost of the project needs to be determined. The mature cost engineer will recognise the following fixed price contracting types:

- Firm fixed price (FFP)
- Fixed price incentive (FPI)

Table 8.3 The risk spectrum for contract types

Contract type	Supplier risk	Customer risk
Firm Fixed Price (FFP)	Very high	Very low
Fixed Price Incentive (FPI)	High	Low
Cost Plus Incentive Fee (CPIF)	Medium	Medium
Cost Plus Award Fee (CPAF)	Low	High
Cost Plus Fixed Fee (CPFF)	Very low	Very high

As well as the following cost plus contracting types, Table 8.3 provides a refinement of the contracting mechanisms and their relative risks to the supplier and customer.

- Cost plus award fee (CPAF)
- Cost plus incentive fee (CPIF)
- Cost plus fixed fee (CPFF)

A mature cost engineer will have a good appreciation of incentive mechanisms. An incentive contract will include clauses which introduce the terms:

- Share ratio
- Ceiling price

There is a very simple formula for the calculation of the profit that will be achieved in an incentive contract, as shown in the following equation.

$$Final\ Price = Final\ Cost + Incentive\ Profit$$

Where:

Final price = the price paid by the customer
Final cost = the cost claimed by the supplier
Incentive profit = the calculated profit achieved

The incentive profit is calculated by an equation which is shown below.

$$Incentive\ Profit = Target\ Profit + Share\ Ratio(Target\ Cost - Final\ Cost)$$

Where:

Target profit = is a fix agreed profit for the effort
Target cost = is a fixed agreed cost for the effort
Share ratio = is a ratio of supplier's level of profit relative to the final cost

The share ratio provides the incentive; it is the mechanism by which a supplier can generate a greater profit, or potentially a loss. The share ratio is usually expressed as 80/20 or 70/30. The interpretation of an 80/20 share ratio is that the contractor earns £2 of profit for each £10 that the final cost is below the target cost. Various scenarios are shown in Figure 8.11.

In addition to this profit sharing formula, a mature cost engineer will be aware that the customer can impose a ceiling price. The ceiling price can be set against the target cost and limits the price to the purchaser, providing an incentive but capping the contracting authority

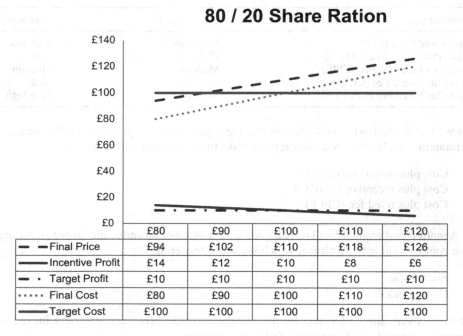

80 / 20 Share Ration	£80	£90	£100	£110	£120
― ―Final Price	£94	£102	£110	£118	£126
——Incentive Profit	£14	£12	£10	£8	£6
― • Target Profit	£10	£10	£10	£10	£10
• • • • • Final Cost	£80	£90	£100	£110	£120
——Target Cost	£100	£100	£100	£100	£100

Figure 8.11 Example of an 80/20 share ratio for an incentive contract

from exceeding a budget limit. The point of total assumption (PTA) is the point at which the costs have risen to a degree that the price is equal to the ceiling price; at this point the supplier assumes responsibility for all additional costs.

8.2.8 How well does the project cost engineer understand the project financial systems?

Financial knowledge is an advantage to a cost engineer for two reasons:

1   To enable them to interpret historical actual costs; and
2   To ensure that they are preparing cost in an appropriate format for budget setting.

Accountants hide behind terms and jargon, so it is important for a cost engineer to be able to understand the difference between raw cost information from a general ledger and accruals information including depreciation. Unfortunately, accounting systems are configured to serve the needs of the finance department and aim to produce balance sheet and profit and loss (P&L) outputs quickly and easily. They are not generally established to deliver the total cost of a project or task without some manual interpretation or manipulation.

Data in financial systems are also not at a level of detail that is commensurate with the cost estimating activity and as such can be of limited use.

It is also important to understand how the costs contained within the financial system have been burdened.

When a customer approaches a cost engineer for figures, it is often the case that the customer does not understand what they need and it is important that the cost engineer is able to guide them. In many cases the customer knows that they require cost information, but requires the cost engineer to direct them in terms of an economic analysis or a financial analysis, both accounting terms:

- Financial analysis (FA) is used to derive the cost associated with a given programme option which must be funded directly by the customer. These financial estimates are being used within the budget planning and within the assessment of affordability within a business case submission. They will typically include the effects of tax and appropriate inflation. They are termed outturn, as-spent or then-year.
- Economic analysis (EA) is based on the total whole life cost to the customer. These estimates will be used for comparison of programme options in a business case. These are used to determine the best value for money (VfM). This is achieved by application of the net present value (NPV) considering the 'time value of money'.

These simple accounting concepts are important for the cost engineer to understand, in addition to constant cost, real cost, discounted cost and so forth.

A mature cost engineer will appreciate that the project, programme or portfolio which they are estimating will have a life cycle. Regardless of whether this is hardware, software or services, there will be a gestation period of discovery, a creation period, a maintenance period and finally a termination period. This all-encompassing concept can be captured in a number of different terms including 'cradle to grave' or 'soup to nuts' in America. At the start of the life cycle there are generally non-recurring activities which lead to recurring activities, as seen in Figure 8.12.

Non-recurring costs are typically due to activities which consume resources once. When achieved, these activities result in a discovery which does not need to be repeated, for example, the design of tooling, the acquisition of test equipment, the building of facilities, the set-up of production machinery and so forth. Recurring costs are typically due to activities which consume resources time after time. Their purpose is to be easily repeatable and their outcome is uniquely valuable each time, for example, the labour required to assemble an engine, the material required to produce a casting and so forth.

There needs to be an appreciation that within recurring costs there can be non-recurring elements which can be amortised across the recurring costs. The most common form of this is the time to set up a machine. The set-up time can be spread across the recurring cost of each of the items produced, thus becoming invisible to the end users of the information (see Figure 8.13).

These non-recurring and recurring costs are direct costs; they can be attributed to a project or product. Typically the direct costs are built up of a few components including:

- Labour cost
- Non-labour costs, comprising:
  - Raw material
  - Purchased parts
  - Sub-contractor costs

The direct labour cost can be comprised of a number of direct labour hours at specific labour rates. Alternatively, the direct labour hours can be multiplied by a composite labour rate

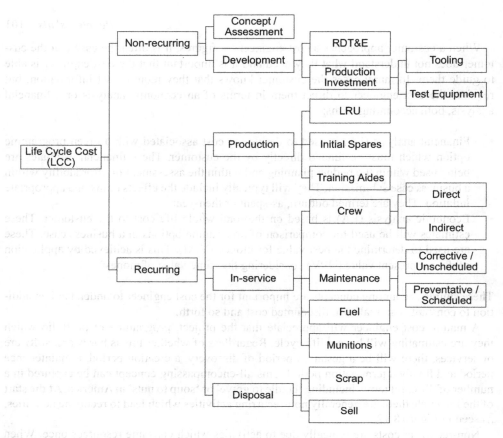

Figure 8.12 Life cycle development of costing

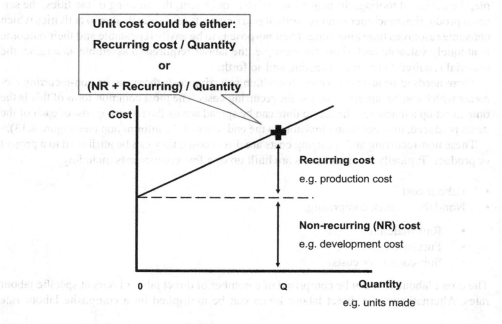

Figure 8.13 Establishing recurring and non-recurring costs

Table 8.4 Detailed and composite labour rates

| Labour grade | Grade title | Labour cost | | |
		Hours	£ / Hr	Cost
US	Un-skilled	64	£ 26.56	£ 1,699.84
SS	Semi-skilled	98	£ 34.80	£ 3,410.40
HS	Skilled	56	£ 45.65	£ 2,556.40
		218		£ 7,666.65

Composite labour rate =
$26.56 \times (64/218) + 34.8 \times (98/218) + 45.56 \times (56/218) = 35.17$

| Labour grade | Grade title | Labour cost | | |
		Hours	£ / Hr	Cost
N/A	Composite	218	£ 35.17	£ 7,666.64

which has been derived from a mixture of the appropriate labour rates for the task, as shown in Table 8.4.

It is usual for overheads and labour rates to be agreed when the organisation has completed a period of transactions. At this point the total labour hours and total salary bill is known and the labour rates can be determined through the division of the total labour bill over the total labour hours. The problem arises when an organisation wishes to bid for work in the future. In this case the proposal will be based upon predicted labour rates and overheads. A mature cost engineer will appreciate forward pricing, where the prospective pricing of overhead and labour rates is utilised in advance of specific contract negotiations and known costs.

The quantity of time required to complete a piece of work can be established by work measurements, time studies or analogous assessments. If the piece of work is repeated regularly, then it can become recognised as a standard time, as defined in the equation below.

$$Time\,Standard = \frac{measured\,time \times pace}{1 - personal\,fatigue + Delay\,factor}$$

Where:

Measured time = nominal time it should take for conducting the work
Pace = a rating factor of how fast or slow a worker is performing (considers safe working, ergonomics of the workspace, etc.)
Personal fatigue and delay factor = decreases or losses in production which might be attributed to worker fatigue (considers toilet breaks, tea breaks, etc.)

This will not consider the effort to plan, design and acquire tools and test equipment for the manufacture of the end item, for example production planners, production engineers, inspectors, supervisors, production controllers and industry and production engineers.

The standard time will be further adjusted by learning curves, and any associated production breaks, the experience of the labour force (sometime referred to as green labour) and any process improvement initiatives that are being implemented.

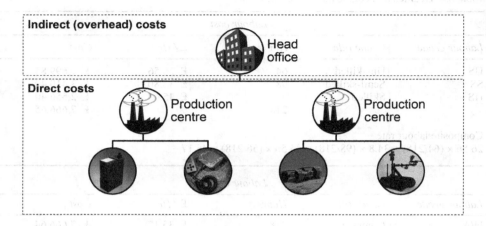

Figure 8.14 Indirect and direct allocation of costs

In addition to recurring and non-recurring costs, a mature cost engineer will appreciate that there are overhead costs. Overheads are costs which consume resources but are unable to be attributed to a specific project or revenue generating task, as shown in Figure 8.14. Alternative terms for overhead are burden or indirect costs. Capital expenditure is a specific type of overhead, when capital machinery is purchased, such as CNC machines, lathes, milling and drilling machines; these are not allocated to specific projects but are depreciated over the term of their useful life. This depreciation is part of the overhead costs.

Many organisations will distinguish cost centres and profit centres. This is common in a matrix organisation where the production centres, which manufacture items, are cost centres, leans and efficient. These are used by system or platform centres, which market, sell, design and integrate items from production centres and other sources, and are profit centres.

When considering the whole life costs of military systems and reviewing options, then overheads are similar in concept, but applied in the context of a military scenario. Fully overheaded costs spread the total cost of an organisation across its deliverable products or other outputs; this is also referred to as absorption costing. Marginal costs are costs arising, or saved, 'at the margin' via small changes in products or other outputs. Marginal costs are well defined but do not add up to the total cost of an activity or operational function. Differences are especially acute when equipping men (Army) rather than manning equipment (Navy and Air Force) since 'overheads' are then large and their attribution arbitrary (see Figure 8.15).

8.2.9 How well does the project cost engineer gather fundamental cost estimating data?

It is not possible to estimate in a vacuum; it is necessary to interact with other members of the project and wider organisation. At the start of this process it is common to identify gaps in their knowledge. The requirements have not been fully developed, the customer is unsure what they want and the engineers have not matured their thinking in terms of the design and

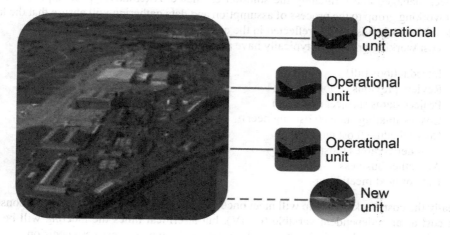

Figure 8.15 How the addition or removal of an operational unit affects the overheads

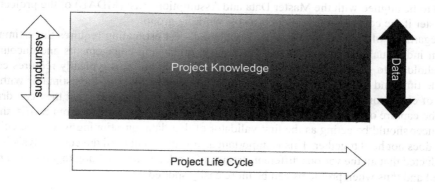

Figure 8.16 From assumption to data over a project life cycle

solution that they are going to recommend. But the poor cost engineer is still required to gather cost data and generate estimates.

It is not uncommon, therefore, for the cost engineer to make assumptions regarding the magnitude of the problem and the complexity of the solution. At the start of the project life cycle the assumptions help to put their estimate into context and provide a safeguard against criticism. As the project life cycle matures (see Figure 8.16), it is imperative that the assumptions are replaced with robust data and facts. A mature cost engineering organisation nurtures the development of these facts before the engineers would naturally be inclined to mature them.

Ideally the assumptions and data for any cost estimate will be gathered in a collaborative environment. The ESA concurrent design facility (CDF) [44] is an extreme example of this type of environment where the whole team including customer and all stakeholders work in a facilitated purpose built facility. In real-time the requirements are explored, design matured, project managed and ultimately the solution estimated. Alternatively, the application of a cost working group to the process of assumption and data gathering will ensure that the latest state of the project is always reflected in the cost estimates.

A cost working group will typically have an agenda as follows:

1   Introductions (all)
2   Review previous action (all)
3   Project status (project manager)
4   Cost estimating status (cost engineer)
5   Cost schedule (cost engineer)
6   Cost deliverables (cost engineer)
7   Any other business
8   Date of next meeting

Ideally the cost working group will meet once per month for project work or when considering cost as an independent variable (CAIV), but at critical times the meeting will be held more frequently, such as during proposals or approaching a business case decision.

The information critical to a project should be recorded in a Cost Data and Assumptions List (CDAL), CARD, CADRe or similar document produced by the cost engineer. This will need to be aligned with the Master Data and Assumptions List (MDAL) of the project. This is easier if the cost engineer conducts a cost working group.

Regardless of which way cost data is gathered, cost estimating requires the estimator to be an individual that is able to take the lead in organising engagements and encouraging stakeholders to get involved and give up their information. This typically requires considerable time and effort and is often facilitated by the credibility of the estimator within the role of estimator, in addition to the professional network of contacts that they can draw on for the capture of information. In gathering such data and assumptions from SMEs, the cost engineer should be acting as the first validator of that data, questioning where the collected data does not hold together. This is important as it is often not until the cost analysis is being conducted that all the various different streams of work begin to be hung together and rationalised and thus when problems can be more easily spotted.

8.2.10   What level of technical proficiency does the project cost engineer possess?

I was once asked, "Why are you an engineer?" I had to stop and really think before I answered, but when I thought about it, it was obvious and I simply answered "because I see things in bits". What I meant was an engineer sees the beauty of items around them in terms of their assemblies, subassemblies and parts and marvels at their construction. When an accountant looks at a laptop they consider it as a tangible asset to depreciated; when an engineer looks at a laptop they see moulding, electronics, interfaces, software and so forth.

Cost engineers need to have the ability to communicate with numerous types of engineers. It can be considered to be a specialist type of systems engineering. The cost engineer needs to be an equal to engineers and understand their language, otherwise the trust will be lost. Engineers spend their entire life solving difficult technical problems. But to enable their solutions to become reality or to 'be born', they need to appreciate the value of the solution regardless if it's hardware, software or a service. This is when the cost engineer comes into their life and asks probing questions.

The cost engineer does not need to have an in-depth knowledge of any one engineering discipline, but they do need a broad understanding of the all engineering disciplines, as they will be inevitably faced with estimating the cost of completely diverse business offerings.

Not only does this enable the cost engineer to ask the correct type of questions in order to elicit the right type of information; as before, it also enables the cost engineer to be the first screen of the data validation process.

This breadth of technical knowledge is typically not learnt from textbooks or taught in classes, but rather gained through experience. It is one reason that development as a cost engineer never really stops. There are always domains, technical areas, systems and new technologies that an estimator must gain a working appreciation of to enable them to be effective in their role.

8.2.11 Does the project cost engineer participate in the wider cost engineering community?

Even the most experienced cost engineer needs to consider the requirement for continuous personal development (CPD). It might be considered that the cost engineering discipline is not developing at a lightning rate with new discoveries every waking moment, and that provided you can convince the boss that you are producing the right answer, then why worry. However, attendance at conferences and workshops pays huge dividends in terms of opportunities to network and discover new ideas.

It is not always the most obvious gatherings that pay the highest dividend. Try attending non-cost related workshops. These are often the places to discover parallel methodologies, theories and ideas that can be adapted for application in the cost engineering domain. For example, the concept of Behavioural Estimating, the study of the psychology of producing cost estimates, came from a study of Behavioural Economics [23].

The cost engineer should write and present papers at events. There is nothing like the deadline of a conference or workshop to focus the attention on the delivery of a piece of work. There is nothing like a conference paper to make you sit down and consider exactly what process you use, what data sources you utilise and so forth. If you are unable to explain it to yourself and write it down, how do you expect to influence and persuade others of your argument or estimate?

There are many specialist cost engineering groups to be explored and joined including:

- International Cost Estimating and Analysis Association (ICEAA)
- Society for Cost Analysis and Forecasting (SCAF)
- Dutch Association of Cost Estimation (DACE)
- Space Systems Cost Analysis Group (SSCAG)
- European Association of Cost Engineers (EACE)
- Association of Cost Engineers (ACostE)
- American Association of Cost Engineers (AACE)

Any mature cost engineer and their organisation will be a member of one or more of these groups and regularly contribute to their proceedings and network at their gatherings to ensure that they are current and up to date on the latest developments in their field to bring these concepts and ideas to the organisation and project in which they work.

In certain instances it may be important for the cost engineer to demonstrate leadership qualities. They should be transformational in their approach to their tasks rather than merely transactional. They should be emotionally competent (self-awareness, self-management, social awareness and relationship management) and understand how their interactions impact the individuals with whom they are engaging and the quality of the output that the interactions generate.

8.2.12 Is the project cost engineer proficient in economic analysis?

One of the most interesting areas that a cost engineer can work in is the area of economic analysis. But unfortunately this is an area that many cost engineers will shy away from. Economic analysis is a method for making evidence-based sensible decisions amongst solutions or options to a particular problem or capability gap. It is too easy to produce an estimate of the number of labour hours required for a task, multiply this by an hourly rate to establish a labour cost, add any non-labour elements like material and declare the task complete, as shown in Figure 8.17, all without any consideration to the profile of the costs. Such an omission would be naïve when wishing to compare options.

In this example, the material and labour costs are established at a particular base year. This gives the cost reference in terms of time. In this case the base year and the spread of the costs are both the same: 2008. But this does not need to be the case. Consider Figure 8.18: in this instance the base year of the estimate remains at 2008, but the constant costs are now at 2011. This requires the application of three years of inflation to bring all the constant costs to the same year.

Constant costs are used in economic analysis and the determination of net present value (NPV). For financial analysis we need to determine the as-spent cost; this is the cost that is needed in each year to pay for the work completed; it is the budget, as shown in Figure 8.19. This requires the estimate at base year to have appropriate inflation applied to it. Depending upon your country or organisation, as-spent cost is also known as outturn cost, then-year cost, real year cost, escalated cost, inflated cost or current year dollars.

It is easy to expect another function to take this unique output and utilise it as required for a decision to be made. But the difficult part has been done; considering the cost estimate at different constant costs only requires the application of economics. Considering the cost estimate in as-spent or outturn only requires the application of in-year escalation factors and taxes. If the cost estimate is going to be used in an options analysis, then a discount rate is

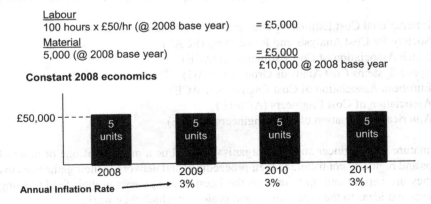

Figure 8.17 Spreading constant cost with the same base year

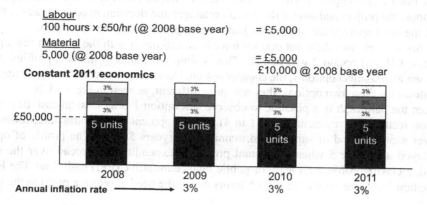

Figure 8.18 Understanding of base year and constant costs

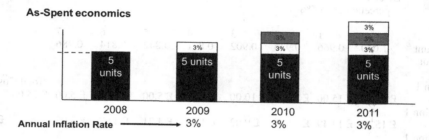

Figure 8.19 Explanation of base year and outturn costs

applied to determine the net present value (NPV); alternatively, if the lifespan of the options are not the same, then an equivalent annual cost (EAC) will be used to ensure that the options are considered on an equitable base.

The net present value of an option, arrived at by discounting its cost profile, can be a reasonably difficult concept to understand, more so for those individuals who may need to use it but who are not regularly involved in estimating, such as a project manager. Discounting is a technique used to compare costs and benefits that occur in different time periods. It is a separate concept from inflation, and is based on the principle that, generally, people prefer to receive goods and services now rather than later. This is known as the 'time value of money' or 'time preference'. For individuals, time preference can be measured by the real interest rate on money lent or borrowed. Amongst other investments, people invest at fixed, low-risk rates, hoping to receive more in the future (net of tax) to compensate for the deferral of consumption now. These real rates of return give some indication of their individual pure time preference rate. Society as a whole also prefers to receive goods and services sooner rather than later, and to defer costs to future generations. This is known as 'social time preference'; the 'social time preference rate' (STPR) is the rate at which society values the present compared to the future [46]. It is important that the concept is understood by the cost engineer and communicated by them to interested stakeholders.

The mature cost engineer will not avoid these concepts, but will embrace the opportunity to support the project and advise the project manager and decision makers to enable them to select the most appropriate option, not just the cheapest option (see Table 8.5).

In this example two different options have been estimated with the forecast that option 1 will cost £75 and option 2 will be £80. This is simply the sum of the cost profiles. At face value we would select option 1, the cheaper option. However, if we consider the timing of the cash flows for these two options, they are quite different, as seen in Figure 8.20.

From the bar graph it is possible to observe that option 1 is a classical cash flow assuming non-recurring investment (years 1 to 4) of development and manufacture, followed by a lower annual period of support and maintenance (years 5 to 8). The profile of option 2 is delayed until year 5 when a constant profile of expenditure is spread over the service period, a classic profile for a lease or public finance initiative (PFI) cash flow. The lease or PFI option 2 is more expensive in cash terms due to the need to return a profit to the bank or

Table 8.5 A discounted cash flow example

	Discount percentage = 3.5%							
Years		1	2	3	4	5	6	7
Discount factor	1.000	0.966	0.934	0.902	0.871	0.842	0.814	0.786
Option 1								Total Cost NPV
Cost – Option 1	£ 15.00	£ 15.00	£ 15.00	£ 10.00	£ 5.00	£ 5.00	£ 5.00	£ 5.00	£ 75.00
NPV – Option 1	£ 15.00	£ 14.49	£ 14.00	£ 9.02	£ 4.36	£ 4.21	£ 4.07	£ 3.93	£ 69.08
Option 2								
Cost – Option 2					£ 20.00	£ 20.00	£ 20.00	£ 20.00	£ 80.00
NPV – Option 2	£ -	£ -	£ -	£ -	£ 17.43	£ 16.84	£ 16.27	£ 15.72	£ 66.26

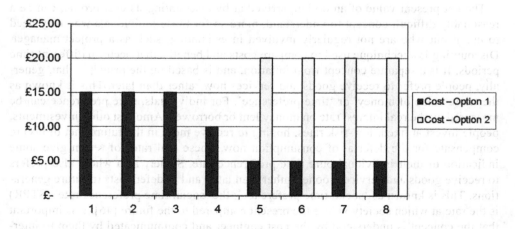

Figure 8.20 The cash flow of example options 1 and 2

institution that acquired the asset during years 1 to 4; the bank needs to make a profit from the money loaned and risk taken.

Now, if you consider the NPV of the options it would seem that our initial selection of option 1 over option 2 is now reversed, as option 2, with its delayed cash flow, is only £66.26 while the option 1 NPV is £69.08; hence, in the eyes of an economist, by selecting the lower NPV option, option 2, there is an opportunity to defer the expenditure.

A mature cost engineer will appreciate that an economic analysis needs to be conducted on a total life cycle cost or whole life cost of the option under consideration. This should include opportunity costs (these are the costs of the options if they could be used elsewhere) and marginal costs (these are the incremental costs resulting in the increase to the overheads as a result of the addition of the options).

However, as this is a comparison of options, there are some costs which can be excluded as they apply to all the options and will not provide discrimination:

- Sunk costs – these are costs that have already been consumed, for example previous studies, technology demonstrators and so forth. The economic analysis recognises that regardless of the option selected, the decision will not recover this money.
- Wash costs or common costs – these are the costs which are common and equal for all options, for example the cost of project management, operating or maintenance staff and so forth. The economic analysis recognises that these costs will not contribute to the decision to select the alternate options.

A mature cost engineer will understand that as well as costs there can be benefits. If costs are a positive drain on resources, then benefits are a source of income for the project. Examples of benefits include the value of the hardware, software or service at the end of its economic life when it's sold, contract terminated or scrapped. This gives rise to the cost benefit analysis (CBA) which seeks to combine these two financial measures. The economic life is usually recognised as the period over which any capital equipment will be depreciated by the finance function. It can also be the duration of the life cycle or whole life cost.

Following the application of discounting, the costs and benefits will become the cost and benefit present values. The application of discounting benefits and costs has the effect of transforming the project gains and losses at different periods during a project to a common unit of measure. The cost and benefits of a number of options can be compared with the concept of net present value (NPV). Net present value has the equation:

NPV = Benefits present value – Costs present value

Where:

Benefits = discounted project financial income
Costs = discounted project financial outgoing

Once the NPV has been calculated it is possible to rank the alternative options. It is good practice to check the assumptions used in the generation of the cost and benefit estimates. A sensitivity analysis will determine the ranking of the cost drivers. A mature cost engineer will analyse the effects of different assumptions on the NPV and any effect that the changes will have on the ranking of the alternatives.

It is usual to select the option with the lowest NPV, provided that the capability or performance is equal across all the options and the spend profile will fit within the budget allocation in terms of affordability.

Beyond the more common NPV analysis highlighted here, a mature cost engineer will appreciate that there are a number of other option comparison techniques that can be utilised. These include:

- Uniform annual cost (UAC)
- Benefit/cost ratio (B/CR)
- Savings/investment ratio (SIR)
- Payback period analysis
- Return on investment (ROI)
- Benefit to investment ratio (BIR)
- Break-even analysis

8.2.13   Is the project cost engineer proficient in probabilistic analysis (i.e. cost uncertainty and risk modelling)?

For the purposes of this book it is possible to define cost estimate, uncertainty and risk using the same parameters: probability and impact.

If we consider the elements of an estimate in this way, it is possible to consider their characteristics as defined in Table 8.6.

A baseline cost element is the smallest element (an atom); because it is part of the baseline plan, it has a probability of 100%, and if an estimate is required the most likely figure will be quoted. The uncertainty around a baseline cost element is a little more complex (a molecule); it will occur as it is part of the baseline plan, but the cost estimate is defined as a three-point estimate consisting of the minimum, most likely and maximum. The minimum and maximum are the worst case and best case, respectively, and their estimated value will have been considered to be so remote that is has no chance of occurring. Finally, risk (a compound) has a less than 100% chance of occurrence, otherwise it would be in the baseline plan and would be costed as such. The probability of the risk occurrence and an estimate of its impact are both determined by a three-point estimate.

The mature cost engineer will have a mature appreciation of these terms, their definition and application. Unfortunately, many engineers use these terms interchangeably, but as you can see in Table 8.6 this should not be the case. The mature cost engineer will be able to articulate the terms and apply them to the project that he or she are engaged with. The qualification of the probability and impact is frequently held in a risk register and assessed by a risk manager, but a cost engineer should not shy away from facilitating a workshop to generate the risks (see section 9.2.9) regarding risk management.

Typically, the cost engineer is left to quantify the risk register from qualitative bondings such as low, medium and high into real figures. It is not possible to aggregate a low probability and a medium impact; you need to establish that there is a 20% probability of occurring,

Table 8.6 Definitions of cost elements, uncertainty and risk

Cost element	Probability	Impact
Baseline cost estimate	100%	Single-point estimate
Cost uncertainty	100%	Three-point estimate
Risk	<100%	Three-point estimate
Mitigation	100%	Three-point estimate

or one project in five will experience this risk. It might be expressed as minimum 10%, most likely 20% and maximum 30% probability.

When we consider the impact, the cost engineer is best placed to quantify this parameter. Consider, for example, the qualitative impact assessment of 'medium', which has been equated to quantitative assessment of minimum £50,000, most likely £100,000 and maximum £150,000. If this definition is global or set at a corporate level and takes no consideration of the size of the project then it is likely that it will have limited applicability to the project and ultimately cause problems when used. Again a mature cost engineer will be aware of this and will calibrate the definitions to the project or assess them individually for each risk.

It has been tempting for customer and government authorities to establish the impact using percentages, for example medium impact is defined as 30%, 40% and 50% for the minimum, most likely and maximum, respectively. This can then be applied corporately across large and small projects consistently. This is a well-meaning attempt to ensure that the risk contingency is adequate. But for the supplier, who is likely to have an anticipation of profit levels on a government contract of 10% to 20% percent, this definition would swallow their whole profit and plunge them into a huge loss. These figures are probably considered very high impact rather than medium impact.

It is also important that a cost engineer can distinguish when it is appropriate to conduct a probabilistic cost analysis. Probabilistic analysis can be expensive to conduct, taking into account the tools required, the time required to collect all the appropriate data, and then the time to undertake and validate the analysis itself. While undertaking a probabilistic analysis always has merit, the cost should be offset against the decision being informed and the relative increase in understanding gained over a more traditional deterministic estimate. A cost engineer should be aware of the point at which undertaking a probabilistic analysis is likely to offer limited value and thus make a recommendation to the project manager to maximise best use of their time by focusing only on developing a robust deterministic analysis. Again, such knowledge is gained through experience rather than textbook learning.

Providing an explanation of risk and uncertainty is easiest through a simple example. Figure 8.21 shows a simple project consisting of two sub-systems. This product breakdown results in a work breakdown structure (WBS) containing eight tasks from Task 0 (e.g. project management) to Task 7 (e.g. integration and test).

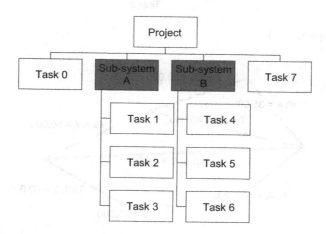

Figure 8.21 Work breakdown structure (WBS)

This simple project can be represented as a simple network of tasks which are necessary to complete the work in the project (see Figure 8.22). This also defines the relationships between the tasks for the purpose of scheduling.

If the tasks are populated with single point estimated costs, as shown in Figure 8.23, the total deterministic cost of the project can be established as the sum of all the costs.

The baseline is the planned work, activities or tasks necessary to complete a project. As this is the planned work, it is 100% probable that these events will occur and the associated resources will be consumed. The resources are estimated as a single 'most likely' point estimate; the most likely can be defined as:

- A genuine expert opinion of the typical resources (or time) required to complete a task.
- The estimate that represents 'normal working practice'; it recognises that we don't get it right the first time.
- Excludes contingency, risk or uncertainty.

The only certainty regarding this estimate is that it will be incorrect. When the project has been completed, and the actual costs are reported, the likelihood that the total actual costs are equal to 330,000 is extremely remote.

Uncertainty, therefore, considers the tolerance around the most likely inputs. It is possible to determine a minimum and maximum cost around the point estimate to determine the three-point estimated cost.

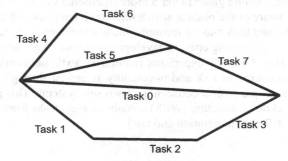

Figure 8.22 Sample network

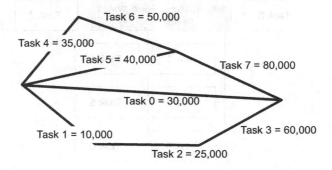

Figure 8.23 Point cost estimate

The maximum cost can be defined as:

• A genuine expert opinion of the worst case resources (or time) required to complete a task; the largest possible estimate.
• It represents zero confidence (0%) that this situation will ever be exceeded; if you can conceivably do the task for this effort (or schedule), then it is not zero confidence.
• It recognises the worst case estimate of the *planned* activities.
• *Excludes* risk events that will cause a deviation from the baseline.

The minimum cost can therefore be defined as:

• A genuine expert opinion of the best case resources (or time) required to complete a task; the smallest possible estimate.
• It represents zero confidence (0%) that this situation will ever be beaten; if you can conceivably do the task for this effort (or schedule), then it is not zero confidence.
• It recognises the best case estimate of the *planned* activities.
• *Excludes* opportunity events that will cause a deviation from the baseline.

For this example, the possible uncertainties for the network are shown in Figure 8.24.

These inputs can be aggregated using Monte Carlo analysis (see Figure 8.23) as shown in Figure 8.25 to provide an S-curve of confidence versus costs.

Typically the 10%, 50% and 90% percentile are reported in the UK to indicate the likely outcome (50%) and the upper (90%) and lower (10%) tolerance on the estimate of forecast.

Considering the S-curve in Figure 8.25, there is only a 10% probability that the project cost will fall below £324,887. If setting a project budget at this level then 9 out of 10 projects would be expected to exceed £324,887 and hence be over budget.

At the other extreme, the 90% confidence figure would provide a budget of 358,717 that would make any project manager happy; 9 out of 10 projects would fall within this budget.

Risks are potential deviations from the planned work, activities or tasks. These events are less than 100% probable; otherwise they would form part of the baseline. In our example, each task in the network is assumed to have an associated risk, as shown in Figure 8.26.

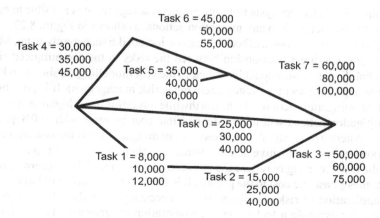

Figure 8.24 Uncertainty quantified as minimum, most likely and maximum

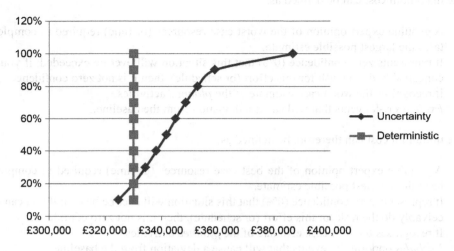

Figure 8.25 Analysis of the uncertainty using Monte Carlo

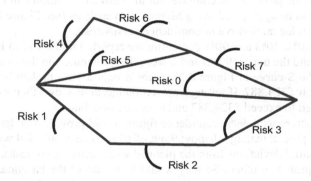

Figure 8.26 Risks or potential deviations for the baseline plan

Taking the quantitative analysis from the project risk register, it is possible to establish the probability and impact prior to any mitigation actions, as shown in Figure 8.27.

In the QinetiQ risk analysis method this can be included transparently using Monte Carlo analysis. There is a direct relationship between the risks in the pre-mitigated risk register and the probability and cost impact identified in the cost modelling, as shown in Figure 8.28.

This open and transparent approach encourages risk management. It is possible to assess the virtue of mitigation actions. Is it worthwhile investing in mitigation actions? These planned mitigation actions will add to the baseline cost estimate with 100% probability of being spent. Alternatively, should the project do nothing and see if the risk occurs?

Mitigation actions are positive actions which are taken in an attempt to reduce the probability of the risk occurring or reduce the impact of the risk once it has occurred. A mitigation action becomes a baseline cost to the project, it is 100% probable and will have a cost impact.

In the application of risk management it is necessary to analyse the merits of mitigation actions, for example a technology demonstration programme (TDP) which will add to the baseline programme of work. This needs to be weighed against not taking action

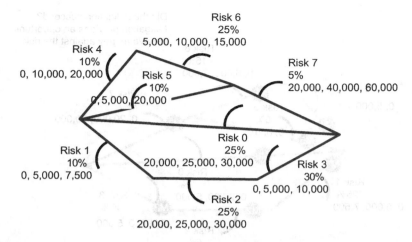

Figure 8.27 Pre-mitigation risks quantified as probability and impact

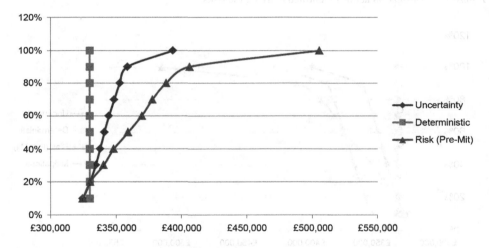

Figure 8.28 Uncertainty and pre-mitigated risk analysis

(e.g. accepting the risk) and taking the chance that the risk could occur, realising that this impact could be more than the cost of the mitigation.

In Figure 8.29 there have been mitigation actions identified for each of the risks in an attempt to avoid their occurrence or reduce their impact. This is an unusual situation as typically there could be multiple mitigation plans and some risks will be considered too low to warrant a mitigation plan. The risks shown are post-mitigation risks; in the case of Risk 5 the mitigation action is deemed effective enough to eliminate the probability and impact completely as a post-mitigated risk.

However, the mitigation actions require funding. The mitigation actions will need to be added to the baseline plan, as shown in Figure 8.30.

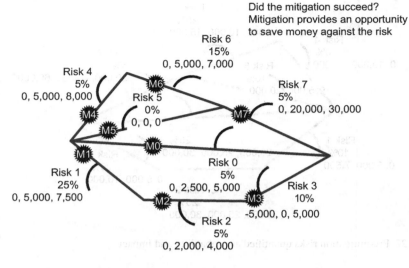

Figure 8.29 Mitigation actions identified to avoid the risks

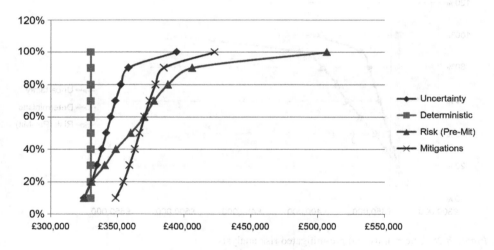

Figure 8.30 Mitigation actions added to the baseline uncertainty

This analysis must realise that the post-mitigated risks are not completely eliminated. In Figure 8.31 it is possible to observe the post-mitigation risks.

In this scenario it is possible to conclude that:

- At lower confidence levels (70% or lower) it would be wise not to invest in the mitigation because pre-mitigated costs are lower than post-mitigated costs.
- At higher confidence levels (70% or above) it would be wise to invest in the mitigation because post-mitigated costs are lower than pre-mitigated costs.

Naturally, other combination of mitigation actions can result in different evidence with which to make management decisions.

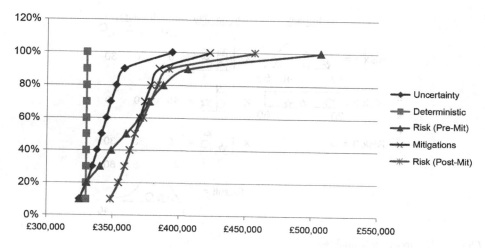

Figure 8.31 Post-mitigation risk analysis

This approach is open and transparent; there is traceability through the S-curve output of the analysis back to the contents of the risk register. The risk register contains the known-unknowns: events that can be foreseen but their probability of occurrence cannot be controlled. The question then arises: "What happens if the risk register does not include all the risks?" or "How do you consider the unknown-unknowns?"

It is desirable to include in the analysis an allowance for the unknown-unknowns to be able to deal with them, if they occur. An approach is to include a risk in the risk register that is proportional to the magnitude of the risk register. As a consequence, if a project is deemed very risky (demonstrated through the risk register), it follows that it is likely to experience many unknown-unknowns during its execution. Conversely, if a project is low risk (again, evidenced through the risk register), then it is less likely to require additional unforeseen funding.

The inclusion of this risk for unknown-unknowns will be transparent and included in the Monte Carlo analysis in the same way as the other risks.

Traditionally in the UK the 50% confidence level has been used to set budgets. The justification for this figure is that, assuming the contracting authority does sufficient volumes of work with a contract, sometimes they will make a loss and sometime they will make profit, but on balance neither will prosper excessively from the other.

The problem with this approach is that not all projects are the same or justify the same level of confidence. Any healthy risk environment requires a portfolio of risk projects. For example, a project which is acquiring another batch of a thousand COTS vehicles can probably reduce the confidence level as they will have experienced risks in previous batches that they have acquired and the maturity of their risk register will be high and baseline costs will have narrow uncertainty tolerances. Conversely, a project that acquires a newly designed satellite with a low TRL and innovative technology should attract a desire for a much higher confidence level.

The utilisation of S-curves with confidence levels provides a decision maker with the opportunity to make a decision. Presented with a deterministic point estimate, they can only take a view on that one number. Presented with an S-curve, the decision maker has the means to set the budget to reflect their appetite for risk on that given project.

Monte Carlo analysis is the technique used to aggregate uncertainty and risk. The analysis utilises a random number generator to simulate the project being conducted multiple times

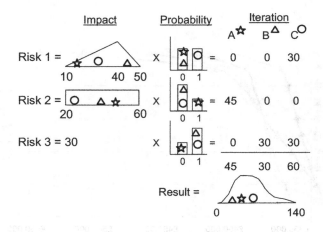

Figure 8.32 Monte Carlo analysis

within the probability distributions defined in the model. Figure 8.32 is a simple explanation of the Monte Carlo analysis technique.

In this simulation the cost impacts resulting in the occurrence of risks 1 to 3 have been defined with probability distributions. For risk 1 the impact has been defined as a triangular probability function to represent a three point estimate having defined the minimum, most likely and maximum outcome of the risk in terms of cost. In the case of risk 1 the distribution is skewed demonstrating that the actual cost outcomes are likely to be lower rather than higher.

The cost impact of risk 2 has a uniformly probability distributed; there is no most likely figure and the cost as equally likely to occur anywhere between the maximum and minimum. In the case of risk 3 the impact is deterministic with no variability on the cost impact.

The probability of the risk occurring is modelled by a discrete function that will result in either an occurrence, represented by the number one, or no occurrence, represented by zero. When this is multiplied by the cost impacts it will calculate the cost of rectifying the deviation from the baseline plan caused by the risk event.

To produce a simulation a number of iterations (1,000 or more) are generated using random numbers within the probability distribution. Each iteration is summed and recorded to produce a total probability distribution.

In Figure 8.32 there are three example iterations, iteration A has generated no probability of risks 1 and 3 occurring, resulting in any cost impact being multiplied by zero, but risk 2 occurred and a random number of 45, representing the cost impact, has been stored in system memory. It is possible to see iteration B and C continue to generate random numbers and sum them; as if the same project was conducted 1,000 times and the totals stored.

From these iterations a total probability distribution is formed and this is cumulated to generate the classical S-curve of confidence versus cost used for decision making.

8.2.14 *Does the project cost engineer have good relationships with the rest of the members of the project team?*

An organisation that values their cost engineers, will place them in a matrix management structure. Their professional development will be overseen by the head of profession or head of function to ensure that their output is technically assured and they are using the best data sources, the most appropriate processes and validated and verified cost models and data. These managers will set their personal objectives and plan their career path.

The other axis in their management will be the team leader for whom they are creating the cost estimate. They will oversee their work load, direct them in terms of their priorities and ensure that they are fully utilised. The 'customer' will set their requirements and have expectations with regards to the outcome of their estimating process. Ideally the cost engineer will be co-located and embedded with the project team and the team leader.

The head of profession will need to maintain focus of the cost engineer on the core skills. They will need to safeguard against requirements creep such that the cost engineer is not asked to conduct non-cost estimating and forecasting tasks. Although they are a resource for the project team, they cannot be utilised for any task other than cost estimating; otherwise they should be re-deployed to a project that has a need.

The team leader needs to have the cost engineer co-located with the team to make sure that they are current with regards to any changes programmatically or technically. They need to be part of the discussion and daily decision making process for the team and make certain that financial matters and value for money is uppermost in the minds of the project team. The cost engineer should be respected and proactive in the promotion of cost engineering in the team environment.

The cost engineer is like other technical members of the team or project: as electronics designers consider the watts, amps, volts and ohms, and the structure designers consider the weight, stress, fatigue and force, a mature cost engineer will consider, with the same reliable rigour, euros, dollars and pounds sterling.

8.2.15 Is the cost engineer motivated by the domain in which the project resides?

Cost engineering is not a career that people choose. At school the career advisor does not suggest to the budding maths student, "You would make a great cost engineer." When you talk to cost engineers, they have a variety of reasons for their ultimate career choice. Many people try cost engineering or pass through the function but don't stop (on their way to a less satisfying career).

Motivation to get to work on time and do a good job when you are there is not unique to cost engineering. It is required of all good employees. So a great cost engineer exhibits behaviours that go beyond just turning up [38]. Good cost engineers require experience; they need to apply their talents to a number of projects and programmes to enable them to gain an understanding of their discipline. They need to volunteer to work on hardware, software and services. Only through doing this will they appreciate and understand the differences between these types of estimates and their relative dependency.

When they are deployed on a project or programme, they need to rapidly become familiar with the hardware, software or services that are the subject of their project or programme. It is not possible to estimate or forecast the cost of something that you don't understand. A good cost engineer reads about the subject and reads into the problem or threat that the project is trying to overcome. This also helps when they are discussing costs with subject matter experts as they are able to demonstrate an appreciation of the project and are more likely to get useful information from the SME.

Finally, a mature cost engineer will wish to further their professional understanding and network through active engagement in the following relevant groups:

- Websites
- News feeds
- LinkedIn groups
- Professional affiliations

9 Process existence and utilisation

9.1 Introduction

This chapter outlines an optimised, evidence-based approach to the defence equipment acquisition process through a logical and analytical structured argument, to the assessment of the options and ensuring value for money for the tax payer. The emphasis is on the financial aspect of the process, starting at the high level and tracing it through to budget setting for projects.

At the time of this book's writing, the 2008 financial banking crisis was still affecting both public and private sectors around the world. The effect of this crisis was a considered and balanced shift towards austerity [16]. Governments are looking to reduce their deficits and reduce budgets across all departments.

There is a renewed emphasis on understanding and controlling budgets with a focus on the processes that are used to allocate funds and distribute budgets. This chapter will consider the budget estimating and forecasting process, its rigour and its mechanisms.

How is a budget allocated? This is a reasonable starting point for this chapter. If we take a defence department within a typical developed country, this process is typically a top-down dissemination of monies, as indicated in Figure 9.1, although this approach is applicable for all departments and large organisations.

At the top level the defence budget is voted for by the government of the day. This defence budget is too large to control as one account and is therefore broken down into a series of programme boards or operating centres. These programme boards have delegated authority to spend the money, but also the responsibility to guide the return on that investment. In other words, they have a vested interest in how the money is spent and on what it is spent. They are also responsible for holding risk contingencies to mitigate low-probability high-impact risks which might occur across the projects they own, for example, exchange rate risk or inflation risk.

Programme budget is allocated to projects to acquire platforms, equipment and services as the programme budget is too large still to control as one account. The projects are allotted funds and directed by the programme board regarding what is required of them.

The dissemination of money is simple; ensuring that it is spent wisely is less easy. The government or shareholders will hold the organisation or company accountable for the way that it spends its money. For this reason, good governance is desirable.

Within government departments it is common to have groups that perform scrutiny roles. They play 'devil's advocate' and are the conscience of the organisation. They will constantly ask "How is the money spent?" Good examples of this are auditors in the private sector or the National Audit Office (NAO) [17] or General Accounting Office (GAO) [18] in the public sector.

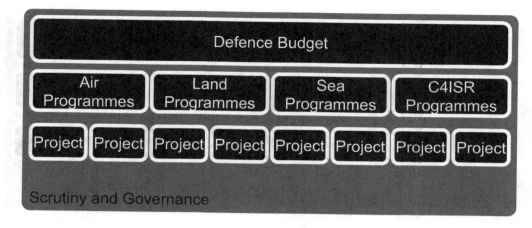

Figure 9.1 A defence budget is too large to handle in one part and hence it is broken down

These groups are the eyes and ears of the tax payer and ensure that they are getting value for money. At a more local level the public sector might have 'policemen' to provide oversight and guidance, for example, the CAPE [19] in the US or the Cost Assurance and Analysis Service (CAAS) [20] in the UK. These organisations will validate cost data and models to ensure that they are appropriate for the use that they are being employed for and verify that the cost models are error free and function according to their specifications and design.

The best defence against the threat of misappropriating budgets is the application of structured arguments for the acquisitions that the organisation embarks upon. In the world of defence this starts at the top level with defence planning. Periodically a Strategic Defence and Security Review (SDSR) is conducted to set defence priorities. This provides an overall context for the expenditure of budgets against a perceived threat in words that the public can understand and that are general enough to enable the threat to be perceived and described as real without the detail that requires security classification.

Typically the organisation will have a planning cycle that will match the lower level project expenditure to the top level. This periodic, usually annual, cross-check is important to audit the budget that is cascaded down to the projects with the expenditure that is necessary.

It is necessary to conduct different levels of analysis at different levels of an organisation, as shown in Figure 9.2.

At the top level a balance of investment (BOI) or strategic model will consider the overall size and shape of the enterprise. In the defence world this will consider the force mix. For example, should you have 10 destroyers, 40 aircraft and 100 tanks, or 5 destroyers, 20 aircraft and 300 tanks?

The BIO activity will provide a high level strategic cost model delivering the capability audit. It will check that the armed forces are balanced in terms of capability requirements. In other words, you don't have a huge navy that is vulnerable from the air as you have little or no aircraft. The BOI step of the process is important as it will ensure that there is a suitable capability mix relative to the perceived threat. This step in the process is essential as it addresses the question "Do the armed forces meet the defence needs?"

At the programme board level there are these and other concerns to address and analyse. At the programme board level the emphasis is the need to sustain the relevant capability

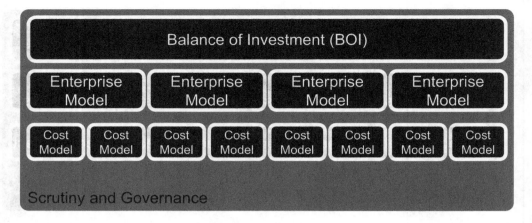

Figure 9.2 Different analysis techniques are used at different levels of the budget

over the longer term. For this reason it is common to deploy an enterprise model. This cost model is aimed at considering the industry capability and sustainment of the capability. If the programme board is going to be able to deliver military capability for the longer term, then it is important to consider the capacity and development for the relevant industry. It could be appropriate to support export initiatives from the industry to ensure that it remains healthy, but not all at the tax payers' expense.

The programme board will be responsible for the investment in appropriate new technology and research applicable across multiple projects. This will be aimed at nurturing the strategic industry to enhance its capability and remain ahead of the threat. This pure and applied research will need to be introduced into a balanced portfolio of projects, some with cutting-edge capability while some remain the lifeblood of the capability.

At the project level the analysis that is relevant will justify the expenditure of the budget on the most cost effective solution. The case has already been established for the need for a capability against a threat in the BIO. The case has been further developed by enterprise cost modelling to justify the typical solution to the capability incorporating the necessary technologies. Now at the project level the release of funding is sought through the analytical modelling leading to a business case.

Options analysis will be considered in section 9.2.10, but will include the combined operational effectiveness and investment appraisal (COEIA). The case will need to be made for the expenditure and release of a budget through a financial analysis (FA), which will demonstrate the affordability of the solution, and through an economic analysis (EA), which will demonstrate that it is the option selected that has the most value for money (VfM).

At the project level, a number of analyses will be used on an ongoing basis to control the progress of the acquisition. Problem solving is resolved through risk analysis of a project risk register using Monte Carlo analysis. Cost and schedule will be controlled through the analysis of earned value through the application of earned value management techniques.

A rigorous process of analysis is necessary to support the acquisition of any capability either in the public or private sector. Shareholders and tax payers are not amused when funds are squandered on unnecessary or frivolous purchases. The process described in Figure 9.3 is an example of a defence acquisition process that would withstand subsequent scrutiny.

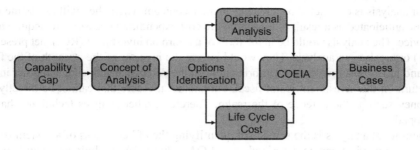

Figure 9.3 The decision making process

Should a capability gap arise, either from the identification of a new threat or the current capabilities becoming obsolete, then this can trigger the process. These requirements can be generated by a change of priorities at the highest level; for example, the defence capability audit indicates a change of policy – we will only acquire nuclear submarines or we will have a single Marines armed force. Generally, the capability gap can be easily identified by a system being scheduled to go out of service date. The more difficult capability gaps to anticipate are the new threats such as terrorism.

Having identified the capability gap, there is a perceived need to do something about it; but what? It is necessary to determine what the exam question is: a simply constructed, easy to articulate statement that encapsulates the reason for venturing down the road of an acquisition. For example, "The nuclear deterrent has been extended beyond its original out of service date without the capacity for further life extensions; with the defence policy for a nuclear deterrent a replacement programme is necessary." This can be the introduction to a concept of analysis (COA). The purpose of the COA is to establish the exam question and document how the argument is going to be developed. The purpose of the document is to ensure that all stakeholders agree on the process and analysis so that when the outcome is presented nobody can argue that the process was not correct. It will describe the analysis methodology and outline the options to be considered.

Identifying the options needs to be conducted in a structured fashion to avoid the criticism that the process is flawed due to options not being considered. It must consider all logical options. One options identification technique is the 'PEMP-M' methodology [21]. This is a structured approach to identifying acquisition options through the consideration of:

- Processes – What is to be done to achieve the declared objectives?
- Environment – Which physical resources and conditions will the new capability require to operate?
- Migration – How will the current system transfer to the new system or service?
- Procurement mode – How will the new arrangements be resourced?

The method involves the solution space being considered in terms of a number of separate 'dimensions' that capture the different acquisition decisions that need to be made. Options are initially identified and assessed with respect to each dimension. The overall solution space then arises from the feasible combinations of options within each dimension.

At this point there is a need to quantify the benefit and the cost of the options that have been identified to enable a decision to be made and justified regarding the system or service to be acquired. To achieve this two dimensional puzzle there are two separate analyses to be undertaken: operational analysis (OA) and investment appraisal (IA). In many industries this type of analysis is conducted by a management accountant where they will assess the profit or revenue anticipated as a result of the whole life cost expenditure necessary to acquire a system or service. The analysis would be in the form of a return on investment (ROI), net present value (NPV) or break-even analysis. They would inform the investor of the strength of the financial case and justify this investment. Unfortunately, in the defence, health care and other industries the return on the investment is not fiscal, but another measure that cannot be directly related to money such as the defence of the realm. Therefore, other analysis techniques have been developed.

Operational analysis is the science of quantifying the effectiveness of a system or service relative to a need. It can be described as soft OA or hard OA. Techniques include war gaming, mission analysis and benefits analysis. The essential outcome is the ability to quantify the measure of effectiveness (MOE) of the options to be acquired on the same basis.

Whole life cost (WLC) or life cycle cost (LCC) analysis needs to cover the entire budget that will be consumed through the life of the service or system. In the UK defence domain this is usually considered to be the CADMID/T and Defence Lines of Development (DLoDs), as defined in Figure 9.4. To ensure that there is confidence in the outcome, multiple methods of estimating need to be employed to form a consensus view of the total cost.

Having determined the measure of effectiveness and the whole life cost in the form of an investment appraisal, then it is possible to compare all of the options. This needs to be considered with the added consideration of uncertainty about the deterministic figures. For this reason, the combined operational effectiveness and investment appraisal (COEIA) results are plotted as a series of points with tolerances indicated, as shown in Figure 9.5.

Ideally the results will be established in the COA as either constant cost or constant effectiveness to make the interpretation of the results simple. Typically boundaries are included on the COEIA plot to indicate the budget constraint, above which there is no funding, and the current MOE, below which the capability already exists or would be ineffective.

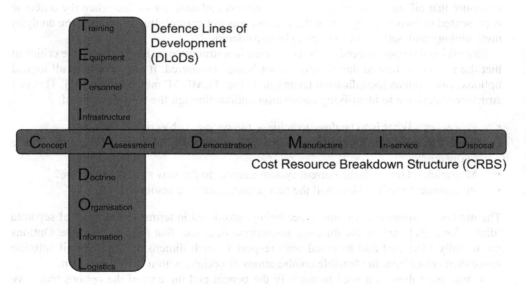

Figure 9.4 The costs need to include all costs necessary to deliver a capability, not just the equipment costs

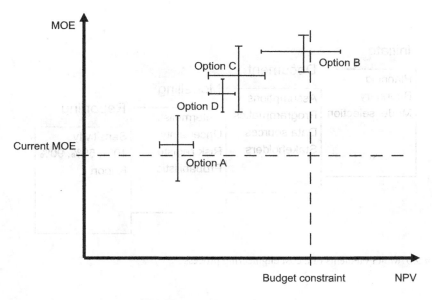

Figure 9.5 The COEIA will replace MOE with benefits when appropriate

In this case:

- Option A = potentially less military effectiveness than current equipment
- Option B = potential to exceed the budget
- Options C and D = result in similar 'bang for buck'; however, option D has more certainty, less risk

Finally, in the acquisition process the business case is produced. If the preceding steps have been rigorously completed, this will be a relatively straightforward process. The question "Why are you acquiring this item?" has been answered in the capability gap analysis. The question "What options have been explored?" has similarly been answered in the options identification process. There should be no concern regarding the question "What analysis was conducted?" as this would have been circulated and agreed at the beginning of the process. The COEIA will be scrutinised but will present the most cost effective option or options to acquire, which, combined with the affordability of those options, should make a compelling case. It just remains to make the recommendations regarding the acquisition, confident in the knowledge that there is a robust trail of analysis for the tax payers or shareholders should they later have any doubts.

Cost engineering processes are like any other project processes in that they should be properly planned, executed to the plan and then subsequently monitored and controlled to ensure they are achieving what they set out to achieve. Effective and efficient cost engineering processes are necessary so that that people conduct an estimate in a rational, repeatable way, ensuring that the outputs are traceable to source data and assumptions.

Cost modelling, in the first instance, will be the responsibility of the project manager; however, in most projects, the scale and required skills means that the project manager must call upon a cost engineering specialist or a team of specialists. Regardless of who undertakes

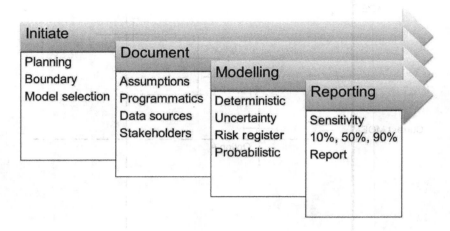

Figure 9.6 Major elements of a cost engineering process

the costing, there are certain aspects of the cost modelling process that will indicate the maturity of the cost modelling capability being displayed. These are covered in the following question sets.

This process can be broken down into four generic work packages as shown in Figure 9.6.

These work packages typically should include inputs, activities, outputs, dependencies and resources allocated.

Work package 1: initiation

Inputs:	• Agreed schedule and milestones for the task
	• Validated and verified cost model
	• Cost modelling requirements
Activities:	• Detail the WLC plan to accommodate the task milestones with resources and furnished information
	• Review of the cost modelling requirements to establish the cost boundaries
Outputs:	• Agreed detailed WLC plan
	• Agreed reporting format
Dependencies:	• Design input from technical lead including product breakdown, make / buy strategy, assembly plan, etc.
	• Historical cost and technical data from previous kindred systems
Resources:	• Cost engineer with cost model
	• Engineers able to interpret requirements into the design

Work package 2: documentation

Inputs:	• Agreed WLC plan
	• Agreed reporting format
	• Validated and verified cost model

Activities:	• Conduct WLC workshops with customer to agree on programmatic, procurements strategy, support strategy, data source and assumptions
	• Agree option to be modelled
	• Write Cost Data and Assumptions List (CDAL) and obtain agreement
Outputs:	• Agreed set of baseline data captured in CDAL
	• Minutes of the WLC workshops
Dependencies:	• Stakeholder ability to agree on CDAL
	• Uncertainty agreed with regard to the input parameters
	• Contributions from all stakeholders
Resources:	• Cost engineer with cost model
	• All stakeholders for customer

Work package 3: modelling

Inputs:	• Cost model for population
	• Agreed Cost Data and Assumptions List (CDAL)
	• Quantified risk register (probability and impact)
Activities:	• Application of cost model as applicable to the requirements
	• Build product breakdown structure (PBS) in cost model
	• Population of the technical parameters
	• Historical trend analysis (HTA) [10] to provide contextual information
	• Monte Carlo analysis of the cost modelling uncertainty and the risk register
Outputs:	• Deterministic cost model results
	• Probabilistic cost model results
	• Independent schedule analysis
	• Risk prioritisation
Dependencies:	• Agreement to risk register
Resources:	• Cost engineer with cost model
	• Risk management consultant with risk register and Monte Carlo risk analysis model
	• All stakeholders for customer

Work package 4: reporting

Inputs:	• Deterministic cost model results
	• Probabilistic cost model results
	• Independent schedule analysis
Activities:	• Iterate the design to accommodate alteration to the requirements with resulting cost impact to enable sensitivity analysis to be conducted and the cost driving requirements to be identified
	• Produce cost modelling summary, cost profiles, S-curves, etc.
	• Document the 10%, 50%, 90% confidence levels and compare to budget
	• Presentation of cost results, risks and requirements to stakeholders
Outputs:	• Risk assessment of practicality of the design and requirements
	• Identified and quantified influence of requirements on design and cost
	• Draft and final cost modelling report
	• Risk prioritisation
Dependencies:	• Agreed risk register
Resources:	• Cost engineer with cost model
	• All stakeholders
	• Risk manager with risk register and Monte Carlo risk analysis model

9.2 Maturity considerations

9.2.1 How well does the cost engineering process align with corporate guidance?

Why is corporate guidance important when generating cost estimates?

In an organisation running multiple projects, it is appropriate that all cost engineering is conducted in a similar manner, to ensure consistency of output across the business unit and that all costs are clearly understood. This acts to ensure that costs from one project can be directly compared with costs from another.

Corporate guidance should articulate if and when any specific cost breakdown structures, cost boundaries and specialist analysis techniques are required (such as probabilistic analysis). For example, it is important that the organisation articulates whether costs should be inclusive of overhead elements, e.g. backroom staff, runways, and so forth.

Corporate guidance should itself adhere to best practice cost estimating methodologies. It should have been developed by individuals that are knowledgeable of the business in which the organisation operates and of cost engineering methodologies. The guidance should be coherent and consistent across all business units such that the organisation can fairly assess projects on a cost basis across its complete portfolio.

If corporate guidance does indeed exist, then it is also important to understand the degree of adherence that a project has exhibited to this, and whether adherence has been independently assessed. It is one thing for guidance to exist and another for a project to adhere to it. A bad situation can be one in which the organisation assumes that a project has followed its guidance when it hasn't. Consider the example of corporate guidance dictating that all estimates being provided to senior management have undergone independent validation and verification. Managers could reasonably expect that any cost information they are provided with has undergone some scrutiny. In such situations, failing to adhere to the guidance and failing to have this discretion noticed could result in decisions being made on potentially poor information.

Where a project has attempted to adhere to guidance but can't, perhaps indicates that the corporate guidance is inappropriately specified and requires amending or updating.

In a mature cost engineering organisation the need for a cost organisation will have cascaded down from the executive management; with this authority the corporate guidance will have been formulated and provided. The mature cost engineering organisation will use this corporate guidance as a basis of engagement with all projects and programmes, and the justification for investment in tools and data gathering, the expenditure on training and staff upskilling, and their existence.

9.2.2 How well does the cost engineering process align with the project objectives?

Why is aligning a cost engineering process with the project objectives important?

This sounds obvious, but it is an important aspect that is often overlooked, especially at the initiation of a costing exercise. Too often costing exercises are begun without a full understanding of how the outputs of the analysis will be used to support the project's other products. What are the project's outputs and how does a cost estimate support this? – i.e. does the cost estimate support either option down selection or is the option in support of an affordability analysis? The types of costs and the analysis that will need to be conducted to satisfy these different aims are different. Hence it is important to establish early on what the intention is such that the cost engineering process can be tailored to create meaningful outputs for the project.

Similarly, is the cost analysis required to support trade studies where modelling should be conducted in a fashion that is sufficiently flexible to address 'what-if' type questions? In fact, all estimating should be conducted with the expectation that 'what-if' questions will be asked. There is nothing surer than when cost information is presented to inform a decision that the receivers of that information will always have permutations to consider. Therefore, it is important that a cost analyst has sufficient knowledge of the domain and of the types of pressures the organisation is facing so that they are in a position to 'future-proof' their cost modelling by anticipating what the next logical question will be, and having the answer either already generated, or easily calculated from an existent model with only minimal manipulation.

Examples for consideration include attention to the labelling and break out of cost by department, by capability being offered, and splitting the recurring and non-recurring costs.

A mature cost engineering organisation will be customer-focused and realise that although they are independent and need to remain unbiased, they have a customer. The project for which they work has a need for their services and their ability to generate costs outputs. It is important for a mature cost engineering organisation to seek the project objectives and understand their context. It will then be the responsibility of the cost engineer to support the project with the services that they need in order to for the project to succeed. It will frequently be the outcome that the cost engineer will deliver bad news: "You can't afford this solution"; but the cost engineering process should support the project objectives to aid the success of the project: "But you can afford a solution like this."

9.2.3 How well is the cost engineering process planned and communicated?

Prior to undertaking a cost engineering activity, the process to be followed should be appropriately planned and scheduled. This is typically achieved via a cost plan. A cost plan is a clear indication of cost modelling intent. Creation of a cost plan at the start of a project, and having it endorsed by all stakeholders, ensures that all stakeholders get the opportunity to buy into the cost modelling process and understand their roles and responsibilities prior to any effort being expended. This is of particular importance when there is a dependence on third parties to provide input, such as data, to the cost estimating process, as it will articulate to them what the expectation is with respect to when data is required, in what format is it required in and, if they are interested, how it will be used. In the case of bidding, this will be part of a master schedule for the bid process.

It is also a useful to have an evidence trail that supports the estimate, by articulating what was done and by whom and when. Linking the cost modelling plan to the project management plan helps ensure coherence of the planning function across the project. Having the plan independently assessed to ensure that good process is being followed and that it adheres to organisational expectation means that estimates generated down the line are likely to be more positively received.

A mature cost engineering organisation will have templates and monitor the progress of the cost engineering activities like any other part of the project. The plan in a mature cost engineering organisation will reflect the needs of a project and adhere to the demands of the corporate guidance. At regular stakeholder meetings the plan will be reviewed to ensure that there are no surprises and that the project will receive the cost output when it was agreed.

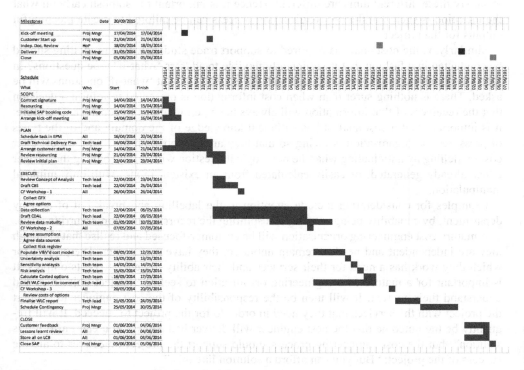

Figure 9.7 Example cost estimating schedule

Figure 9.7 is an example of a cost engineering schedule implemented using MS-Excel, the tool of choice for cost engineers.

9.2.4 Do the cost engineering processes align with the project's other analysis processes?

Requirements analysis, operational analysis, revenue modelling, risk analysis, schedule analysis, integrated support modelling, cost analysis. All these are typical analysis processes associated with the development of project products. Each of these analysis processes are interlinked, that is, each provide or are dependent upon outputs from at least one of the other processes. Typically, though, due to the specialist skill sets each of these processes require, they will be conducted by different teams of individuals. To ensure consistency between the different analysis streams, all the processes should be based on the same set of assumptions. The management of a coherent set of project assumptions is of particular importance to the successful delivery of comprehensive and consistent analysis output, as costing typically requires that what is to be defined and fully scoped by other teams prior to completion of the finished item.

Figure 9.8 is a simple flow diagram which indicates some of the interactions between analysis and the cost modelling for a simple defence project.

A mature cost engineering organisation will be cognisant of the needs for consistency throughout the analysis set, but also aware that they are not responsible for it. The cost

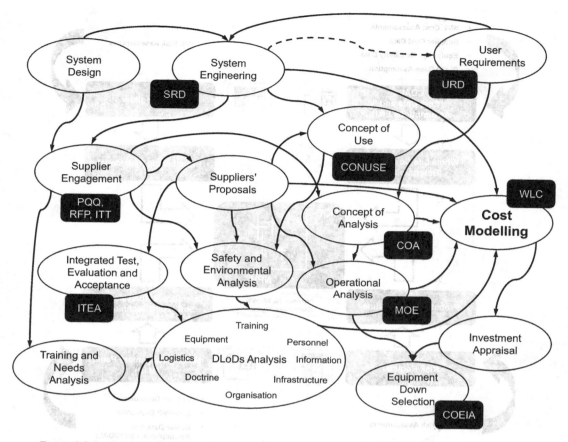

Figure 9.8 Integration of costing with other project analysis processes on a typical defence project

process element needs to be a subset of the overall analysis, integrated within the whole analysis, influencing it and influenced by it, but the cost process needs to be able to stand alone in its own right for scrutiny. In the UK defence domain this is achieved by the utilisation of a Cost Data and Assumptions List (CDAL), which remains independent from, but also augments the Master Data and Assumptions List (MDAL), which frequently used by the operational analysis and other functions.

Figure 9.9 shows the need for alignment of processes between cost and operational analysis to generate a combined operational effectiveness and investment appraisal (COEIA) in the defence domain in an economic analysis.

9.2.5 Is there appropriate allowance within the schedule for cost engineering activities?

Producing an estimate is like a project in itself. It requires a purpose, resources, tasks and naturally a schedule. There is a wonderful saying in the world of estimating: "There is never enough time to do an estimate properly, but there is always enough time to do it twice!"

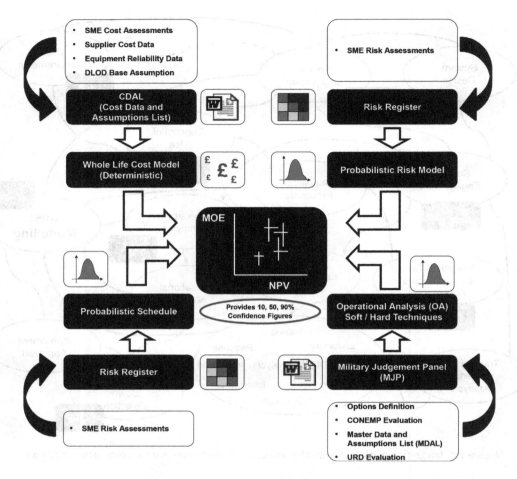

Figure 9.9 Interlinking of project processes to generate a combined operational effectiveness and investment appraisal

It's interesting that an estimate is very time dependent. If your CEO requires the answer that afternoon, then they will have an estimate but the quality and tolerance around the estimate will be suitably caveated. If they give you a week to compile the estimate, then it will be more refined. The week-long estimate will come with more certainty and hopefully a reduced tolerance as there has been more time to consider all the alternative cost methodologies. Ask for the estimate in a month and again the result will be more refined and considered. The level of credibility and justification will be higher still.

Estimating is a discipline that can be adjusted to fit with the time allocated, but the quality of the result will be compromised as the time becomes reduced. Ironically, the estimate is commercially the most critical part of any proposal; without it the proposal price cannot be offered. But it is likely to be the final task on the proposal schedule. When the technical volume and other parts of the proposal slip, it is the estimate which gets compressed, but as we have just established, accelerating the estimate compromises the quality.

For these reasons it is essential that a mature cost engineering function has a well-developed schedule which is used to plan the estimate as part of the overall master plan. All cost engineering activities are appropriately identified within the project schedule, reflective of the cost engineers' duration estimates; sufficient time has been allowed for their satisfactory completion and the interdependencies to other tasks are clear. In the best cases the schedule has been independently verified.

It requires a cost engineer to be firm in requesting that adequate time is made available for them to do their job to the required quality standards. They should not allow themselves to be pressured into unrealistic deadlines because other functions have failed to keep to their schedules. Realism should also be inserted in the schedule with respect to the requirement for a number of iterations of the cost analysis. It is almost certainly a given that any estimate generated will likely come in for some criticism and time should be made to conduct sensitivity analysis and 'what-if' scenario modelling. These types of activities and their associated outputs will help build stakeholder confidence in the numbers and should help close out any points of contention. An experienced cost engineer will be sufficiently battle-scarred to anticipate such requests, and allow adequate time for these types of activities within their schedule.

A mature cost engineering organisation will practise what they preach. They will have historical information on the time it took to produce previous historic cost estimates, and these will be incorporated in a calculator (see Figure 9.10) or cost model to provide consistent estimates of the time required to produce an estimate of a particular type. It would be inconceivable for a mature cost engineering organisation to guess the amount of time required to complete the activities required for a cost estimate or forecast.

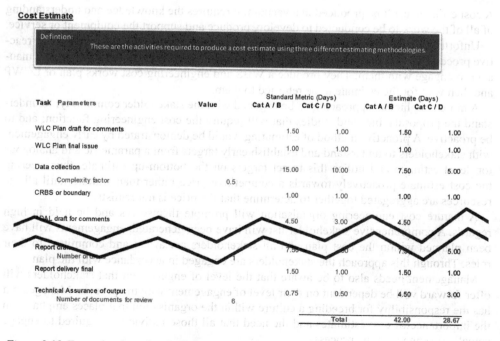

Cost Estimate

Defintion:
These are the activities required to produce a cost estimate using three different estimating methodologies.

Task Parameters	Value	Standard Metric (Days) Cat A / B	Cat C / D	Estimate (Days) Cat A / B	Cat C / D
WLC Plan draft for comments		1.50	1.00	1.50	1.00
WLC Plan final issue		1.00	1.00	1.00	1.00
Data collection		15.00	10.00	7.50	5.00
Complexity factor	0.5				
CRBS or boundary		1.00	1.00	1.00	1.00
DAL draft for comments		4.50	3.00	4.50	
Report draft / Number of	1	7.50		7.50	5.00
Report delivery final		1.50	1.00	1.50	1.00
Technical Assurance of output / Number of documents for review	6	0.75	0.50	4.50	3.00
Total				42.00	28.67

Figure 9.10 Example of a task calculator for cost engineers

9.2.6 How are cost engineering responsibilities carried out within the project team?

With the advent of spreadsheets anyone who is able to find the =SUM() function thinks they can be a cost engineer. It's not until they fully engage with the process and all the disciplines required that they realise that there is more to cost engineering than just adding up!

Within small projects it is appropriate that a member of the project team, such as a systems engineer, fulfils the role of a cost engineer. In the case of a study this is often the case; the systems engineer as part of their technology options assessment and design will consider the cost along with the performance of their design. In the 1990s the American DOD began an initiative called 'cost as an independent variable', or CAIV. This promoted the idea of considering the cost – for example pounds, dollars and euros – as equal characteristics to trade as thrust, volts, speed and weight. It was the role of the project team as a whole to conduct CAIV studies.

In larger projects it is more appropriate to have a cost engineer allocated to the project to support the initial proposal and then subsequent cost to completion (CTC) exercises and costing any contract change notices (CCN).

Within a mature organisation the cost engineer role is identified and endorsed within the organisation. This role is clearly empowered with a terms of reference (TOR). Finally, in a mature organisation the role will have been identified as a permanent post and a suitably qualified individual will have been allocated to the role and they will have accepted responsibility to deliver the required deliverables.

9.2.7 How well are other stakeholders engaged with the cost engineering process?

A cost estimate can't be produced in a vacuum; it requires the knowledge and understanding of all of the work to be conducted to develop, produce and support the equipment or service.

Unfortunately, in many organisations the cost estimating process is a firefighting or reactive process. The cost estimating department waits for the proposal manager or project manager to engage with them. They produce a WBS and engineering cost works plan or ECWP and then wait for the estimate to be returned to them.

A more enlightened approach is to be engaged with the stakeholder community; to understand the proposals, bids and studies that will require the cost engineering function; and to be proactive. A proactive method of estimating would be demonstrated by early engagement with stakeholders to understand and establish early targets from a parametric and analogous top level estimate and utilise this to set targets on the bottom-up estimate, thus steering the cost estimate proactively towards a competitive price rather than waiting until all the resources are aggregated together to determine that the price is not realistic.

A mature cost engineering organisation will promote themselves and be held in high regards. A comprehensive stakeholder list will have been generated, engagements will have been planned within the cost plan and all stakeholders are aware and committed to their roles. Through this approach the stakeholders are engaged in accordance with the plan.

Management needs also to be aware that the level of engagement that stakeholders will offer forward will be dependent on their level of engagement with the process. Management has the responsibility for breeding a culture within the organisation that places emphasis on the importance of cost estimates and the need that all those individuals required to engage actually do engage in the process.

9.2.8 Is the process implemented in accordance with the plan?

We have already established that a cost estimating plan and schedule is good practice. But it is not useful if it becomes shelf-ware.

The cost engineering plan needs to be utilised, and even for long duration studies or major bids there needs to be monitoring against the plan. In the extreme it is possible to conduct earned value management (EVM) techniques to the plan to determine the likely schedule at completion. Within a mature cost engineering organisation the cost engineering plan exists, it is adhered to and adherence has been assessed by an independent body.

The organisation has the responsibility for ensuring that all individuals are appropriately briefed and trained in any mandatory aspects of the cost estimating process as this is likely to foster adherence to the plan. Similarly, the organisation needs to emphasise the importance for all stakeholders to fulfil their commitments as listed within the plan or else the process is likely to fail. Any significant deviations from the plan should be escalated through the management channels, and management should take action as required to ensure their speedy resolution.

9.2.9 How does the cost process interact with the risk management process?

The risk management process is a well-established project management tool in mature organisations. In this age project managers should not be monitoring clocking on and off or personal issues; their focus should be on the project problems, and the formal mechanism to manage problems is the risk management process. Figure 9.11 is a typical example of a mature risk management process with the application of a risk maturity model around the process to ensure good governance.

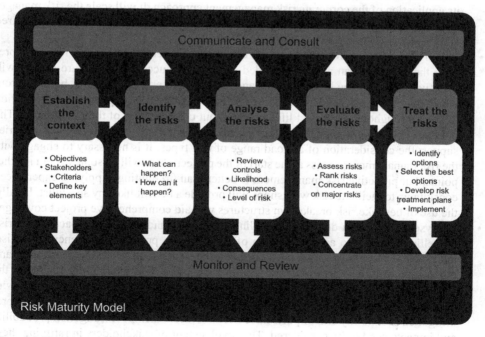

Figure 9.11 A risk management process with governance

The cost engineer requires a strong, mature risk management process to provide a risk register which can be relied upon. The risk manager will depend on the cost engineer to quantitatively assess the impact of risks. Through this approach it is possible to determine if mitigation actions are justified. If the cost of the impact is low compared to the cost of the mitigation action, then the mitigation action is not worthy of investment. Hence, the risk and cost engineering processes are interwoven.

The cost and risk processes in a mature cost engineering organisation are fully synchronised, and the cost engineer is consulted for the purposes of risk identification and for the evaluation of cost impacts. Cost risk analysis is conducted in accordance with corporate guidance and is independently assured.

Where risks have been quantitatively assessed, a prudent cost engineer will conduct a review of all risks with their respective risk owners to ensure that the risks have been assessed appropriately for their impact on cost. Care needs to be had with respect to those risks that have been identified as having a cost impact but where this is limited to 'marching army' costs. These may already be accounted for depending upon the way in which schedule delay has been included within the cost analysis. It is also worth checking that the cost impacts are sensible in relation to the baseline costs.

Cost risk profiling is also very important, especially if the cost analysis is informing budgets that are controlled on a yearly basis.

A mature cost engineering organisation will require a mature risk management process to interact with. This risk management process will have a number of formal steps including:

- Establish the context – the project will determine the risk objectives in the context of wider programme and enterprise aims. It will identify what successful risk management looks like and recognise industry best practice. However, it will need to be practical in its application of the corporate risk management approach. It will scale the risk management approach to best balance the needs of the project with the level of effort required and the potential value achieved.
- Identify the risks – before a project can consider the potential deviations, it must appreciate the baseline plan and the intended strategy for success. The mature project will effectively identify the baseline plans and controls and estimate a robust baseline from which to identify risks and opportunities. Risk prompt lists can support the identification of risks throughout the project life cycle without consideration of their magnitude. The political, economic, social, technological, environmental and legal (PESTEL) categories support the consideration of a broad range of risk types. It is necessary to engage with the risk management process at the start of the project; there will be some benefit at other points, but proactive risk management is better than firefighting. Applying experienced consultants to facilitate risk workshops will provide a benefit like any specialist. Finally, the use of bespoke risk breakdown structures will aid comprehensive project coverage.
- Analyse the risks – a deep understanding of the cost and schedule impact on the risk modelling is a key to an appreciation of the effect on project contingency. Likewise, the probability of the risk occurring needs to be understood. Both the probability and the impact need to be clearly understood in the context of estimating uncertainty in the project budget and schedule. For this reason there needs to be a close interaction with cost estimating and planning staff to develop robust risk impact values. Once the pre-mitigation probability and impacts have been assessed, then post-mitigation probability and impacts need to be considered. The involvement of stakeholders in ratifying these estimates is invaluable.

- Evaluate the risks – once the risks have been quantified and agreed, the mature cost engineering organisation will have higher quality, more meaningful data to support an analysis of both the cost and schedule. Increased risk maturity improves the understanding of analysis results supporting key decision makers. Ranking the risk in terms of their criticality will help decision makers to make informed decisions whether to invest in a mitigation action, or whether to permit the risk to mature and deal with the impacts.
- Treat the risks – there will be a number of mitigation options to consider; once assessed there will be a need to gain approval for the mitigation action and then execute it. Typically, there will be mitigation actions that act to address the probability of the risk occurring and those that address the impact should the risk occur. The former will seek to prevent the risk from occurring and the latter will seek to reduce the impact of the risk once the trigger event or date has been reached. Alignment with cost and project controls brings informed decisions relating to risk responses. A robust process for the approval of responses ensures budget availability and inclusion in the baseline approach. There will be a need to liaise with stakeholders to gain support and ideas for improved risk responses.

This process needs to the conducted in an open environment where communication and consultation are encouraged. All stakeholders need to be approached to gain insight and new ideas relating to the treatment of risks. At the same time, there needs to be monitoring of the risk process performance against the project aims and the review of the risk process against external advances in risks methodologies.

A mature cost engineering organisation will understand that a sensitivity analysis will provide a cost engineer with a focus for the uncertainty analysis.

The tornado plot (see Figure 9.12) provides an indication of the cost drivers which will make the largest difference to the total cost. If these cost drivers are not well defined, or based

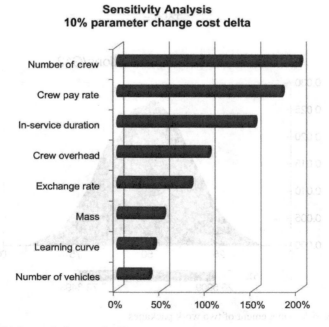

Figure 9.12 Sensitivity analysis tornado chart

upon assumptions, then they will have an impact on the total cost. In terms of uncertainty, the risk management process should concentrate on maturing these cost drivers first. The quantification of the uncertainty around an estimate either can be derived from expert opinion or can be historically based. The expert opinion will require the bottom-up engagement with stakeholders, while the historically based assessment will be a top-down review of past analogous projects with known costs or schedule outcomes. In addition to the quantification of the probability and the impact, it will be necessary in the risk management process to quantify the correlation. Correlation is the relationship between risks and has an impact on the distribution of the resulting risk analysis. It is therefore the role of a mature cost engineering organisation to request correlation information to accompany the risk register and uncertainty analysis.

In Figure 9.13 it is possible to determine that the total deterministic cost of two identical work packages is 50. An aggregation of two work packages using Monte Carlo analysis has resulted in a probability distribution with a mean of 50 and a range of $73.8 - 26.6 = 47.2$.

Now if the work breakdowns structure was more detailed and broke these two packages of work into four rather than into two, the same analysis (see Figure 9.14) would result in a mean of 50 again, but a range of $67.0 - 32.8 = 34.2$. So the simple act of sub-dividing these work packages into more detail has had the effect of reducing the range from 47.2 to 34.2.

Two Work Packages / Years

	Min.	ML	Max.	
WP 1	0	25	50	**25**
WP 2	0	25	50	**25**
			Total =	**50**

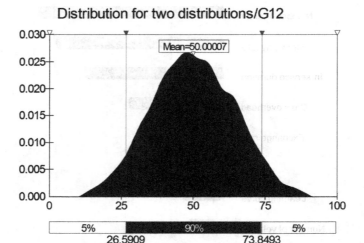

Figure 9.13 The risk management of two work packages

Four Work Packages / Years

	Min.	ML	Max.	
WP 1.1	0	12.5	25	**12.5**
WP 1.2	0	12.5	25	**12.5**
WP 2.1	0	12.5	25	**12.5**
WP 2.2	0	12.5	25	**12.5**
		Total =		**50**

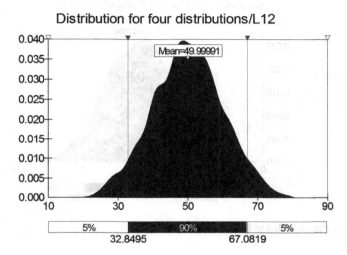

Figure 9.14 Two work packages split into four work packages

Let's consider the impact of correlation. In Monte Carlo analysis a mature cost engineering organisation will understand that positive correlation will influence the random numbers in the analysis to act together, rather than completely at random. So if one work package tends towards the maximum in the probability distribution, then a correlated work package would also favour a random number towards the top end of the range. For example, if a design office is correlated to a detailed drawing office, and if the design office is overspending, it would seem justified that the detailed drawing office will also be experiencing a cost overrun.

If the work packages were negatively correlated, then the opposite will apply. When one work package is high, the correlated work package is equally low and vice versa.

In Figure 9.15 the work packages have been grouped into two correlated pairs of work packages. Now the mean is still 50 when Monte Carlo analysis is applied, but the range is now 73.6 − 25.5 = 48.1, which is similar to the original two-work package scenario.

Hence, a mature cost engineering organisation will appreciate that sub-dividing an estimate or forecast into more detail can give the perception of a more detailed knowledge of the project, but it can also have the effect of narrowing the range of the resulting probability distribution unless corrected with correlation.

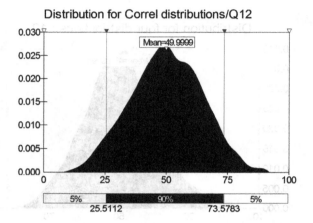

Four Work Packages / Years

0	12.5	25	**12.5**
0	12.5	25	**12.5**
0	12.5	25	**12.5**
0	12.5	25	**12.5**

Total =   50

Distribution for Correl distributions/Q12

Mean=49.9999

5%   90%   5%
25.5112   73.5783

Figure 9.15 Correlation added to four-work package

A mature cost engineering organisation will appreciate the benefits of risk management. It will be seen as a means of proactive problem management in projects, programmes and portfolios rather than a burden. Benefits will include:

- Increased stakeholder confidence through improved visibility of risk information, decisions and management activities
- Enhanced buy-in of senior stakeholders, helping to increase the likelihood of project success
- Greater alignment of project team aims, activities and approaches
- Improved ownership of risk, driving a more proactive team culture, and increasing morale and team support to risk management activities
- Increased value obtained from quantitative risk analysis
- Improved project performance to cost, time and quality

9.2.10 Are the cost outputs used to inform decision making?

There is no point conducting a cost estimate or forecast if it goes nowhere. Part of the skills of a mature cost engineer is the ability to 'sell' their estimate. In these terms there is a fine line between being awkward and being persuasive.

Communication is key to this area of cost engineering; it is not uncommon for a cost engineer who is delivering the results of their many man-days of analysis to start with the statement "I'm not here to make you happy; I'm here to tell you the truth". It's just a problem when the truth is unpalatable to the project or study team. It is this point when the relationship between the cost engineer organisation and the project or bid team can come under considerable pressure as the project or bid team will seek to discredit the cost estimate. For this reason the communication of numbers needs to be dealt with professionally and sensitively.

Difficulties and challenges only really occur when the cost engineer delivers bad news and walks away. In a mature cost engineering organisation the cost engineer will seek to deliver a justified and credible cost estimate but be aware of the difficulties that this might cause the bid or project team. They will therefore be prepared with alternatives of cheaper courses of action. They will offer value engineering solutions which could reduce the cost of the equipment, project or services. An example of this proactive approach is the QinetiQ Austerity Handbook [8], which offers practical advice on "Hints and tips on how to make a project affordable", as shown in Figure 9.16.

Figure 9.16 Austerity Handbook: "Hints and tips on how to make a project affordable"

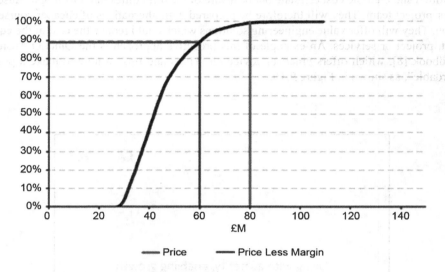

Figure 9.17 Price to win

In a mature cost engineering organisation the consideration of cost commences from the point at which the need for the project was identified. As the project matures, cost and affordability are key attributes considered in any project options analysis. Ultimately, as the project matures and becomes funded, the actual costs are reconciled against the baseline estimate and differences are documented and fed back into the cost engineering process to ensure that the quality of future cost forecasts is improved.

Does the cost estimate quantify the amount of inherent risk? S-curves quantify risk and enable decision makers to set budget or price according to the level of risk appetite. For example, the model highlighted in Figure 9.17 makes it easier for a budget maker to position the prices of their products low if they have an understanding of the likelihood that they will make a loss.

9.2.11 Does the project maintain a cost baseline?

Projects that don't change over the course of their life cycle are very rare. By the very nature of engineering we are seeking to solve a problem, whether that's a bridge across a river or the ability to fly into space commercially. As a result, the initial solution conceived during the bidding process or the original studies will be very different from the final solution. In the same way that the technical configuration of the evolving solution needs to be maintained, so does the cost estimate of the final solution need to evolve.

It is important, therefore, at the start of any project to clearly identify a cost baseline, and to be very explicit as to what is in and out of scope of this baseline.

During the course of the project execution the customer and supplier will both propose changes to the project. The customer will desire more capability for the same cost, looking to take advantage of the changing landscape of the solution, while the supplier will seek to propose changes to the contract to recover costs resulting in the change to the technical solution not considered during the proposal. These changes will need to be cost estimated and negotiated throughout the course of the project. In terms of the cost baseline this will require a process to deal with contract change notices (CCNs).

In a mature cost engineering organisation, the baseline view of the projects within their portfolio will need to be estimated. These estimates of the delta changes in costs will need to be maintained, updated regularly and a record of deviations from one iteration to the next maintained. The mature cost engineering organisation will utilise these records in future proposals and bids to ensure that lessons are learnt and these changes are considered comprehensively in future proposals.

9.2.12 Is the importance of cost iteration understood?

During the execution of a project, the task of monitoring the actual costs generally migrates to the cost controls or project control department. These organisations will deploy earned value management (EVM) and other project control processes to bring harmony to the cost and schedule actuals when compared to the cost and schedule plans. A significant element of this work is to establish an independent baseline review (IBR). For the cost engineer this will mean that they need to appreciate EVM as a process and understand how to align their cost estimate with the needs of the EVM process. At the control account the cost engineer will need to furnish the project control manager with cost resources to a level of fidelity that is required.

Within a mature cost engineering organisation the cost estimate creation is viewed as an iterative process that evolves as the project's technical understanding of the solution evolves.

The uncertainty (or precision) associated with an estimate should be reflective of the certainty in the technical solution, and the underlying technical and cost data and assumptions. At the early stages of design this will typically be limited and as a consequence the estimate generated should also have associated with it a large uncertainty range. As the project matures the estimate should become more refined. This creates the typical 'estimating funnel' as shown in Figure 9.18. Interestingly, though, the articulation of certainty is often something that an estimator struggles with. They often face pressures from management to reduce the uncertainty in an estimate, even when the associated assumptions and data do not lend to this.

Critical to the establishment of a justified estimate capable of being utilised for EVM purposes are stakeholders who are given the opportunity to review and provide comments on estimates prior to formal release or use.

The classical interpretation of Figure 9.19 is a great project: the work performed (EV) is ahead of schedule and the actual cost expenditure is less than anticipated. But the picture

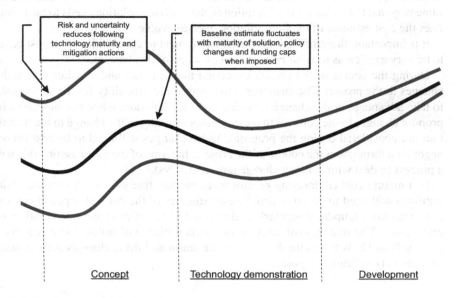

Risk and uncertainty reduces following technology maturity and mitigation actions

Baseline estimate fluctuates with maturity of solution, policy changes and funding caps when imposed

Concept   Technology demonstration   Development

Figure 9.18 Estimating uncertainty funnel

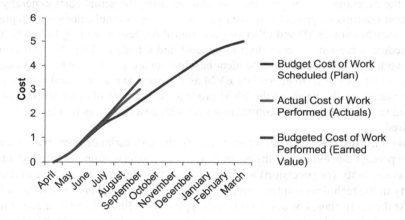

- Budget Cost of Work Scheduled (Plan)
- Actual Cost of Work Performed (Actuals)
- Budgeted Cost of Work Performed (Earned Value)

Figure 9.19 A typical EVM chart of a plan, actual and progress

could be very different if the baseline plan was updated with significant contract changes: the actual and EV will not change, but the planned work could be significantly higher. It is imperative in a mature cost engineering organisation to keep the cost changes in hand.

9.2.13 Does the cost engineer make use of multiple estimation approaches to arrive at a suitable estimate (i.e. triangulation)?

A single estimate is at best an opinion; it's 10 million pounds at 2014 economic conditions. The utilisation of probabilistic estimates through the application of uncertainty and risk analysis change an opinion into a range; it's between 8 and 15 million pounds with a most likely of 10 million at 2014 economic conditions. This provides a decision maker with a decision to make, whether it's based upon a confidence which they desire or a budget which is competitive. The S-curve provides them with the ability to balance cost and probability of the outcome of the project. However, it does not provide them with confidence.

Some organisations try to provide confidence to the decision maker through the use of analytical estimating. In this sense the stakeholders are required to sign their resource estimate as if it were a contract. The decision maker has a level of comfort that their subordinates have committed on paper to perform the work or tasks for a set amount of resources. The problem with this approach is that the level of detail required in the binders and folders and spreadsheets aggregating these detailed costs together are no measure of accuracy. At best it provides the decision maker with the satisfaction that they can fire the person responsible, but that's not going to make the project better.

Confidence can be provided by the relentless requirement for multiple methods of estimating. The presentation of multiple methods enables the decision maker to question the difference between the range of estimates presented [49]. They have the ability to request a reconciliation between the methods: top-down and bottom-up. What might be missed in the bottom-up estimate due to the sheer quantity of data being processed may be captured by the top-down, birds-eye view of the project estimate (see Figure 9.20).

In a mature cost engineering organisation the staff all have knowledge of, and access to, a broad spectrum of estimating techniques, but for each estimation activity they will down select those methodologies (i.e. parametric, analogy, bottom-up) that are most appropriate and then use these to arrive at a triangulated value as shown in Figure 9.21.

9.2.14 Are the quality of the outputs assessed?

It is difficult to generate good will, but it's very easy to lose it. The banking industry has gone from a position of respect and honesty to the current situation where they have become

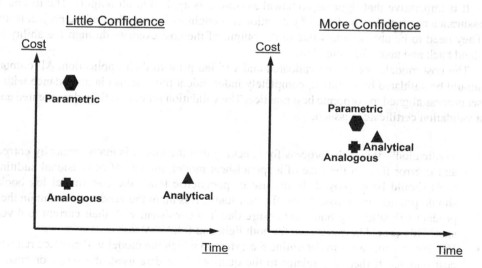

Figure 9.20 The use of multiple estimating methods provides confidence to the decision maker

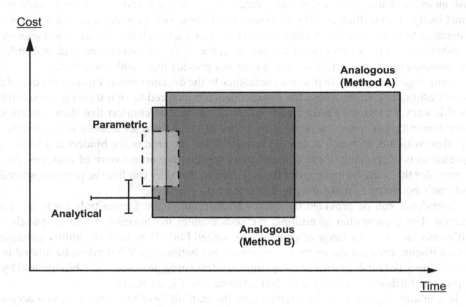

Figure 9.21 Multiple estimating methodology approach

the source of endless jokes. Rebuilding that reputation will take a lot of time and marketing budgets.

The same can be true for a cost engineer. The stakeholders will put their trust in your results until the day that your approach is proved to be flawed. There only needs to be one occasion when you have added dollars, euros and pounds without considering the exchange rates, and your credibility will be in ruins.

It is imperative that rigorous technical assurance is applied to all outputs. The technical assurance needs to be conducted by a senior cost engineer independent of the project team. They need to be able to add value to the output of the cost exercise through the ability to stand back and take a holistic view.

The cost models need to be validated and verified prior to their application. All outputs should be validated by qualified, completely independent third parties in accordance with a set process aligned to corporate best practice. The validation process is fully documented and a validation certificate is issued.

- Verification – this is the process for checking that the model is mathematically correct and is error free. In the case of a spreadsheet model, the use of professional auditing tools should be employed. In the use of parametric tools, the cost model log books should provide an up-to-date verification status. It is up to the vendors to maintain their product validation log book and ensure that it is consistent with their current tool version. This should be conducted for both light and full V&V tasks.
- Validation – this aims to determine the extent to which the model will produce realistic cost outputs. It therefore relates to the quality of the data used, the scope or costing

boundary of the estimate and the skill of the analyst in interpreting and using the cost model and any supporting tools. Is the model answering the question being asked? Was the correct question asked in the first place? (See Figure 9.22.)

In addition to the cost model, the cost data needs to be assessed for maturity. There needs to be a review of the data entered into the model as no amount of clever cost modelling will make poor data into good data.

9.2.15 How is the efficiency and/or ongoing viability of the process assessed?

People like change! I like to change my car and to go on holiday to have a change of scenery. People don't like change which is unplanned and not communicated effectively.

This is the same situation in the cost engineering process. The process needs to be pre-planned an aligned with every major deliverable. The basis of the cost assessment is clearly pre-defined and then regularly reviewed for the need to enhance it. The results

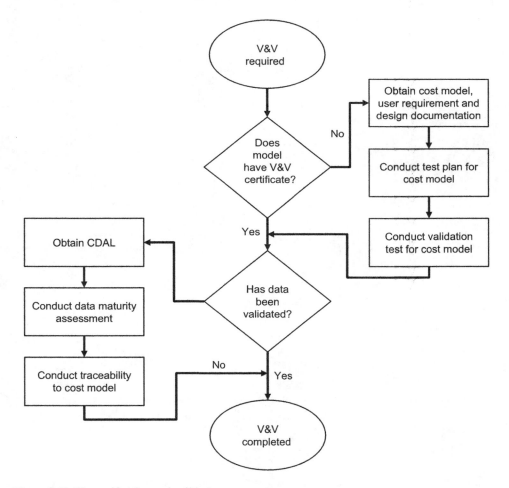

Figure 9.22 The verification and validation process

of these reviews are socialised to ensure that all stakeholders are in agreement with the proposed changes. When changes are deemed necessary, there is training associated with the change and the improvement changes are fully enacted and their impact monitored and evaluated.

Undertaking the CEHC is itself an indicator that the organisation is being proactive in improving the capability of its processes.

10 Culture, leadership and management

10.1 Introduction

The culture in which the cost engineering is conducted makes a difference to the end product. Is the cost estimate welcome or is the cost engineering function constantly fighting to be heard? If the culture is welcoming to the output of the cost estimating function, then it is likely that the cost engineers will feel able to add value through confident application of their trade. However, if the culture is such that the cost engineering function has to fight for a place at the table, then their energy is not best utilised and by the time they offer forward the output of their analysis, it is likely that it will be less than optimum.

Organisational cultural leadership must come right from the very top of the organisation. I was once asked my advice regarding how to implement risk analysis into an organisation. Should there be an organisation-wide training course? Would there be a benefit if there was a help desk? There were lots of alternative suggestions. My response was simple. The culture needed to be changed such that it was understood that risk analysis would be required at each project and bid review. The solution was easily implemented. We advised the CEO to ask one question: "Where is the S-curve?" If the necessary work had been done to generate an S-curve with Monte Carlo analysis, which could be explained, then the change in culture had been achieved. There were a few projects that came forward for review by the CEO that thought they could circumvent the new requirement, but after being pushed back they and other projects got the message that adherence to the rules was not negotiable. This consequently generated a demand for help and support from the cost engineering function to support satisfying the new analysis requirement. In this example, strong leadership from the very top of the organisation drove positive change within that organisation.

Changing the culture of an organisation is most challenging, but first the behaviours of an organisation need to be assessed. If you don't know your starting point, then how can you judge if the changes that you are making are for the better or worse? Culture includes the organisation's vision, values, beliefs and habits. For a number of years I worked in a satellite company which had two sites. One site made recurring communications satellites and the other made unique scientific satellites for the European Space Agency (ESA). We observed that the communications site had a culture of producing the cheapest common modular satellites. It was instilled in their beliefs that to drive costs down, reuse of existent technology wherever possible should be made. This had the effect of creating an evolutionary satellite product that became increasingly efficient to produce. The other extreme was the scientific site, which had a culture of science, research and development. Each instrument and satellite was unique to the mission for which it was being developed. Each satellite was packed with new mission systems. The culture required that the requirements of the systems to meet the scientific goals of the missions, and the schedule of the project to meet the designated launch window, should be all prevailing. Whilst cost was undoubtedly a constraint, it was of minimal concern to anyone involved within the engineering function. Consequently, the cost of these satellites proved to be eye-wateringly expensive, with cost overruns being common. To introduce a new cost-conscious culture within this organisation, it would be necessary for senior management to lead this change from the top and act to ensure that all personnel, especially those involved with design, understand that cost is a prime constraint that must be designed out of their products.

When new members of staff are introduced to the organisation, they absorb the culture in which the cost engineering function works. Organisational culture affects the ways in which people and groups interact with each other, with clients and with stakeholders (see chapter 11).

10.2 Maturity considerations

So what does a mature cost engineering function look like? How do they function? It is possible to assess the culture by looking at the answers to the KBE questions. From these answers it is possible to gain an understanding of the culture without having to ask specific questions regarding culture.

Before conducting a Cost Engineering Health Check (see chapter 5), it is good practice to request and review any documented evidence of the processes that the organisation has put in place with respect to cost engineering. It is also good practice to request and review evidence of the organisation's cost engineering function's outputs. This is done to achieve two things: first, to familiarise the assessors with the company to be assessed and the terminology that they use, for example, acronyms; second, to establish the culture. If the organisation is unwilling to cooperate with the Cost Engineering Health Check, then that must tell you something about the organisation to begin with!

10.2.1 People culture

Culture is all about the people in an organisation, and for the cost engineering function, that needs to start with them. Cost engineers that are actively participating in the wider cost engineering community – like through the involvement with societies and associations, both as attendees and active contributors – would be an example of an organisation that is mature. If the cost engineering function is presenting to audiences outside the organisation, and those audiences are finding the presentations relevant and interesting, then perhaps the organisation should take heed and listen to what their own people have to say.

At another level the cost engineer needs to have an interest in the project and industry in which they are working. A healthy culture is one in which individuals have an interest in the work they conduct, not just as a means of earning money but as a genuine interest in the topic. It needs to stimulate them.

10.2.2 Data culture

Of course it's not just about the cost engineering function. They need support from other parts of their organisation that are motivated by the organisation's culture to support and help them. So, for instance, if the cost engineer arrives in the finance department to gather historical

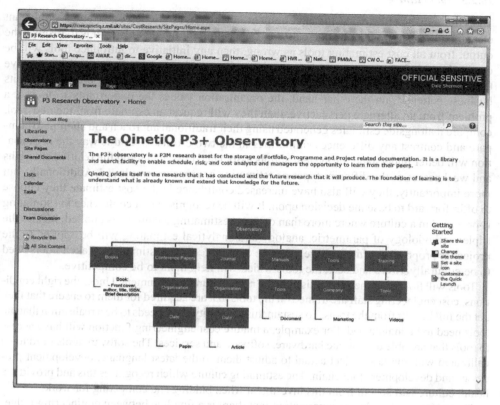

Figure 10.1 The storage of data in an accessible format is an indication of maturity

financial data for cost estimating purposes, they are supported. Similarly, if they arrive in the project management and technical department to gather master schedules and milestones or technical information, respectively, for the purposes of future cost estimates, they should get a similar positive welcome as their purpose is understood and appreciated.

To reciprocate, the cost engineering function needs to have a repository for all this information (see Figure 10.1) for the purposes of sharing the knowledge that they have in an easily accessible format.

However, it's not just about the internal data; cost engineers also require information from outside their own organisation to enable them to make analogous estimates or benchmark their organisation against others. Culturally it can be difficult for staff outside the cost engineering function to understand why it is important to buy, swop or volunteer data. Data is the lifeblood of the cost engineering function; without it the function will die. A healthy cost engineering culture will provide time for staff to research the cost of near neighbour organisations and competitors.

Once data has been gathered in a consistent manner, then a healthy cost engineering culture will provide resources to normalise it and classify its maturity and boundary. The most cost effective way to achieve this is through the heathy promotion and nurturing of a stakeholder working group or equivalent.

10.2.3   Tool culture

Tools are only as effective as the environment in which they are deployed, and a significant element of this environment is the culture. If the culture of the organisation is to dismiss the output from all cost estimating tools as wrong, then any initiative to introduce tools will be destined to fail from the very outset as it will not have had a reasonable opportunity to prove the tools' value. Consequently, the organisation also fails to realise an opportunity to do its business better. If, on the other hand, the organisation values the opportunity to look at a problem from an alternate perspective, then they will request an estimate from the new tool, compare it alongside estimates generated using their traditional approach and attempt to compare and contrast any differences/similarities in the two estimates. In this way the organisation will better understand the system and its associated cost, including the relative strengths and weaknesses of the different types of estimating approaches employed. Additionally, but more importantly, they will also have increased confidence in the cost estimate they choose to offer forward to base the decision upon. It will be recognised that confidence in estimating is provided in a culture where more than one cost estimating technique is applied. Ideally the triple methodology of parametric, analogy and analytical estimating will be applied to the project or proposal in order to have a culture of confident cost estimating. Stakeholders need to be culturally aware and seek the tools which will help them to be competitive.

Tools will flourish if they are utilised in the right cultural environment. Under the right conditions, cost engineering staff are trained on the tools that are acquired for them to ensure that they get the full benefit from the tools. To sustain this capability there needs to be a realisation that the tools need to be maintained. For example, a mature cost engineering function will have access to tools that are able to estimate hardware, software and services. The software tools need to be calibrated with the last project actual to adjust them to the latest language, development processes and development tool chain. The estimating culture which recognises this and provides a health culture will benefit from this investment when bidding and competing for work.

There also needs to be an appreciation that there is a fine line between engineering judgement (guessing) and professional cost engineering. In a mature culture the management will not expect a deterministic point estimate, but an estimate with a tolerance. The combination of uncertainty within the estimate based upon past history and normal working practices, then adjusted for the unique risks which cannot be mitigated in this project, will lead to the realisation that accuracy is not a possibility in cost engineering as it may be with other engineering disciplines.

10.2.4   Process culture

A strong culture is said to exist where staff respond to stimulus because of their alignment to the organisation's values. In such environments, strong cultures help firms operate like well-oiled machines, engaging in outstanding execution with only minor adjustments to existing procedures as needed. Conversely, there is weak culture where there is little alignment with organisational values, and control must be exercised through extensive procedures and bureaucracy. This is when the processes of the cost engineering function are required.

Starting from the outside, there is a need in a mature cost engineering function to align the cost processes with corporate guidance. The cost engineering function should be acting to promote the corporate direction, not oppose the corporate direction of travel. Next, the cost engineering function should be working in harmony with the project objectives. They need to have an independent mind and not be persuaded by the project team's opinion of the cost, but working closely with them and their processes.

There is no point in having wonderful processes if these are not planned and communicated. The processes need to be socialised with the rest of the organisation to be effective. This will enable the rest of the organisation to accommodate the cost engineering function planning and make allowance for the resources to be included in the planning. This could be a dedicated cost engineer or a member of the project staff working in this role; however, the terms of their cost engineering role should be clearly understood and planned. There are some advantages to the project staff conducting the cost engineering role specifically due to being particularly well placed to have a combination of good project, technical and wider project risk knowledge. Conversely, though, the problem with project team members taking on this role is with respect to their independence. Will an entrenched project team member be happy to present costs which mean the project is not viable?

The mature cost engineering organisation will have a culture that implements the plan without fail. This will result in the cost outputs being used for decision making within the organisation; decision makers will have confidence in the figures that they are being supplied with and the accuracy of the information. The mature organisation will track the contract changes over the course of the project execution and map the outcome of the project to the initial estimate to check accuracy and make adjustments for the next estimate.

In addition to the cost estimating accuracy, the mature cost organisation will regularly seek comments and feedback from their customers regarding the quality of the service that they provide.

10.3 Transformation plan

So what can be done to change a culture? This is not an easy proposition. When an organisation discovers that there is a problem, it will try to implement a 'get well plan' itself or bring in external third-party support to nudge it in a different direction. In the short-term this can seem to be easy, but the problem is corporate memory. Staff can be introduced to new ideas through staff briefings, training courses and facilitator-led workshops, but such sessions do not necessarily lead to acceptance. Staff need to share the understanding that the old ways are not working, and that change is a necessary step for the organisation to remain competitive and viable. When this occurs it is likely that new ideas will be more readily accepted, they will be more easily rolled out and embedded within the organisation, and that the tendency to revert back to the old ways of doing things will be minimised.

When an organisation does not possess a healthy cost engineering culture, the change process can be daunting. One major reason why such change is difficult is that organisational cultures show remarkable inflexibility and exhibit remarkable levels of inertia. Culture change may be necessary to influence the organisation's behaviour, make improvements to the cost engineering function, refocus the cost engineering objectives, resize the cost engineering function, provide better cost engineering service and achieve improved company goals and results. Culture change is impacted by a number of factors including:

*   The external environment and industry competitors;
*   Change in industry standards;
*   Technology and cost model changes;
*   The size and nature of the cost engineering team; and
*   The organisation's history and management.

Prior to a cultural change initiative, a needs assessment is required to identify and understand the current organisational culture. This can be done through the QinetiQ Cost Engineering

Health Check, which uses workshops and a maturity framework with electronic voting to establish a baseline. This will enable the organisation to identify areas of culture that require change. The organisation must then assess and clearly identify the new, desired culture, and then design a change process.

The following steps can be used to guide the change or transformation of the culture that is desired.

1   Strategic vision – the first step is to establish a clear cost engineering vision of the organisation. This will include a new strategy, shared values and behaviours. This vision provides the intention and direction for the culture change.

2   Display of commitment – senior management at the top of the organisation need to demonstrate leadership and a willingness to change themselves. The senior management of the organisation should be very much in favour of the change to the cost engineering function in order to actually implement the change in the rest of the organisation.

3   Model change – as the first level of the organisation, the management needs to exemplify the changes to the culture. They need to demonstrate by example that the change has been bought into and is real. The management team should take every opportunity to demonstrate faith in the cost engineering function and request their support to signal change. The behaviour of the management needs to demonstrate the kinds of values and behaviours that should be replicated in the rest of the organisation. It is important that the management shows the strengths of the non-cost engineering culture as well; it must be made clear that the current organisation does not need radical changes, but just in the area of cost engineering. This step may also include creating working groups, change managers or similar. Change managers need to possess courage, flexibility, excellent interpersonal skills, knowledge of the organisation, and patience; these individuals need to be catalysts, not dictators.

4   Change the organisation – this includes identifying what current organisation systems, policies, procedures and rules need to be changed in order to accommodate the new cost engineering desired values and culture. This may include a change to accountability introduced through a RACI analysis. This may lead to adjustments to individuals' benefits and rewards under the new culture.

5   Workforce adjustment – ultimately individuals need to make a decision whether they like the new culture or not. Employee motivation and loyalty to the organisation is important and will result in a healthy culture. The senior management and change managers should be able to articulate the connections between the desired behaviour and how it will impact and improve the company's success, to further encourage buy-in in the transformation process. Training should be provided to all employees to understand the new processes, systems and culture. Changes in culture can lead to tensions between the organisation and individuals, which can result in ethical and legal problems. This is particularly relevant for changes in employee integrity, control, equitable treatment and job security.

6   Maintenance – it is beneficial to include an evaluation process, conducted periodically to monitor the cultural change progress and identify areas that need further development. This step can also identify obstacles to change and resistant employees. It may be helpful and necessary to incorporate new change managers to refresh the process. Outside consultants can be useful as surge resources, in facilitating the change process and providing employee training. People often resist changes, and hence it is the duty of the management to convince people that likely gain will outweigh the losses.

11 Stakeholders' engagement and acknowledgement

11.1 Introduction

It is possible to define cost engineering stakeholders as "organisations and individuals with an interest in the input and output of the cost engineering process", which means that we can categorise stakeholders into:

1 Those providing input to the cost engineering process; and
2 Those receiving the output from the cost engineering process, or who are impacted by the decisions made based on the outputs of the costing function.

The first category of stakeholders is often the hardest to engage with as these individuals have no vested interest in the output of the process. For the first category, the cost engineer is a person who consumes their time with no obvious added value. In this category we can consider designers, scientists, researchers, engineers and other technical professionals. Of course, a cost engineer does have added value for this class of stakeholder, as cost estimates generated are likely to impact either their work or profession down the line; it is just that this link can be somewhat removed from the stakeholders' day-to-day work. Consequently, it is the responsibility of the cost engineer to help this set of stakeholders understand the link between their work and the cost estimate, and why it is important for them to positively participate in the cost estimating process.

The second category has a vested interest in the output of the cost engineering process. For these people, the cost engineer has a curious fascination: they admire the output that they produce, but don't necessarily understand how it is produced. In this category we can consider proposal managers, project managers, finance staff, commercial staff and other business professionals.

Figure 11.1 provides some of the psychological and social influences ideally surrounding the cost engineer together with the moral standing of the ideal cost estimator. These influences are frequently placed under pressure from the stakeholder community in an attempt to sway the cost estimates which they create.

The cost engineer has to interface with all stakeholders in order to gather the information necessary to produce cost models and create cost estimates. It is necessary to approach the first category of staff with a view to creating a long-term enduring relationship. In doing this the cost engineer needs to make the effort to ensure that they are able to speak the stakeholders' language. There is nothing worse than a cost engineer requiring help, but is unable to converse in the language of the technical guru. Learning the abbreviations and acronyms is a good first start. The providers of information need to see the long-term benefit of supporting the cost engineering function. A well-furnished cost engineering function can provide long-term prosperity to the organisation, and as a result everyone benefits.

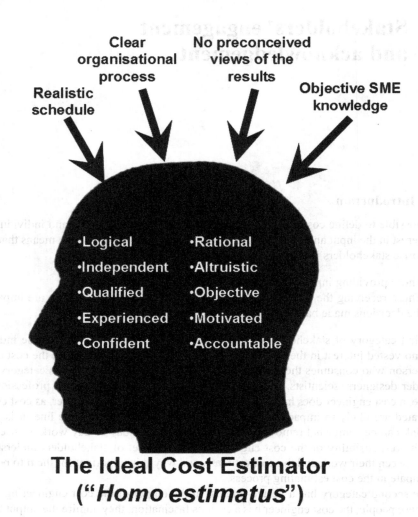

Realistic schedule

Clear organisational process

No preconceived views of the results

Objective SME knowledge

- •Logical
- •Independent
- •Qualified
- •Experienced
- •Confident

- •Rational
- •Altruistic
- •Objective
- •Motivated
- •Accountable

The Ideal Cost Estimator ("*Homo estimatus*")

Figure 11.1 The perfect cost engineer experiences considerable stakeholder pressure

11.2 Maturity considerations

So what does a mature cost engineering function look like when considering stakeholders? Well, they really need to be a 'jack of all trades and master of none'. By this we mean that a cost engineer needs a broad education, and they need to have good interpersonal skills.

As we can see in Figure 11.2, the cost engineer needs to have the ability to communicate at all levels. At the bottom of the spectrum they should be able to pass on their trade to the next generation of cost engineers: junior staff who will one day take their place in the department. They need to be able to communicate the excitement of understanding the complete or whole life of a project or programme. At the other extreme they will need the ability to withstand scrutiny from the most senior members of staff. When presenting their costs to the CEO or MD, they need to be able to speak with authority and confidence regarding the costs they are presenting.

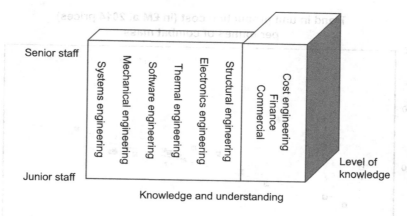

Figure 11.2 The dimensions of the cost engineering stakeholder community and knowledge

Across the spectrum of knowledge and understanding, they need to have a technical background to enable them to move from project to project quickly and to be able to conceive the technical solution presented to them resulting from the requirements of the customer. This knowledge does not require depth – we don't expect the cost engineer to execute the work – but it does need to be sufficient to understand some of the more relevant specifics and intricacies of the work. This is an area where a lot of individuals coming from a purely accountancy or financial background have difficulties; they can appreciate the financial manipulation required by cost engineering, but are unable to engage with technical staff on a common footing.

More in-depth knowledge and understanding is required in the area of business stakeholders. A deep knowledge of cost engineering is essential, but also finance and commercial issues.

11.2.1 People

Stakeholders are people; it's that simple.

The problem is engaging with people. Do they see the value of the cost engineering function? To that end it is a sales task. In a mature cost engineering organisation, senior management has bought into the function and have made an investment in the function. They are proactive in seeking the opinion of cost engineers when considering bids and project costs. They value the insight provided by Monte Carlo risk analysis in terms of setting realistic prices with transparent contingency and management reserves. When bid, project or programme managers engage with the cost engineering function in a mature organisation, they have the same opinion as senior management; they see the value as a stakeholder.

Internal stakeholders are typically easier to influence and get onside. External stakeholders are typically more difficult, but key to getting them onside is the ability of the cost engineer to generate good will. Generating good will isn't easy; it takes time to create respect from an external stakeholder, and can be all too easy to loose. One poor estimate or mistake and the external stakeholder will dismiss all estimates as flawed. You only need to forget to apply an exchange rate once and present a dollar value as a pounds sterling value, and the stakeholders will forever be sceptical.

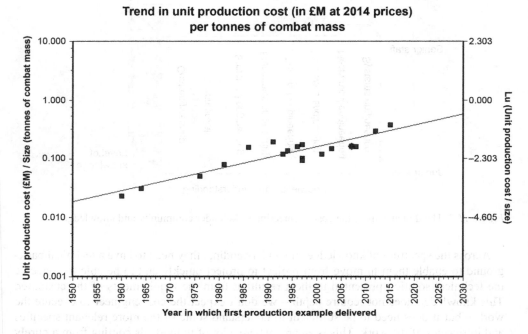

Figure 11.3 The reassuring presence of data gives stakeholders a warm feeling

All stakeholders will be reassured by the presence of unequivocal hard data, and a sound analysis process for the interpretation of that data. Figure 11.3 is taken from the QinetiQ Family of Advanced Cost Estimating Tools (FACET) system.

The graph presents a plot of historical project costs versus the year in which the system was introduced to service. Historical costs are presented as square boxes. Past projects whose actual costs are shown are: Bradley, CV-9030CH, CV-9035, CV-9040, DAF YPR-765, Desert Warrior, LAV III (Canada), LAV III (New Zealand), M-113, M-113A2, Pandur II (IFV fit), Piranah IIIC (IFV variant), Pizarro, Type 89, and Warrior. The dot is the budget or estimate put in context of these historical projects. When the stakeholders are presented with data such as this they can visually understand why an estimate is what it is and they understand that it is grounded in defendable evidence. Consequently their opportunity to disagree with the estimate is reduced and they will feel more compelled to agree with the conclusion the cost engineer has produced.

11.2.2 Data

In a mature cost engineering function it is possible to find stakeholders who are volunteering data to the cost engineers as they appreciate the value of the function. Within the organisation, on completion of projects or delivery of services, stakeholders will actively seek out cost engineers to provide them with their trusted data. Their motivation for this effort is, firstly, to learn for themselves from the lessons of the project, and secondly, to ensure that the cost engineering function has the latest data upon which to base their current estimates.

Information and data from outside the immediate organisation is more difficult generally. Finding external stakeholders who are willing to provide information is challenging,

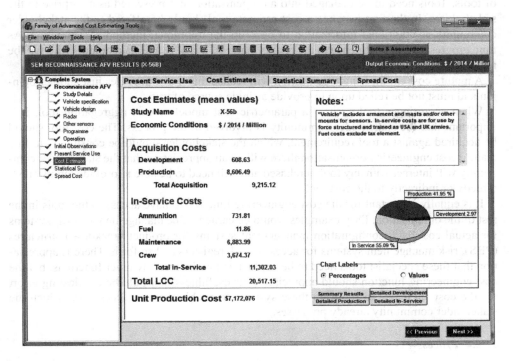

Figure 11.4 An example output from the FACET cost model

particularly in the private sector. In the public sector there have been instances when the government stakeholders have provided data to cost engineering organisations, for instance in the case of a widely used parametric cost model. The data was provided by the stakeholder on the understanding that the information was used to improve the accuracy of the parametric cost model for the good of the user community, but the data was not to be released in its raw form.

A mature cost engineering function will have a regular meeting with stakeholders to consider and agree on the manner in which data is used in the estimates they produce. This is particularly important in a regulated industry or when scrutineers are likely to be part of the stakeholder community. These meetings will consider a broad number of topics, including normalisation of historical cost data for quantity effects; the cost boundary for the project; and the potential impact of escalation rates, currency exchange rates and so forth. A stakeholder working group or equivalent should meet regularly throughout the creation of a cost estimate to ensure that the latest assumptions are being made and that the most appropriate and current data sources are being utilised. This is an opportunity for stakeholders to influence the cost engineering function, thus facilitating a mature and mutually respectful and ultimately beneficial relationship.

11.2.3 Tools

It is very common for stakeholders to be sceptical about cost estimating tools. The typical response of a stakeholder when they are presented with an estimate from a cost estimating tool (see Figure 11.4) is "It's a black-box, I don't believe it." This is particularly true when the estimate presented does not reflect the answer required by the stakeholder. This is a reflection of the maturity of the organisation and stakeholder with regards to the application of tools. Tools need to be managed into an organisation, not presented as a surprise to the stakeholders. In the first instance a cost estimate tool should be offered to the stakeholder community as additional information to back up the traditional method of estimating. As time progresses and confidence in the results matures, it will be the stakeholders who will be requesting the cost estimating output from a tool.

A mature cost engineering organisation will realise that a tool provides just another opinion and must not be relied upon to provide a single source of truth.

When acquiring a tool such as a parametric cost model or cost aggregation tool, it is important that the stakeholder community is involved in the process. The cost tool should be acquired against a tool requirement, which the stakeholder should be consulted on. In a mature cost engineering organisation there will be an appreciation that the stakeholder community will interact with any tool purchased and will need to be able to provide inputs either directly or indirectly to the cost tool.

It is equally important for the cost engineering function to have access to the tools in the rest of the organisation. Easy examples would be earned value management (EVM) systems for actual cost data, configuration management systems for product breakdown structures (PBS), risk management systems for access to risk registers and so forth. There is appreciation that these specialist tools need to be applied and maintained by other functions, but the cost engineering function should appreciate their usefulness. It would be duplicating effort for the cost engineers to replicate these systems to enable them to access data which the stakeholder community already possesses.

11.2.4 Process

If the cost engineering function is mature in its approach to estimating and forecasting, it will have a process which includes stakeholder engagement (see Figure 11.5); but this is only one aspect of the process. To be fully implemented it is necessary for the stakeholder community to include the cost engineering function in their processes also.

The stakeholders need to understand that cost estimating is not confined to the cost engineering function and that their input is essential. The cost engineering process is inevitably iterative. The first estimate is exactly that, a first pass. This should be reviewed and discussed amongst all stakeholders with assumptions clarified. Following this review process there is likely the need to conduct further iterations of the analysis to consider things like affordability or what-if design to cost trade-offs. These iterations will be guided by the cost modelling conducted by the cost engineers, but to ensure that the solution estimated is still compliant with the customer requirements the iterations will need to be advised by the stakeholder community. There is no sense in the cost engineers' achieving an affordable estimate if the solution doesn't fly – literally!

A mature cost engineering organisation will have stakeholders that seek support for their cost engineering needs. The process and capability that they will seek from the cost engineering organisation will include, but is not limited to:

- Design-to-cost
- Cost-effectiveness analysis
- Cost-performance trade-off analysis
- Target costing
- Total ownership cost (TOC)
- Life cycle costing
- TOC reduction and cost management
- Cost as an independent variable (CAIV)

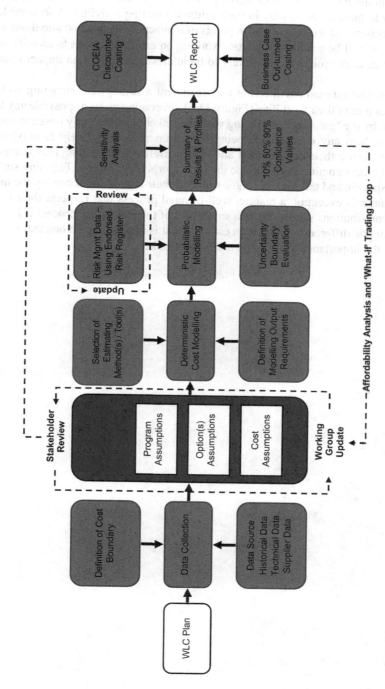

Figure 11.5 Cost engineering process with stakeholder reviews clearly identified

To summarise what is evident coming from all KBE pillars is that a mature cost estimating function should be proactive in identifying as early as possible all groups of stakeholders that are likely to have a role to play in their future estimating activities. A forward leaning estimating function will work to establish points of contacts or 'gateways' into those groups. Such 'gateways' will be used by estimators working on estimating tasks to identify specific individuals from each group who are likely to be interested and have an impact upon their estimates.

A proficient cost estimator will create and document a strategy for engaging with these stakeholders as part of their Cost Plan (Figure 11.5), leveraging as far as possible any knowledge provided by the 'gateway'. Engaging with the stakeholders as early possible and making explicit to them any expectations being placed upon them is likely to maximise the opportunity to secure their commitment and obtain useful contribution. This is especially true for stakeholders coming from outside the estimator's organisation. Targeting such individuals with specific and tailored messages suited to their interests will convey the message that the estimator is executing a mature, well-planned process that respects their time and values their contribution. Whilst this is a softer part of the estimating process it is one that can often mean the difference between an estimate that is successful and one that is not, and consequently the importance of it should not be overlooked.

12 Conducting assessments

12.1 Introduction

QinetiQ has conducted a number of maturity assessments using the Cost Engineering Health Check. The customers for these have ranged from internal QinetiQ, to other commercial organisations and government bodies, right through to professional cost estimating/forecasting bodies. The specific reasons for conducting the assessments varies from organisation to organisation, but the common theme is a desire to understand the state of current costing capability in that organisation, with the overriding goal being to draw out areas of weakness and thus focus intervention to improve those low capability areas within the organisation being considered.

The following provides a view on a selection of the results of the assessments conducted. All data has been aggregated together. The graphs present two different views of the data. Specifically, these are:

- A view on the range of scores as provided by individuals that have undertaken the CEHC.
- The ranges of average organisational scores (min, average and max) for each indicator contained within the database.

All results have been anonymised so that deductions cannot be made concerning the costing capability of those organisations that have undergone the CEHC. The following analysis provides a summary of the responses to two indicators from each of the four KBE pillars of Data, Tools, People and Process. The analysis enables some conclusions to be drawn concerning the comparative strengths/weaknesses of the international costing community as a whole and also international organisational costing capability. Note also that these results present a snap shot of the assessment database at a point in time [32]. As more assessments are undertaken, the underlying trends in the database may alter.

12.2 Individual perspectives

People

Indicator A1: What is the nature of the senior management's involvement in cost engineering?

Section 8.2.1 draws attention to the importance of management involvement in the estimating process. Specifically it discusses the importance for management to:

1   Use and value the outputs of the cost estimating function to inform their decisions.
2   To understand how those outputs have been generated to ensure they are making decisions fully aware of the limitations of the information with which they are being provided.

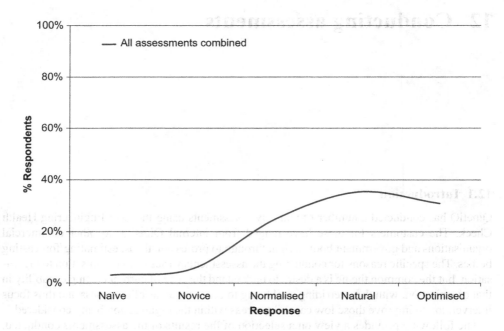

Figure 12.1 CEHC database – indicator A1 – senior management involvement – all individuals'
perspectives

Within the database of all CEHC assessments conducted, across all the individuals sampled
and across all the organisations, less than 10% considered their management's involvement
to be Novice or Naïve combined. About 25% considered it to be Normalised, whilst 35%
rated it as Natural and 31% as Optimised, as shown in Figure 12.1.

When these results have been discussed with participants, the message that has been received
is that the management teams within both industry and government bodies have been taking an
active role with cost estimating and analysis. Indeed, by virtue of the CEHC having been authorised and funded by management, that in itself indicates that management recognises the importance of its costing function and wants to act to ensure that it is sufficiently capable to inform their
decision making process. It is possible that for organisations that have not conducted a CEHC
assessment the results are likely to be somewhat lower, on account of their management not
recognising the importance of understanding the capability of their internal estimating function.

Although not presented in the chart, individuals within government bodies indicated a
greater level of management involvement in the cost estimating process than industry. This
is explained by the typical bureaucratic nature of government bodies where there are very
clear lines of authority.

Indicator A5: How well does the cost engineer understand their project and the way that
it functions?

Section 8.2.5 discusses the importance of the cost engineer's understanding of the whole life of
a project and equipment type within the project. They need to understand the costs associated
with design, development, testing, manufacturing, operation and disposal. Additionally, they
also need to understand the project environment, the various different decision points and who

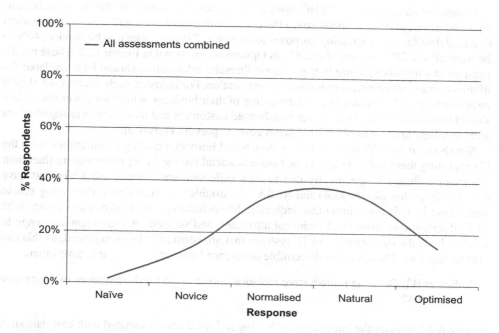

Figure 12.2 CEHC database – indicator A5 – estimators' understanding of project – all individuals' perspectives

makes them. They need to understand who has responsibility for funding the project across the different phases, who their stakeholders are and the different behaviours of the funding streams.

Within the database of all CEHC assessments conducted, across all the individuals sampled and across all the organisations, only 2% consider their engineers to be Naïve, only 14% consider them to be Novice, 35% to be Normalised, 35% as Natural and 14% as Optimised, as shown in Figure 12.2.

Although not presented on the graph, competency varied internationally. The US reports higher levels of technical competency than Europe. Counterintuitively, there was no discernible difference between industry and government. It would be expected that government contains a mixture of cost generalists who have an awareness of developing, buying and supporting equipment through projects than industry, who are typically suppliers of equipment. Examination of why the difference wasn't more distinct in the underlying data was attributed to government bodies having individuals who have specific interests in different domains and project phases and the need to match those with the most appropriate skill sets to the costing tasks as they arise. Notwithstanding this, there was a general consensus by almost all individuals sampled that gaining exposure to domains outside individuals' immediate comfort zones was necessary to become a rounded estimator.

Data

Indicator B1: Does the project gather historical financial data for cost estimating purposes?

Section 6.2.1 highlights the important role that historic cost data plays in making projections about future costs. The importance of understanding where that data has come from and the confidence level that can be attributed to it is also emphasised.

Within the database of all CEHC assessments conducted, across all the individuals sampled and across all the organisations, 11% consider their gathering and storing of historical financial data for cost estimating purposes to be Naïve, 23% consider it to be Novice, 40% to be Normalised, 20% as Natural and 6% as Optimised, as shown in Figure 12.3. These results paint quite a negative picture in that historic financial information should be considered the lifeblood of any government or industrial organisation. For industry, such information should be acting to give them complete understanding of their business, whilst for government they should be used to enable them to act as informed customers and used to inform negotiations with suppliers in an attempt to drive down costs or prevent entry-ism.

Not shown is the difference between the US and European costing communities, with the US reporting their ability to gather and store financial data as being more mature than their European colleagues, specifically due to data collection and storage initiatives that have been run by bodies like the DoD and NASA. The trouble with such data is then being able to understand it. This plays into other indicators like schedule, cost breakdown structure with defined definitions, associated technical attributes, and so forth. A significant challenge to this has been the development of IT systems that are constantly being replaced, as this can lead to data loss. There was no discernible difference between industry and government.

Indicator B3: Does the project store technical information for the purposes of future cost estimates?

Section 6.2.3 stresses the importance of having technical data associated with cost data such that the cost data can be used to make projections about the future. It also emphasises the importance of collecting the technical data in a meaningful manner such that it can be easily retrieved and reused. It recommends that an organisation develops a data dictionary, linked

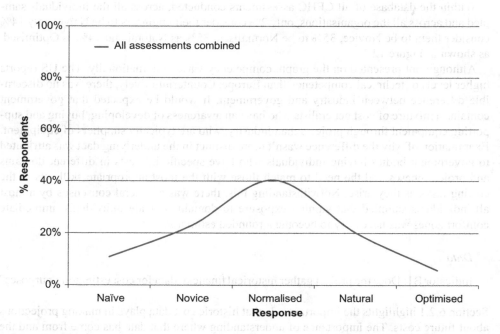

Figure 12.3 CEHC database – indicator B1 – historical financial data – all individuals' perspectives

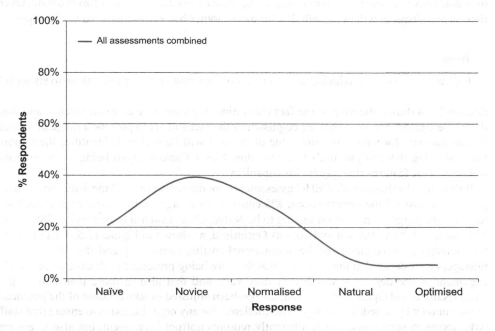

Figure 12.4 CEHC database – indicator B3 – historical technical data – all individuals' perspectives

to some form of cost, product or work breakdown structure such that data from various different projects can be sourced in a consistent manner and compared meaningfully.

Within the database of all CEHC assessments conducted, across all the individuals sampled and across all the organisations, 21% consider their gathering and storing of historical technical data for cost estimating purposes to be Naïve, 39% consider it to be Novice, 28% to be Normalised, 7% as Natural and 5% as Optimised, as shown in Figure 12.4.

Similar to the way cost data is being stored, these results paint a negative picture of the way organisations are valuing their internal knowledge. A significant challenge in this instance is understanding upfront what information is worth saving and putting the structures in place that allow it to be stored and easily retrieved for future reference. It also may require such data structures to span a multitude of different bodies, all who may be quite far removed from the estimating function. Gaining the cooperation of a multitude of different bodies, and ensuring that they share the desire to record data accurately, may prove to be challenging.

Within the underlying databases there were some marked differences. Individuals within industry reported scores that were typically more mature than that of their government colleagues. This could be explained on the basis that organisations typically should understand their products in more detail than the government bodies to which they are being sold. Additionally, within government organisations there was some variation, this being attributed to the different contractual mechanisms that governments are using to buy and support equipment. As such, especially where equipment is being sourced on an availability type contract, governments don't necessarily get access to the level of detail concerning the technical characteristics or performance of the system as this is all rolled up as part of the contract with the supplier. Care must be had with such a situation, as ultimately this puts the government customer in a much weaker position the next time it becomes necessary to re-cost the project as they don't have at hand the information they necessarily need to arrive at a cost estimate. Over time such a situation will eventually lead to the customer becoming easily led by the supplier.

Tools

Indicator C4: When producing an estimate, does the cost engineer use risk analysis tools?

Section 7.2.4 draws attention to the fact that estimating cannot be an exact science and that the best estimates are those that are cognisant of the fact and act to provide a range of values for the estimate for which the true value of the cost will lie within. It identifies the importance of using risk analysis tools to enable this, Monte Carlo analysis being a key analysis technique that features strongly in this capability.

Within the database of all CEHC assessments conducted, across all the individuals sampled and across all the organisations, 8% consider their organisation's use of risk analysis tools for the purposes of cost estimating to be Naïve, 6% consider it to be Novice, 28% to be Normalised, 31% as Natural and 26% as Optimised, as shown in Figure 12.5. This presents a reasonably positive picture of the international costing community and should act to give managers confidence that the estimates that they are being presented with have an acknowledgement of the degree to which they may vary, and that also in more than half of the cases (Natural and Optimised) the estimate has been adjusted to take account of the potential impact upon it by schedule slippage. The challenge for any organisation is to ensure that staff have access to such tools, which inherently requires upfront investment, but also to ensure that they are appropriately trained and skilled in using them. Additionally, it then becomes important for the organisation to ensure that its decision makers have been trained in how best to interpret such information and how best to use it to maximise its value to the business.

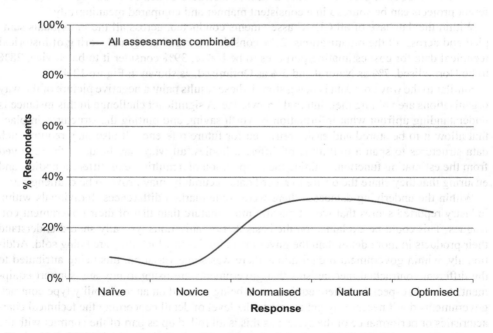

Figure 12.5 CEHC database – indicator C4 – risk analysis tools – all individuals' perspectives

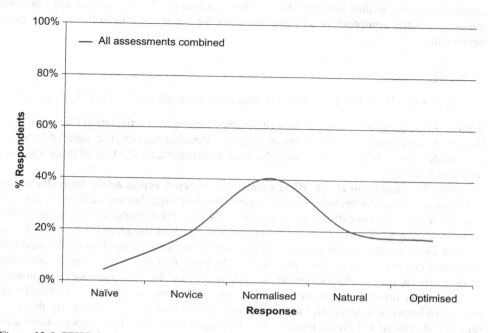

Figure 12.6 CEHC database – indicator C5 – software estimating tools – all individuals' perspectives

Figure 12.5 does not display the fact that the database suggests that the use of risk analysis is greatest with government bodies, presumably because of the level of investment required.

Indicator C5: Does the project consider software estimating tools necessary?

Section 7.2.5 makes reference to the move towards greater use of software and hence an increased need to be able to accurately cost software projects. It also draws attention to some of the 'fear' associated with software costing, stemming from the fact that it is not something tangible that can be seen or touched. A critical aspect to costing software capability is an ability to quantify the size of the software code to be developed. The section points towards a number of the different, more commonly accepted methods for sizing and costing software.

Within the database of all CEHC assessments conducted, across all the individuals sampled and across all the organisations, 4% consider their organisation's use of software estimating tools for the purposes of cost estimating to be Naïve, 18% consider it to be Novice, 41% to be Normalised, 20% as Natural and 17% as Optimised, as shown in Figure 12.6.

Software projects in the past have seen notorious cost overruns and continue to do so. There still remains the miscomprehension that software development is not expensive and is minimal risk.

There is a marked difference across the international community in this instance. There is significantly greater uptake of software costing tools by the US than in Europe. Again, uptake is greater within industry than within government bodies, presumably because industry is better equipped to generate estimates for the size of the software code to be developed.

Process

Indicator D3: How well is the cost engineering process planned and communicated?

Section 9.2.3 discusses the importance of clearly planning and articulating the cost modelling intent prior to the commencement of the cost estimating activity. The value of obtaining stakeholder buy-in is highlighted, as is the need to develop an audit trail of what was done and how it was done.

Within the database of all CEHC assessments conducted, across all the individuals sampled and across all the organisations, 4% consider their organisation's ability to plan and communicate their cost estimating process to be Naïve, 9% consider it to be Novice, 35% to be Normalised, 34% as Natural and 18% as Optimised, as shown in Figure 12.7. Whilst the bulk or respondents indicate that their organisations recognise the importance of developing and communicating a cost plan, only 18% think that this is endorsed by all stakeholders prior to the commencement of the costing activity. This is somewhat disappointing as stakeholder involvement from the very outset of the costing activity can often be the difference between a successful costing activity and one that is not. Certainly there is a reduced likelihood for the estimate to be challenged at the end if all stakeholders have bought into the process upfront and have contributed as required. The challenge for an organisation is to develop guidance on how best to plan and communicate the costing

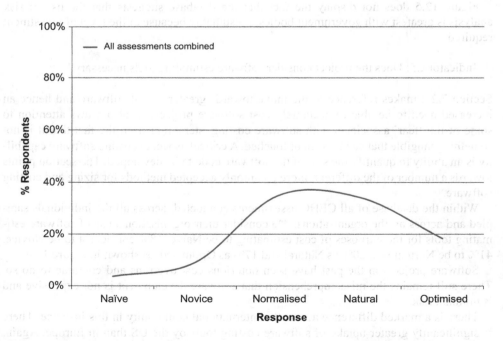

Figure 12.7 CEHC database – indicator D3 – planning and communication – all individuals' perspectives

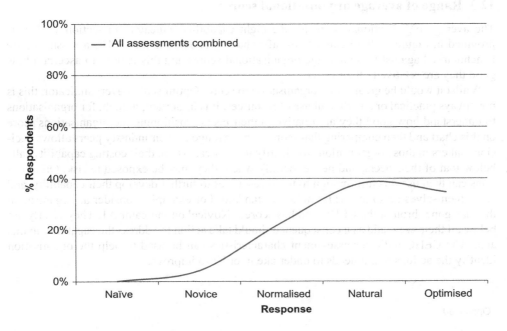

Figure 12.8 CEHC database – indicator D13 – use of multiple estimating processes – all individuals' perspectives

process, but then to also ensure that estimators adhere to that guidance and implement it appropriately. There is a fine line between overburdening a cost estimator with bureaucratic process and letting them get on with the job.

> Indicator D13: Does the cost engineer make use of multiple estimation approaches to arrive at a suitable estimate (i.e. triangulation)?

Section 9.2.13 highlights the importance of using multiple estimating approaches to gain confidence that an estimate is in the right ballpark. This is particularly useful for a decision maker if a detailed bottom-up estimate has been provided to inform a decision and they want to be confident that no major aspect of cost has been omitted.

Within the database of all CEHC assessments conducted, across all the individuals sampled and across all the organisations, 0% consider their use of multiple estimation approaches to be Naïve, 4% consider it to be Novice, 23% to be Normalised, 38% as Natural and 35% as Optimised (see Figure 12.8). Whilst the awareness of multiple estimation methods across respondents is good, it is disappointing that 61% (Normalised and Natural) believe that these are not entirely appropriately applied as individuals stay with what they know best or are not provided with tools to conduct estimates using alternate methodologies. There is a need therefore for organisations and management to recognise the importance of 'sanity checking' any estimate by approaching the problem from a different perspective, and thus providing the appropriate tools and training to do this. Similarly, there is a need for the estimators themselves to be proactive in their working practices and to have some professional pride in ensuring that the information that they offer forward has been tested to the maximum extent possible.

12.3 Range of average organisational scores

The average organisational score for the eight capability indicators in section 12.2 is as provided in Figure 12.9. Organisations, after having undergone the CEHC assessment, are benchmarked against these average organisational scores and this is used to ascertain how good they are relative to their peers.

Whilst it would be great for an organisation to score 'Optimised' in every indicator, this is not always practical or an efficient use of resources. It is important, though, for organisations to understand how good they are relative to their peers. Positioning the organisations score on this chart and then comparing that score with the range of their industry peers allows decision makers in those organisations to identify those areas where their costing capability falls below that of their peers, and hence identify where they may be exposed to risk. Organisations can then use this information to focus resources to further develop their capability, and bring themselves up to the wider industry standard. For example, consider an organisation that has gone through the CEHC and has scored 'Novice' on indicator A1. They clearly are below all their peers and as a consequence should take action to address the capability in this area. The CEHC indicator assessment characteristics can be used to help the organisation identify the actions that it needs to undertake in order to improve.

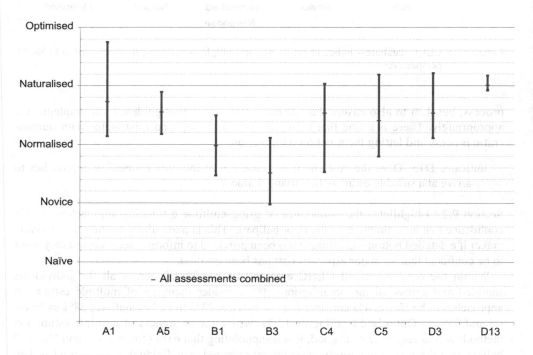

Figure 12.9 CEHC database – multiple indicators – range of average organisational scores

13 Summary

13.1 Introduction

This book begins to explore the concepts of a Cost Engineering Heath Check with a simple question: "How good are your estimates?" If you are a senior manager, decision maker or head of a cost engineering function, then this question should make you wake up and pay attention. The decisions and future of your career depends upon the answer.

13.2 Conclusion

When the Cost Engineering Health Check has been completed, it will provide you with a set of results in graphical format and a dialogue of the comments and observations. Each Cost Engineering Health Check capability area is scored against exemplars relevant to the capability area to provide context. The maturity is ranked as follows:

*   Naïve = process design or application flawed and probably not adding value
*   Novice = some added value, but weakness in process design or implementation
*   Normalised = newly formalised process, implemented systematically and adding value
*   Natural = formalised process, implemented systematically and adding value for a reasonable duration
*   Optimised = applied at strategic levels in driving objectives and optimising outcomes for a considerable length of time

This provides the sponsor with an indication of the level of maturity of their organisation. This is an indication of how good your estimating capability is. It will indicate and assess the quality and consistency of cost engineering implementation in the organisation. It will also provide understanding of the effectiveness of cost engineering and its impacts across the enterprise and on the interactions between customer and supplier.

For senior management, the Cost Engineering Health Check will provide an indication of how you compare with your peers. It will enable the improvement of cost engineering when informing decision making across the organisation. Where the cost engineering function is weak relative to peer organisations, the Cost Engineering Health Check will provide guidance regarding how you can improve. Figure 13.1, for example, provides an indication of the six categories of the Cost Engineering Health Check relative to the assessing organisation, indicated by the diamond. The quartile ranges of the competitor organisations are indicated by box plots for the 25%, 50% and 75% percentiles of the benchmark, with error bars indicating the 0% and 100%.

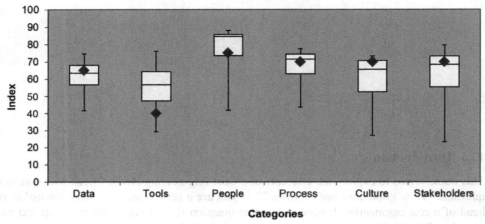

Figure 13.1 A dashboard showing the organisation relative to the quartile ranges of the competition

It is not necessary for the cost engineering function to obtain a maturity score of 100 on the index. It is only necessary for them to be ahead of the competition. So, for example, in the tools category an index score of 80 would put them ahead of the competition; unfortunately, the present maturity score is 40, which puts them in the 0% to 25% quartile and this is the area which requires investment and further maturing.

For decision makers, the Cost Engineering Health Check will address the question: "What does good look like?" The outcome of the transformation programme will improve coherency and alignment, and share good practice. This will lead to improved communications, where common issues are identified, and reduce duplication of effort across the organisation.

13.3 Benefits

The QinetiQ CEHC has a number of benefits beyond those obtained through implementing the ideas in this book. These include:

- The QinetiQ CEHC is a tried and tested approach.
- It produces rapid results that are easy to understand.
- The QinetiQ CEHC is conducted by experienced consulting professionals with a detailed knowledge of cost engineering.
- It will result in independent, objective and comprehensive cost estimating advice.
- The e-voting will conclude in a group evaluation approach.
- It is based upon previous homogenous database comparisons with industry standards and peer organisations.

David Lewis, the chairman of the European Aerospace Cost Engineering (EACE), described the QinetiQ CEHC workshops: "The Cost Engineering Health Check (CEHC) was a professionally facilitated workshop and the results will guide the future direction of capability development for the cost community in the EACE Working Group."

13.4 Synopsis

QinetiQ CEHC provides:

- Evidence of weaknesses in the cost engineering capability of an organisation.
- Focus for improvement programmes.
- Greater confidence for decision makers that their decisions are made on credible and justified financial information.

Observation from the SCAF [39] [40] and EACE [41] [42] assessment workshops:

- Vote on each question: re-votes can be taken if necessary.
- Debate is very useful in exploring rationale behind assessments.
- Be honest and positive; differences of view are acceptable and helpful.
- Encourage open discussion with points non-attributable to any individual.

Greater confidence in cost estimates increases your competitive edge and funds more projects within the same budget.

Austerity means that there is a bigger demand for good cost engineering – begin the assessment today!

References

1 https://www.gov.uk/government/news/west-coast-main-line-final-report-of-the-laidlaw-inquiry
2 Bolten J G, Leonard R S, Arena M V, Younossi O, Sollinger J M, "Sources of Weapon System Cost Growth – Analysis of 35 Major Defense Acquisition Programs", RAND report, 2008, ISBN 978-0-8330-4289-7
3 The Comptroller and Auditor General, "The Major Projects Report 2008", National Audit Office, 18 December 2008
4 Hopkinson M, *The Project Risk Maturity Model: Measuring and Improving Risk Management Capability*, Gower Publishing, Farnham, UK, 2011, ISBN 978-0-566-08879-7
5 The Comptroller and Auditor General, "The Major Projects Report 2013", National Audit Office, 10 February 2014
6 Chinn D, Dowdy J, "An Expert View on Defence Procurement", McKinsey on Government, Spring 2010
7 The Comptroller and Auditor General, "Forecasting in Government to Achieve Value for Money", National Audit Office, 31 January 2014
8 Shermon D, etc. "Austerity Handbook: Living with Austerity, Enabling Growth" QinetiQ Corporate Marketing, July 2014
9 Shermon D, *Aspects of Complexity: Managing Projects in a Complex World*, Chapter Six "The Impact of Complexity on Project Cost and Schedule Estimates", PMI publication, 2011, ISBN: 978-1-935589-30-3
10 Shermon D, "Historical Trend Analysis Analysed", *The International Society of Parametric Analysts (ISPA) Journal*, Jan–June 2011, Volume 4, No 1, Taylor & Francis, ISSN: 1941-658X
11 Wright T P, "Factors Affecting the Cost of Airplanes", *Journal of Aeronautical Sciences*, February 1936
12 Smit M C, "Normalization of Costs for Multiple Currencies and Multiple Base Years", ISPA conference Brussels, Belgium, May 2012
13 ICEAA BoK, module 07 – learning curves
14 Butterfield J, Curran R, Watson G, Craig C, Raghunathan S, Collins R, Edgar T, Higgins C, Burke R, Kelly P, Gibson C, "Use of Digital Manufacturing to Improve Operator Learning in Aerospace Assembly". Paper Number: AIAA 2007-7865
15 Shermon D, *Systems Cost Engineering*, editor and major contributor, Gower Publishing, Farnham, UK, July 2009. ISBN: 978-0-566-08861-2
16 Shermon D, "Austerity – Is It All Bad News?" ICEAA World, Issue #3, 2014
17 www.nao.org.uk
18 www.gao.gov
19 www.cape.osd.mil
20 www.gov.uk/ministry-of-defence-commercial
21 Pickburn G, Dstl, "Choosing the Options: Mystery or Method?", Society for Cost Analysis and Forecasting (SCAF), April 2010

22 Shermon D, "Those Who Can, Do: Those Who Can, Teach", "The Project Professional" *The Journal of the Association of Cost Engineers (ACostE)*, July 2014, Volume 52, No 4

23 Shermon D, Gilmour M, "Can Psychology and Sociology Teach Us to Be Better Estimators?" ICEAA World, Spring 2014

24 Shermon D, Gilmour M, "Data, Tools, People and Process: But the Most Complex Is People!", "The Project Professional" *The Journal of the Association of Cost Engineers (ACostE)*, March 2014, Volume 52, No 2

25 Shermon D, Gilmour M, "Making a Financial Decision? How Good Are Those Cost?", "The Project Professional" *The Journal of the Association of Cost Engineers (ACostE)*, May 2013, Volume 51, No 3

26 Shermon D, Nicholls A, "The System of All Systems?", "Defence Management Journal" *The Management Journal for the United Kingdom (UK) Ministry of Defence (MOD)*, December 2007, No 39

27 Shermon D, "The Problem with Marketing and Selling Cost Engineering to Organisations", "ISPA World" *The New Letter of the International Society of Parametric Analysts (ISPA)*, Fall 2006, Volume 25, No 4

28 Shermon D, "Historical Trend Analysis", "Project" *Magazine of the Association for Project Management (APM)*, July 2006, Volume 19, No 2

29 Shermon D, "Standing Up to Scrutiny", "Project" *Magazine of the Association for Project Management (APM)*, February 2003, Volume 15, No 8

30 Shermon D, "Benchmarking British Industry", "ISPA Parametric World" *The New Letter of the International Society of Parametric Analysts (ISPA)*, Spring 2003, Volume 22, No 1

31 Shermon D, "Knowledge Management in Parametrics", "The Cost Engineer" *The Journal of the Association of Cost Engineers (ACostE)*, July 2002, Volume 40, No 3

32 Shermon D, Gilmour M, "A Cost Capability Maturity Analysis of the US and European Costing Communities", International Cost Estimating and Analysis Association (ICEAA), June 2015

33 Shermon D, Barnaby C, "Macro-Parametrics and the Applications of Multi-Collinearity and Bayesian to Enhance Early Cost Modelling", International Cost Estimating and Analysis Association (ICEAA), June 2015

34 Shermon D, "The Challenge of Forecasting the Cost of Complex Military, Aerospace and Weapons Projects", 16th Australian International Aerospace Congress, February 2015

35 Shermon D, "Cost Estimating in These Times of Austerity", APM, June 2014

36 Shermon D, Gilmour M, "Behavioural Estimating – Observations on the Psychology of Cost Estimating", International Cost Estimating and Analysis Association (ICEAA), New Orleans, June 2013

37 Shermon D, Gilmour M, "Cost Engineering Heath Check – How Good Are Your Numbers?", International Cost Estimating and Analysis Association (ICEAA), New Orleans, June 2013

38 Shermon D, Gilmour M, "Behavioural Estimating – Can Psychology Teach Us How to Be Better Estimators?" Society for Cost Analysis and Forecasting Winter Workshop, Royal Institute of Naval Architects, London, February 2013

39 Shermon D, Gilmour M, "Cost Engineering Health Check – Results of a Limited Survey for Society for Cost Analysis and Forecasting (SCAF)", December 2012

40 Shermon D, Gilmour M, "Identification of Strengths, Weaknesses and Assertions within the Costing Community", Society for Cost Analysis and Forecasting (SCAF), BAWA, Bristol, UK, November 2012

41 Shermon D, Gilmour M, "Cost Engineering Health Check – Results of a Limited Survey for European Aerospace Cost Engineering (EACE) Working Group", November 2012

42 Shermon D, Gilmour M, "Cost Engineering Health Check", 24th Workshop of the European Aerospace Cost Engineering (EACE) Working Group, University of Bath, Bath, UK, October 2012

43 Shermon D, "UK MOD Up-Skilling in Parametrics", International Society of Parametric Analysts (ISPA), Brussels, May 2012

44 ESA, CDF, http://www.esa.int/Our_Activities/Space_Engineering_Technology/CDF

45 Shermon D, Scire J, "Implementing Parametric Discipline to Performance Based Contracting (PBC) in Through Life Projects", International Society of Parametric Analysts (ISPA), Brussels, May 2012

46 HM Treasury, Green Book

47 Shermon D, Curran S, "Operating and Support Cost Analysis Modelling" Society of Cost Analysts and Forecasters (SCAF), BAWA, Bristol, April 2011

48 International Society of Parametric Analysts (ISPA), *Parametric Estimating Handbook*©, 4th Edition, April 2008

49 Shermon D, "Parametric Cost Estimating, What Is It and How Is It Useful to You?", Dutch Association of Cost Engineers (DACE), The Netherlands, March 2010

50 Shermon D, "Cost Benefit Optimisation to Achieve Affordable Force Structures", Department of Defence Cost Analysis Symposium (DODCAS), Williamsburg, USA, February 2010

51 Shermon D, Eilingsfeld F, "Estimating the Potential Cost Benefits of State-of-the-Art Software Engineering Methods and Tools for on-Board, EGSE and Simulators" European Aerospace Cost Engineering (EACE) Working Group, ESA/ESTEC, Noordwijk, September 2009

52 Association for Project Management. *Earned Value Management: APM Guidelines*, 2nd edition

53 Shermon D, "Estimating Through Life", International Society of Parametric Analysts (ISPA), St. Louis, 2009

54 Shermon D, "Creating Early Conceptual Cost Models in Partnership with the UK MOD", Defence iQ, IQPC, London, Through Life Support and Costing, June 2009

55 Shermon D, "Implementing Early Concept Cost Models", Department of Defence Cost Analysis Symposium (DODCAS), Williamsburg, USA, February 2009

56 Shermon D, "Applications of Parametrics: A Historical Perspective", Space Systems Cost Analysis Group (SSCAG), ESTEC, Noordwijk, The Netherlands, 2008

57 Shermon D, "Independent Cost Estimating (ICE) Should Cost Could Cost", Society of Cost Analysts and Forecasters (SCAF), DPA, Abbey Wood, Bristol, February 2008

58 Shermon D, "Applying Parametric Cost Modelling Technology Insertion", International Society of Parametric Analysts (ISPA), New Orleans, 2007

59 Shermon D, Razzaq S, "Virtual Cost Engineering Studio (V-CES)", International Society of Parametric Analysts (ISPA), Denver, 2005

60 Shermon D, "PFG Spine Feasibility Study", International Society of Parametric Analysts (ISPA), Denver, 2005

61 Shermon D, Jones G, "Operating and Support Cost Data Collection Made Simple", International Society of Parametric Analysts (ISPA), Frascati, Italy, 2004

62 Curran, R, Gilmour, M, Kundu, A K, Raghunathan, S. "Cost Optimisation of Tolerances and Manufacturing Capability for Aircraft Surface Features", *International Journal of Manufacturing Technology and Management*, 2008, Volume 1, Nos 3/4

63 Shermon D, "Experience of Top Level Calibration of UK Submarine Platforms", PRICE Systems Symposium, Cambridge, UK, 1999

64 Shermon D, "CCES Centralised Cost Engineering System", PRICE Systems Symposium, Nice, France, 1994

Index

abbreviations 157
accuracy 9, 13, 43, 91, 155, 161
acronyms 152, 157
activity-based costing 44
adaptive maintenance 63
add value 148, 151
analogous 33, 73, 77, 85, 147–8
analysis of alternatives 6
analytical 8, 33, 70, 77, 78, 85, 147, 154
Association of Cost Engineers 84, 107
Association of Project Managers 86, 93
as-spent 45, 101, 108
assumptions 32, 38, 41, 105, 132, 163
austerity 5, 122, 177
Austerity Handbook 143

balance of investment 123
baseline 55, 64, 79, 89, 112, 116, 138, 145
basis of estimate 66, 91
behavioural economics 107
benchmark 3, 10, 15, 23, 72, 77, 86, 153, 174
benefits 6, 19, 35, 81, 111, 125, 142, 176
bill of material 91
bivariate 28
black-box 161
Boeing curve 36, 85
book of anomalies 25
bottom-up *see* analytical
budget estimate 7, 54
budget setting 72, 100, 122
business case 15, 43, 71, 82, 101, 106, 124, 163
business case analysis 6
business leader i, 3

CADMID xi, 126
calculator 50, 135
calibration 52, 71, 72, 77
capability gap 108, 125
capital expenditure 104
catalogue prices 55
causation 74
CBS *see* cost breakdown structure
ceiling price 99

central tendency 34, 96
chief executive officers (CEOs) 134, 151, 158
COCOMO 61
coefficient of variation 34, 75, 95
combined operational effectiveness and
    investment appraisal (COEIA) 124, 127,
    133, 163
commercial cost models 72, 77
common cost 111
communicate 51, 72, 85, 106, 131, 158, 172
composite inflation 46
composite labour rate 101
compounding errors 32
concept of analysis 125, 133
concepts 5, 32, 42, 51, 69
concurrent design facility 105
confidence 48, 147, 163
constant cost 25, 45, 101, 108, 126
constants 74
consultants 15, 138, 156
consumer price index 46
contingency 7, 98, 113, 138, 159
continuous personal development 107
contract change notices 136, 145
corporate direction 154
corporate memory 7, 155
corrective maintenance 63
correlation 33, 74, 95, 140–2
cost 4, 30
cost analysis requirement description
    (CARD) 39
cost analyst 4, 17, 26, 28, 131
cost as an independent variable 106, 136, 162
cost benefit analysis 6, 111
cost breakdown structure 28, 31, 40, 130, 168
cost centres 104
Cost Data and Assumptions List (CDAL) 38, 41,
    106, 133
cost database 9, 73
cost driver 7, 32, 60, 90, 111, 139
cost engineer 4, 5, 7, 81, 83, 87, 158
cost estimating relationship 26, 46, 73, 93
cost forecaster *see* cost engineer

cost improvement curves *see* learning curve
cost model 26, 53, 61, 67, 71, 77, 124, 150, 161
cost of ownership *see* whole life cost
cost plus 98
Cost Plus Award Fee 99
Cost Plus Fixed Fee 99
Cost Plus Incentive Fee 99
cost portal 73
cost research 26, 51, 72
cost tool 52, 69, 162
cost working group 106
Crawford 36, 85
culture 5, 47, 151–6
cumulative average learning 37
current year dollars 108
customer price index 35

dashboard 19, 176
data 3, 5, 25–49, 53, 65, 74, 85, 105, 152, 160, 166
data dictionary 28, 31, 41, 168
Data Protection Act 33
decision makers 3, 176
defence budget 122
defence lines of development 42, 126
definitions 4
Delphi technique 17
dependencies 38–40, 128
detailed estimating *see* analytical
direct cost 31, 86, 88, 101, 104
discounted cash flow 7, 85, 110
discounting 109
doctrine 42, 126

EAC calculation 66, 90, 109; *see also* equivalent annual cost
earned value management (EVM) i, 3, 54, 64, 67, 124, 137, 162
economic analysis 6, 101, 108, 124
education 158
electronic voting/e-voting 15–17, 156, 176
employee motivation 156
engineering judgement 154
equipment 1, 10, 31, 40, 42, 78, 92, 122, 126
equivalent annual cost 109
error sum of squares 75
escalated cost *see* outturn
ESLOC 61
Estimate at Completion (EAC) 54, 64, 66–7
estimated cost works plan (ECWP) 79
European Space Agency (ESA) 39, 151
evolution 32, 63–4
evolutionary 63–4, 151
Excel 23, 50, 69–70, 76, 79, 84
exchange rates 35, 47–8, 148, 159
exclusions 38–9, 79

executive level 51
experience curves *see* learning curve
expert opinion 53, 55, 114–15, 140
external customer 17, 82, 90

Family of Advanced Cost Estimating Tools (FACET) 70, 160
facilitator 15–19, 155
factor 35, 52, 61, 70, 103, 110
feedback 52, 90, 155
financial 29, 100
financial analysis 6, 101
financial data 29
firm fixed price 99
first theoretical piece 36
fixed price 98–9
fixed price incentive 98–9
foreign nations 47
function points 60

gate keepers 81
General Accounting Office (GAO) 122
general ledger 45, 67, 100
get well plan 155
governance 7, 53, 88, 122–4, 137
government 1, 24, 42, 81, 113, 122, 161, 165–72
grass roots *see* analytical
group evaluation 176

hardware 6, 41, 60–3, 87–8, 91, 98, 121, 154
head of profession 120–1
healthy culture 152, 156
historical data 5, 8, 32–8, 72, 95, 163
homogenous database 176
homogenous dataset 38, 73, 96
hypothesis 94, 96–7

incremental 63, 111
independent baseline review (IBR) 146
independent cost estimate (ICE) 7, 54, 72, 77
indirect cost 88, 104
inflation rates 45, 108–9
infrastructure 41–2, 126, 133
intellectual property 34
International Cost Estimating and Analysis Association (ICEAA) 27, 84, 107
interoperability 42
interpersonal skills 156, 158
ISO9001 27
iterative 146, 162

key performance indicators (KPI) 97
key user requirements (KUR) 68
Knowledge Based Estimating (KBE) i, 3, 5–9, 152, 164
knowledge transfer 18–19

learning curve 36–8, 50
lease 47, 110
lessons learnt 19
life cycle cost (LCC) *see* whole life cost
linear 74–6, 96
LINEST 76
logistics 42, 126, 133

management information systems (MIS) 73
management level 51
management reserve 66, 159
marginal costs 104, 111
Master Data and Assumptions List
    (MDAL) 39, 106, 133; *see also*
    Cost Data and Assumptions List
master schedule 29, 131, 153
mathematic 29, 33, 50, 70, 76, 83, 93–7, 148
matrix structure 120
mean 34, 75, 95–7, 140
median 34, 95
meta data 94
Mil Std 881 39
milestones 47, 97
mitigation 58–9, 79–80, 112–19, 138–9, 146
mode 34, 95
Monte Carlo analysis 34, 55, 79, 84, 115–24,
    140, 151, 159, 170
motivation 13, 121, 156
multicollinearity 76
multiple estimation 44, 77, 146, 173
multivariate 28, 76

naive 20, 166–75
National Audit Office 10–12, 122
natural 166–75
net present value 6–7, 85, 101, 108–9,
    111, 126
nonlinear 76
non-recurring 25, 48, 91, 101–2, 104, 110, 131
normalised 25–6, 29, 31, 35, 45–6, 73–4, 93,
    96, 166–75
not to exceed 55
novice 166–75
NPV *see* net present value
null hypothesis 96

operational analysis 15, 125–6, 132–3
opportunities 1, 3, 17, 38–9, 66, 81, 90, 107, 138
optimised 20, 122, 166–75
ordinary least square 76
organisation 3–8, 17
organisational breakdown structure 65, 79
outturn 25, 29, 45, 101, 108–9, 163
overall maturity 43
overheads 25, 29, 41, 52–3, 88, 103–5, 111

parametric 5, 7, 32–3, 71–3, 77–8, 154,
    161–2

parametrician 4, 71–2
people 81–121
perfective maintenance 64
performance based contracting 97
personnel 42, 54, 72, 126, 133, 152
planning cycle 123
point estimate 43, 54–5, 58, 79–80, 95, 112,
    114, 119–20, 154
predictive object points 60
price 1, 7, 45–6, 55, 66, 98–100, 144
primary data 8, 28–9, 44
PRINCE 2 93
probabilistic analysis 112–13, 130
probabilistic estimate 54, 146
process 122–50
product breakdown structure 31, 40, 129, 162
product improvement functions 37
profile 163
profit 66, 99–100
programme budget 122
project objectives 130–1, 154
proposal 1, 7, 35, 54, 64, 106, 133–4,
    136, 145
ProPricer 70
psychological 91, 157

quantity effects 25, 36, 37, 161; *see also*
    learning curve
quartile 20, 175–6
questionnaire of method of allocation of
    costs 25, 31

RACI analysis 72, 156
range 34, 93, 95, 140–1, 145, 147
rates 35–8, 45–7, 70, 101–3, 108–9
ratio 70, 74, 99–100, 112
raw material 29, 34, 41, 87, 101
reactive 81, 136
recommendations 18, 20–2, 127
reconciliation 8, 78, 147
recurring 25, 36–7, 48, 91, 101–2, 104, 110,
    131, 151
regression analysis 29, 73–5, 93, 97
regression sum of squares 75
requirements: CEHC implementation
    requirements 18, 23; estimation requirements
    49, 67–71, 121, 128–9, 162–3; project
    requirements 5, 7, 54, 104–5
residual 59, 75–6
results 165–76
retail goods 46
retail price index 35
revenue 98, 104, 126, 132
risk analysis 55–9, 64, 83–4, 97, 116–17, 119,
    132, 138–9, 142
risk, definition 38–9, 80, 91, 111–20
risk management 10, 30, 56, 66, 112, 116,
    137–41

risk manager 112, 129, 138
risk maturity model 10–12, 137
risk register 79–80, 85, 112, 116, 119,
    129; within cost estimate 54; within
    pricing 66, 98–9
rough order of magnitude 7, 44, 53

satellites 151–2
scatter graphs 33, 75
scatter plot 95
science 42, 55, 74, 80, 93–4, 122, 126,
    151, 170
scrutineers 161
s-curve 58, 115, 119–20, 129, 144, 147, 151
secondary data 8, 28–9, 44
secondary sources 29
sell 87, 102, 104, 142
selling 90
senior management: involvement in CEHC 17;
    role in estimation process 66, 78, 87–90, 152,
    156, 159, 175
sensitivity analysis 111, 129, 135, 139, 163
share price 1
share ratio 99–100
should cost 7, 54, 77
skew 95, 120
SLOC 60–1
Society for Cost Analysis and Forecasting
    84, 107
software: cost database 73; estimating software
    costs 41, 59–64, 87–8, 91–2, 98, 101, 106,
    111, 121, 159; estimation software 5, 26–7,
    39, 41, 58, 60–1, 69–70, 154, 170–1; other 6
spiral 63–4
stakeholder community 18, 23, 136, 157, 159,
    161–2
stakeholders: CEHC methodology 17, 20–1,
    23; culture 152; data gathering 41, 44, 49;
    example assessment 167, 172; KBE Pillar 5,
    8, 13, 157–63; people 83, 89, 105–6, 109;
    process 125, 129, 131, 136–9, 142, 147–8;
    tool development and usage 53, 59, 68–70
stakeholder working group 41, 49, 153, 161
standard deviation 34, 95–6
standard time 103
statistical relationship 32, 74
statistical tools 5, 73–4, 77
statistician 93–4
statistics 34, 76, 93–7
Strategic Defence and Security Review 1, 123
strategic vision 156
subject matter experts 1, 44, 55, 92, 121–2
sunk costs 111
super users 51
suppliers 34–5, 55, 73, 81–2, 90–1,
    133, 167–8

task related activities 30
technical department 153
technical information 21, 31–2, 35, 73, 153, 168
terms and conditions 33, 97
terms of reference 136
then-year 45, 101, 108
three-point estimate 58, 79, 80, 95, 112, 114, 120
through life cost 7, 78
TickIT 27
time preference 109
tools: culture 154; data gathering 30, 43;
    example assessment 170–2, 173, 176; KBE
    Pillar 3, 5, 50–80; people 19, 84, 88, 103,
    113; process 130, 148–9; stakeholders 161–2
total ownership cost 4, 162
total sum of squares 75
trade-offs 6–7, 90, 162
training: costs 41–2, 102, 126, 133; upskilling
    19, 21, 51–2, 59, 88, 149–50, 150–1, 155–6
transformation 18–21, 76, 155–6, 176

uncertainty 55–6, 58–9, 79–80, 91, 95–7,
    112–20, 138–9, 145–6
unit learning 37
univariate 28
unknown-unknowns 119
use case conversion points 60
user level 51

value for money 10, 35, 77, 86, 101, 121–4
variance 34, 37, 67, 75, 95, 97
VBA 69
V diagram 62–3
vendor quotes 55
verification and validation 27, 67, 69, 71–2, 77,
    82, 130, 148–9

wash costs 111; *see also* common cost
waterfall 62–3
West Coast Main Line 3
White Review 65; *see also* lessons learnt
whole life cost: definition 4, 7, 41; economic
    analysis 101, 111, 126; overheads 104; process
    59, 128–9, 133, 163; skills 81, 86, 92
will cost 55
work breakdown structure 31, 40, 65, 79, 113, 169
work package description 79–80
work packages 31, 40, 65–6, 79, 128, 140–2
work performed 67, 146
workshops: conducting CEHC assessments
    15–19, 155–6, 176–7; as part of estimation
    process 49, 112, 129, 138; as part of thought
    leadership 90, 107
would / could cost 7, 54

X-Y graphs 33, 95; *see also* scatter graphs